# Institutionalization of Micro-finance Through Self-help Group and Bank Linkages

## Problems, Challenges and Actions

# Institutionalization of Micro-finance Through Self-help Group and Bank Linkages

## Problems, Challenges and Actions

K. Ramakrishnan
Susanta Kumar Barik
Prof. B. Appa Rao

AKANSHA PUBLISHING HOUSE
NEW DELHI • GUWAHATI • VISAKHAPATNAM

**AKANSHA PUBLISHING HOUSE**
4649-B/21, Ansari Road
Darya Ganj, New Delhi - 110 002
Ph.: 23263193 / 9811582579 / 09435116718
Fax: 011-23263193
Email: ektabooks@yahoo.com
www.akanshapublishinghouse.com

*Institutionalization of Micro-finance Through Self-help Group and Bank Linkages*



First Published 2012
ISBN 978-81-8370-315-4



PRINTED IN INDIA

---

Published by Akansha Publishing House, New Delhi and Printed at Harmain Offset Press, Delhi.

# Contents

# Preface

Financing the poor to take up avenues of income generation through feasible livelihood activities for survival with dignity, taking care of household essentials, meeting requirement of family members and leading a life with self-esteem is the indeavour persistently being visualized by the national and global economics. This initiative is being adopted since establishment of 'Human Civilization' though informally and adopted sporadically in a manner and form suitable to the community and communities involved to realize the potentiality of available resources and its utilization for better survival.

However, with the passage of time microfinance in the form of services such as savings and uncollateralized credit extended to the poor has been louded as a powerful vehicle for reducing global poverty and thereby empowering women. Microfinance got its recognition as an instrument to eliminate poverty through bridging the supply-demand gap for money in rural and geographically cut off areas to take up livelihood activities in line with the resources available in the area and locality.

Rooting finance through microfinance route and especially under the aegis of formal and non formal institutional arrangement has therefore accepted globally as a sustainable approach to the fight against Poverty, Malnutrition and Hunger.

All formal financial institutions, non-formal financial institutions and semi-formal financial institutions have extended credit support to the needy families organized into groups and interested to take up income generation activities.

The Reserve Bank of India and International Monetary Fund have also made mandatory for all form of financial institutions to liquidate part of their transactions supporting the needy families involved in generating income through IGPs and maintaining their *status quo*.

Rastriya Mahila Kosa (RMK) through the non-governmental organizations pumped in cash to self help groups (SHGs) across all states of India. DWCRA group, formation at a wider scale and extending fund support to take up avenues of income generation is the outcome of the initiative for rooting micro finance for poor.

This publication is amplifying the replica role of Andhra Bank involvement is disbursement and/or extending fund support to peoples of Andhra Pradesh across three regions. It is cross examining the effectiveness of formal institutional micro credit injection and its multi-layer effect on the goal of poverty elimination and women empowerment. It is thoroughly summarizing the length and breadth of formal institutional financing in the context of India and in particular to the state of Andhra Pradesh which is otherwise known as "*Macca as well as Madina*" of micro-finance.

**K. Ramakrishnan**
**Susanta Kumar Barik**
**Prof. B. Appa Rao**

# Acknowledgements

We have received generous help from a number of people to carry on our research work. Without their co-operation & encouragement we could not have completed the work. We acknowledge our irredeemable debt to them.

We wish to express our sincere thanks to Sri. A.L. Nageswara Rao, General Manager of Andhra Bank & Convener SLBC for his help and support in this work. We have received much help from Andhra Bank staff, Lead District Managers of Andhra Pradesh, NABARD Officials, SERP Officials, MEPMA Officials & staff of other banks in collecting the data and we express our sense of gratitude to all of them. We are thankful to Mr. Ramesh Santhanam, Vice President Ashok Leyland Projects Ltd and Director Ashley Biofuels Ltd Hinduja Group for his valuable suggestions in the study.

we are thankful to all the staff members of Priority Sector Policy Department for the support rendered in various aspects.

**Authors**

# List of Abbreviations

| | |
|---|---|
| A.B. | Andhra Bank |
| A.P. | Andhra Pradesh |
| ABRDT | Andhra Bank Rural Development Trust |
| ADB | Asian Development Bank |
| AIRCS | All-India Rural Credit Survey |
| AKRSP | Aga Khan Rural Support Programme |
| APCOB | Andhra Pradesh State Cooperative Bank |
| APBIRED | Andhra Pradesh Bankers' Institute of Rural and Entrepreneurship Development |
| APDPIP | Andhra Pradesh District Poverty Initiatives Project |
| APITCO | Andhra Pradesh Industrial Technical Consultancy Organization |
| APMAS | Andhra Pradesh Mahila Abhivridhi Society |
| AML | Anti-Money Laundering |
| APREGP | Andhra Pradesh Rural Employment Generation Programme |
| ASA | Association for Social Advancement |
| ASCA | Accumulating Saving and Credit Association |
| ATM | All Time Money |

| | |
|---|---|
| BC | Business Correspondent |
| BCSBI | Banking Codes and Standards Board of India |
| BF | Business Facilitator |
| BIRD | Bankers Institute or Rural Development |
| BRI | Bank Rakyat Indonesia |
| CAAP | Capital Adequacy Assessment Process |
| CAGR | Compound Annual Growth Rate |
| CBO | Community-based Organizers |
| CBs | Commercial Banks |
| CDF | Cooperative Development Foundation |
| CDP | Community Development Programme |
| CDSL | Central Depository Services (India) Limited |
| CF | Community Facilitator |
| CGAP | Consultative Group to Assist the Poorest |
| CIF | Community Investment Fund |
| CJFS | Cooperative Joint Farming Societies |
| CMG | Credit Management Group |
| CRAFICARD | Committee to Review Arrangements for Agriculture and Rural Development |
| CRI | Critical Rating Index |
| CRAR | Capital to Risk Asset Ratio |
| CRR | Cash Reserve Ratio |
| CSO | Central Statistical Organization |
| CSP | Customer Service Point |
| DCCBs | District Central Cooperative Banks |
| DP | Depository Participant |
| DRDA | District Rural Development Authority |
| DWCRA | Development of Women and Children in Rural Areas |

| | |
|---|---|
| ECA | Eastern Europe and Central Asia |
| EGS | Employment Guarantee Scheme |
| FCRA | Foreign Currency Regulation Act |
| FFW | Food For Work |
| FSS | Farmers' Service Societies |
| GCC | General Purpose Credit Card |
| GNI | Gross National Income |
| GoAP | Government of Andhra Pradesh |
| GOI | Government of India |
| GRT | Group Recognition Test |
| HLA | Housing Loans Activity |
| ICECD | International Centre for Entrepreneurship and Career Development |
| ICRC | Indian Credit Review Committee |
| ICT | Information Communication Technology |
| IFC | International Finance Corporation |
| IFT | Instant Fund Transfer |
| IKP | Indira Kranthi Patham |
| IPCB | Indonesian People's Credit Bank |
| IRDP | Integrated Rural Development Programme |
| ISO-IEC | International Organization for Standardization-International Electro technical Committee |
| JLGs | Joint Liability Groups |
| KCC | Kisan Credit Cards |
| KYC | Know Your Customer |
| LGD | Loss Given Default Model |
| LPG | Liberalization Privatization and Globalization |
| MACS | Mutually Aided Co-operative Societies |

| | |
|---|---|
| MCP | Micro-credit Plan |
| MCO | Micro-credit Organization |
| MCS | Micro-credit Scheme |
| MD | Managing Director |
| MFD | Micro-finance Development –Fund |
| MFIs | Micro-finance Institutions |
| MIS | Management Information System |
| MIX | Micro-finance Information Exchange |
| MNES | Ministry of Non-conventional Energy Sources |
| MMS | Mandal Mahila Samakhya |
| MYRAD A | Mysore Resettlement and Development Agency |
| NABARD | National Bank for Agriculture and Rural Development |
| NBFI | Non-Bank Financial Institutions |
| NGO | Non-Governmental Organization |
| NIRD | National Institute of Rural Development |
| NII | Net Interest Income |
| NISIET | National Institute of Small Industry Extension and Training |
| NPA | Non-Performing Assets |
| NSDL | National Securities Depository Limited |
| ORMC | Operational Risk Management Committee |
| OPS | Other Priority Sector |
| PACS | Primary Agricultural Credit Society |
| PAIS | Personal Accident Insurance Scheme |
| PAR | Portfolio at Risk |
| PIN | Personal Identification Number |
| PLPs | Potential Linked Plans |

| | |
|---|---|
| PMRY | Prime Minister Rozgar Yojana |
| POS | Point of Sale Terminal |
| PRADAN | Professional Assistance for Development Action |
| PRIs | Panchayati Raj Institutions |
| PSBs | Public Sector Banks |
| RBI | Reserve Bank of India |
| RCTP | Rural Credit and Training Programme |
| RFA | Revolving Fund Assistance |
| RIDF | Rural Infrastructure Development Fund |
| RL | Retail Lending |
| RMG | Rythu Mitra Group |
| RMK | Rashtriya Mahila Kosh |
| ROSCA | Rotating Savings and Credit Associations |
| RRBs | Regional Rural Banks |
| SAP | Standard Accounting Package |
| SBDI | Small Development Business Initiative |
| SBL | Self-help group-Bank Linkage |
| SC | Scheduled Caste |
| SC | Solar Cooker |
| SCBs | Scheduled Commercial Banks |
| SERP | Society for Elimination of Rural Poverty |
| SEWA | Self-employed Women's Association |
| SFMC | SIDBI Foundation for Micro-credit |
| SGSY | Swarna-Jayanti Gram Swarjgar Yojana |
| SHGs | Self-help Groups |
| SHPI | Self-help Promoting Institution |
| SIDBI | Small Industries Development Bank of India |

| | |
|---|---|
| SKS | Swayam Krishi Sangam |
| SLBC | State Level Bankers Committee |
| SLR | Statutory Liquidity Ratio |
| SME | Small and Medium Enterprise |
| SMERA | SME Rating Agency of India Ltd. |
| ST | Scheduled Tribe |
| TPA | Third Party Administrator |
| TTDC | Training and Technology Development Centers |
| UNDP | United Nations Development Programme |
| VaR | Value at Risk |
| VO | Village Organization |
| VSS | Vana Samarakshana Samithis |
| ZMS | Zilla Mahila Samaikshya |

# 1

# Introduction and Design of the Study

## Rural Credit System in India

Rural credit has today metamorphosed into a larger animal from what it was a say, in the 1950s, of the hay days of the famous All-India Rural Credit Survey. Rural credit has now acquired new dimensions because of a number of factors. First, the inclusive growth strategy in the real sector embodied in the 11th Five-year Plan (2007-20012) has important implications for rural credit policy. Second, Reserve Bank of India (RBI), on its past, is pursuing vigorously its policy of financial inclusion. Third, recognizing the potential of micro-finance to positively influence the up-liftment of the poor, RBI has been making efforts to create an appropriate environment for its orderly development. Fourth, it has become fashionable to argue, especially by some NGOs involved in micro-finance , that the rural borrower does not mind paying a high rate of interest. What is important is the quantum and timeliness of the credit. This is a dangerous argument. Viability or profitability of an enterprise is as important in the case of rural borrowers as it is for urban borrowers. Financial sector reforms introduced in the 1990s seem to have been designed to pamper the private corporate sector and the net result has been the emergence of an inequitable interest rate structure, biased against agriculture and rural borrowers. RBI's Report on Currency and Finance 2005-06, admits that to compensate for sub-BMPLR lending, other segments are changed higher rates of interest, thus leading to cross subsidization of economically poor borrowers. Correcting this distortion is critical to the success of inclusive growth. Market technology should not be allowed to turn MFIs into glorified money-lenders. It is thus new constellation of factors which would shape the future of rural credit.

The dynamics of the rural economy have resulted in rapid sectoral changes of far-reaching magnitude. The service sector has been growing at a very fast rate and the rural marketing emphasis of MNCs and Indian companies is now paying off. Cable TV and transport operators, hotels and public call booths are all growing in rural areas. The rural-urban divide is slowly crumbling due to the reach of television and increasing mobility of labour, capital, products and also credit for the rural and urban sectors. Commercialization of agriculture with increasing emphasis on cash crops has given way to a new breed of moneylenders in the rural economy. The traders and commission agents are now the major money-lenders in the rural economy with seeds, fertilizer and pesticides being supplied by traders on credit or on deferred payment basis. Commission agents advance money towards purchase of output from farmers and include elements of forward trading. These credit arrangements are all on voluntary basis, as the formal banking system does not readily finance these types of transactions. There is also proliferation of non-banking finance companies providing loan services in rural areas and could be better described as 'blade' companies. Another need of the rural people is consumption credit for meeting urgent religious, so-cial, educational and medical needs and banks do not normally give loans for such purposes. There appears to be a mismatch between the services provided by the formal rural finance sector and the loan requirements of the rural people and hence emerged a parallel credit system to meet the genuine credit needs of rural people.

The All-India Credit Survey Report in 1951-52 advocated the policy of extending formal credit through institutions while viewing local, traditional and informal agencies as usurious. In 1952-87, despite a multi-agency approach, the formal credit institutions have been unable to cover large sections of the rural poor despite massive expansion of the banking network. Efforts were concentrated on developing and strengthening co-operative credit structures. Re-finance was also provided as also financial contributions to cooperative institutions by the Reserve Bank of India (RBI). The State Bank of India (SBI) Act was passed in 1955 for the purpose of extending banking facilities on a large scale, more particularly in rural and semi-urban areas and SBI was an important agency for extending rural credit to supplement that given by cooperative institutions. In 1969 and again in 1980, 14 and six major commercial banks respectively were nationalized with the objective of 'controlling the commanding heights of the economy'. The nationalized banks also became important instruments for advancement of rural banking in addition to cooperatives and SBI. Another step to supplement the efforts of cooperatives and commercial banks was the establishment of 196 RRBs since 1975 in various states with equity participation by Central/State governments and commercial banks. To further supplement the institutional mechanism, 10 Local Area Banks were licensed since 1996-97. There are over 1,05,735 cooperative societies, 12,590 branches of 365 DCCBs, 11,825 rural and 2,153 semi-urban branches, 445 branches in urban/metropolitan areas of 196 RRBs (pre-merger), 20,253 and 12,522 rural and semi-urban branches of 99 commercial banks.

Thus, there are about 1,50,000 retail rural credit outlets for a rural population of 680 million giving a population per credit outlet ratio of 4,155. There is now a reasonably extensive formal banking institution network available and capable of meeting the financial needs of most of the rural population. But over 45 per cent of the members of Primary Agricultural Cooperative Societies (PACS) are not borrowing members and over 65 per cent of the 1,01,245 PACS are dormant or in poor financial health due to insufficient recycling of funds and other weaknesses.

It is a matter of record that failures of the rural credit delivery system have been sought to be addressed by creating yet another set of institutions rather than trying to identify the problems and setting them right. With the financial sector reforms in post-1991 and introduction of prudential norms, the commercial banks are concentrating more on urban areas and on profitability, while RRBs are following the investment route to profitability. All banks are conscious of the need to restrict NPAs but in view of the GOI directive for doubling of agricultural credit by March 2007, all banks were trying their best to meet targets. However, there is a need to strengthen cooperative banks in the country besides redeploying funds in the rural areas, unlike commercial banks and RRBs. The Vaidyanathan Committee Report, 2005 is a step in this direction.

As regards rural credit agencies, the cooperative banks and RRBs are weak due to under-capitalization and high level of NPAs. The cost of financial intermediation of rural financial institutions is high and the interest rates charged on loans by cooperative banks are also high. Also, institutional credit is being cornered by the better-off sections of the rural people and the poorer sections have little or no access to rural credit at regulated rates of interest. The relatively less endowed or backward regions also have less access to institutional credit. In adequate availability of credit, accompanied by cumbersome procedures of loan sanction and documentation, are problems for bank customers, whether in rural or urban areas. The poverty-alleviation and government-sponsored schemes in banks have problems in implementation, with more NPAs than for other schemes. Thus, the rural banking institutions are out of step with the changing rural credit requirements and are unable to come up with systems and credit/savings instruments as required by the rural clientele.

From 1969 various experiences of lending has been witnessed through Government supported schemes like IRDP, Antyodaya etc. The self-help group-bank linkage (SBL) approach has the potential to make a decisive impact on the security and empowerment of the most disadvantaged. The uniqueness of Self-help groups lies in the fact that to a large extent they are self-supporting self-governing organizations, free from bureaucratization and politicization. The process empowers the poor and enables them to control direction of own development by identifying their felt needs.

## Indian Poverty Scenario

The post-economic reform period evidenced both setbacks and progress. Rural income poverty increased from 34 per cent in 1989-90 to 43 per cent in 1992 and then fell to 37 per cent in 1993-94. Urban income poverty went up from 33.4 per cent in 1989-90 to 33.7 per cent in 1992 and declined to 32 per cent in 1993-94. The official estimate of poverty for 1999-2000 was 26.1 per cent, a dramatic decline that led to much debate and analysis. The NSS Survey for 2004 shows poverty at 28.3 per cent in rural areas, 25.7 per cent in urban areas and 27.5 per cent in the country as a whole. In fact, the reduction in poverty is only after the year 2000, before that there had been fluctuations in the levels of poverty in India. Over the period poverty is reduced due to policy decisions of Government of India. Approximately 400 million people consisting of 75 million households are living below or close to the poverty line in India and out of which 60 million are from rural household. Poverty thus in India has predominantly rural in character. While there are several structural dimensions attached to rural poverty, it is generally accepted that it arises due to the lack of capital or surplus. The rural poor lives in perpetuating poverty and is the victims of the "vicious cycle of poverty"

Vicious cycle of poverty

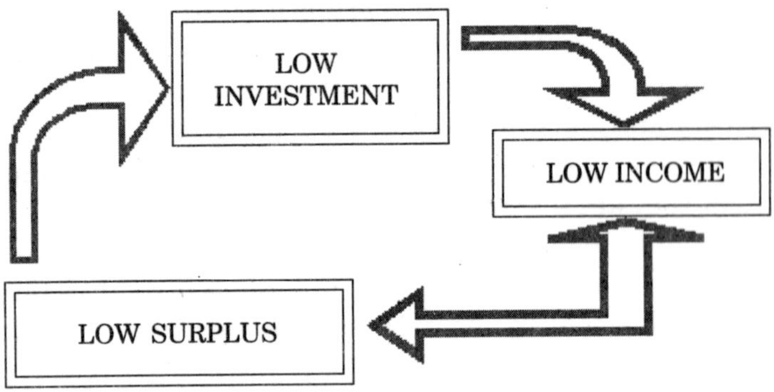


### *Poverty Alleviation Interventions*

The established policy prescription to break the 'cycle of poverty' is through infusion of multiple doses of credit. Hence, credit is a major policy thrust for rural poverty alleviation. Three major components are common in all institutional rural credit system, which remained constant since the 1950s. The Rural Credit Programme has three important components:

1. Institutionalize credit,
2. Enlarge coverage and
3. Provide timely and adequate finance.

Increased involvement of banks in rural credit in post-nationalization era is essentially viewed credit as an integral part of the socio-economic developmental efforts in the rural area and the network of commercial banks were used especially to enlarge coverage. During the period, banking network has reached a spectacular expansion in the rural India. However, the formal financial systems are not been able to benefit more than half of indebted rural households, despite having a vast network of 1,50,000 commercial, co-operative, rural banks and non-banking financial institutions.

After Independence, policy-makers recognized the criticality of people's participation in the development process. To ensure the peoples' participation, the Government intensified banking activities by opening large number of co-operatives in rural areas to provide credit inputs and marketing facilities to farmers. The other attempt made by the Government was setting up and strengthening of Panchayat Raj institutions through 73rd and 74th amendment of the Indian Constitution. However, many of these institutions are being bugged by financial non-viability. Local level politics inconvenienced with bureaucracy saw these institutions relegated to power centers of the local elite.

The picture would not be completed if one does not mention about the largest poverty alleviation programme-Integrated Rural Development Programme (IRDP) in this context. The IRDP was launched in the year 1979-80 with an aim to target group alleviation of poverty in the rural areas. The programme aimed at reaching the people below poverty line in rural areas through subsidized credit for asset creation. Block level governmental machinery played a key role in implementation of this programme to dispense credit through banks. However, it is estimated that only about 20 per cent of the borrowers have crossed the poverty line after assistance. The main causes of failure could be put as:

1. Credit dispensing bodies, in this case the banks did not have any role in identification of activities and borrowers. Partisan local political interests had dominated the process. This patronage led to emergence of middlemen at all levels.
2. In this permissive atmosphere, it is no wonder that repayment ethics goes for a toss.
3. By the time joint identification committees were set up, the bankers lost interest in the programme. With the introduction of prudential norms of asset classification since the early 1990s, bankers started citing the default as the major reasons of non-adherence to implementation target of the programme (it is a different matter that a recent study published in the Journal of Rural Development, April-June 1999, has put a very insignificant correlation between poor recovery performance of banks and their exposure IRDP and weaker section loans).
4. Opportunity cost of foregone wage because of the repeated visits to government officers and the bankers neutralizes the cheap credit and capital subsidy. According to a World Bank study on transaction costs in availing a loan of average size of Rs 7000, the poor borrowers incur about 18.9 per cent towards informal expenses and wage loss.

Even after considering all the small loans of the banking system, the situation is still in the nascent stage of access to credit by the people. Small loans account for nearly 93.6 per cent (0.56 million accounts in 1994) of total number of loans and 18 per cent of the total amount. Of these, 80.5 per cent of the total accounts loan is loan outstanding less than Rs. 7,500. Purpose wise, small agricultural loans accounted for 45.8 per cent, tiny manufacturing 20.2 per cent. By 1998, the total number of small borrowers is 50 million households.

The micro loans cover 40 million households in 2000 (assuming per centage of micro loans below 7500 remaining constant). The remaining 35 million households are perhaps meeting their credit needs from informal sector-landlords, moneylenders, pawnbrokers, traders, relatives etc. Apart from a large unreached people, it implies a process failure and as a result the institutions failed to address issues on distributional social justice.

## Emergence of Micro–finance Institutions

The mechanism of directing credit to the poor through sponsored programmes has suffered from poor recovery rates that had made an adverse impact on the recycling of credit. Also, there has been a mismatch between what the poor people needed, particularly in terms of products and product delivery mechanisms and what conventional financial institutions could offer. Micro-finance Institutions (MFIs) have emerged to fill the gap.

MFIs can be broadly defined as institutions other than banks that are engaged in provision of financial services to the poor. The term "micro" literally means "small". But, the task force has not defined any amount as a ceiling. However, as per the micro-credit special cell of RBI, the borrowal accounts up to a limit of Rs. 25,000 could be considered as micro-credit products and this amount could be gradually increased up to Rs. 50,000 over a period of time. Micro-finance refers to the entire range of financial services such as savings money transfers, insurance, production and investment credit as also housing finance and includes the need for skill up gradation and entrepreneurial development that would enable them to overcome poverty. Micro-finance provides credit support in small doses along with training and other related services to people who are poor but and are able to undertake economic activities.

### *From Micro-credit to Micro-finance*

Micro-finance is being practised as a tool to alleviate poverty through out the world. Since alleviation of poverty is one of the primary objectives of economic planning of any country, it becomes imperative to formulate situation specific poverty alleviation policies and programmes for generation of a minimum level of income for the rural poor. One such initiative is credit infusion in the rural sector. Micro-finance rests on the following principles:

1. Self/employment/enterprise formation is a viable means for poverty alleviation.
2. Access to capital assets/ credit is a constraint for existing and potential micro enterprises.
3. The poor are able to save despite their low and sporadic incomes.

In India, at the end of the Ninth Five-year Plan, 26 per cent of the population was living below the poverty line. The overall unemployment rate was estimated to be 7.32 per cent. The female unemployment rate was 8.5 per cent. The rate of growth of women unemployment in the rural area was 9.8 per cent. This is because of the low growth rate of new and productive employment. The Draft Approach Paper to the Tenth Five-year Plan (2002-07) suggested the adoption of a "monitorable target" relating to the reduction of poverty ratio. It has indicated a target of reducing the poverty ratio to 20 per cent by 2007 and 10 per cent by 2012. Therefore, the Union Government has implemented various schemes to reduce poverty and to promote gainful employment. But the most attractive scheme with less effort (finance) is the "Self-help group" which is a tool to remove poverty and improved rural development.

India's share in the global micro-credit market in 2006 was 13 per cent of all clients and 16 per cent of the poorest clients. NABARD has an ambitious plan of covering 100 million poor through the SHGs by 2008. The Economic and Social Council of the United Nations Proclaimed the year 2005 as the International Year of Micro-credit. In the literature on the subject, the terms micro-finance , micro-credit, micro-enterprises are inter-changeably used which differentiate each other. The term micro-finance is used in its broadest sense.

In fact, lack of finance is seen as a crucial impediment to the transaction from micro to small enterprises and from informal to formal sector. Exceptions to the primacy of credit are found in extremely backward areas or economics which are not integrated into the market economy. Where the degree of magnetization is very low and where demand is severally depressed. However, while micro-credit refers to purvey of loans in small quantities, the term micro-finance has a broader meaning covering in its ambit other financial services like saving, insurance, etc. as well.

### *Towards an Operational Definition of Micro-finance*

Attempts to formally define micro-credit/micro-finance programmes usually refer to the objective of such programmes viz., reaching the poor with small amounts of credit and other micro financial services so as to promote income generating activities. The declaration of the Micro-credit Summit held in Washington, D.C. in 1997 defined micro-credit programmes as those that "extend small loans to poor people for self-employment projects that generate income, allowing them to care for themselves and their families" (Micro-credit Summit 1997). The Task Force on micro-finance established by NABARD defines micro-finance as the "Provision of thrift, credit and other financial services and products of very small amounts to the poor in rural, semi-urban or urban areas for enabling them to raise their income levels and improve living standards" (NABARD 1999).

The range of services is expanded in the Asian Development Bank's (ADB) definition which defines micro-finance as the provision of a broad range of services such as deposits, loans, payment services, money transfers and insurance to poor and low income households and their micro-enterprises (ADB 2000). Micro-finance , by definition, refers to the entire range of financial and non-financial services, including skill upgradation and entrepreneurial development, rendered to the poor for enabling them to overcome poverty.

***Beginning of Micro-finance System***

The origin of micro-finance could be traced back to the beginning of the co-operative movement in Germany, where the movement was started in 1944 in the field of cooperation-based credit system by the Raiffeisen Societies as well as Rochdale Pioneers in England. Similarly, the enactment of the Cooperative Credit Societies Act, 1904, could be considered as the beginning of micro-finance in India. The syndicate bank, started in 1921, concentrated on raising micro-deposits in the form of daily /weekly savings and also sanctioned micro-loans for its constituents. The formation of long term co-operative credit institutions to meet investment needs of farmers started in 1928. The concern for the weaker sections of the society by providing access to credit was first expressed by the All-India Credit Review Committee (1966) by making categorical pronouncement that the credit must be made more accessible to small farmers.

After the failure of the multiplicity of development programmes in India in rural areas to focus on the core issue of poverty alleviation through creation of sustainable income generating opportunities, and on the recommendations of the Hashim Committee, the Government of India, therefore, restructured all the poverty alleviation programmes under one-umbrella scheme "Swarna-Jayanti Gram Swarojgar

Yojana (SGSY)" from April 1999. The focus of scheme, among other things, is on group approach and organizing the poor into SHGs.

Experiences of different anti-poverty and other welfare programmes implemented throughout the world have shown that the key to their success - lies in the evolution and participation of community-based organizations at the grassroots level. People's participation in credit delivery and recovery and linking of formal credit institutions to borrowers through intermediaries of SHGs have been recognized as a supplementary mechanism for providing credit support to the rural poor. NABARD is a pioneer in conceptualization and implementation of the concept of SHG through the SHG-bank linkage programme since 1992. The concept of micro-finance was first developed by Mohammad Yunus - the Noble Prize winner and a U.S.-educated professor of economics from Chittagong University Bangladesh.

### *Micro-finance and Global Poverty Agenda*

#### *World Bank Group Operations*

During 1990s the World Bank and International Development Association (IDA) financed some 185 projects or components involving micro and rural finance and 96 in small enterprise development, and 55 of these projects included both aspects. While rural development had the largest share of these projects, they were spread across a wide range of sectors, including social, financial urban and public sector management. Many of these included a focus on improving the policy, regulatory and institutional environment for private business, including small enterprises.

#### *CGAP*

The establishment of the Consultative Group to Assist the Poorest [CGAP] in 1995 as a multi-donor consortium by nine founding members, including the World Bank, with the mandate of providing financial and technical support to micro-credit programmes world-wide. It is a reflection of the massive global drive behind the micro-credit movement. In the context of designing programmes for the poor, micro-finance is recognized and accepted as tone of the new development paradigms for alleviating poverty through social and economic empowerment of the poor, with special emphasis on empowering women. The concept of micro-finance essentially rests on the premise that:

(a) Self-employment/enterprise formation is a viable alternative means of alleviating poverty

(b) lack of access to capital assets / credit acts as a constraint on existing and potential micro enterprises; and

(c) They are capable of saving despite their low levels of income.

*SBDI*

The new Small Business Development Initiative (SBDI) brought the expertise of the World Bank and the International Finance Corporation (IFC) together to operationalize best practices in small business development, in partnership with other stake holders. The key areas of focus included: the policy and business enabling environment; business development services; financial services; private participation in municipal services; and internet services for SMEs. A survey of regional conferences on business development services for small enterprise supported by the Donor Committee for Small Enterprise Development brought together knowledge on supporting the private sector's provision of small business development services. An objective of the SBDI is to translate this emerging consensus into sustainable interventions and policies, leveraging its impact and quality by partnering with other organizations supporting small enterprise development.

### *Micro-credit Summit*

The Micro-credit Summit was hosted by the Government of Bangladesh, sponsored by the World Bank and other organizations and attended by over 2600 delegates in February 1997 in Washington, D.C, USA, which was considered the first step of a decade-long campaign that sought to ensure delivery of credit for self-employment by 2005 to 100 million of the world's poorest families especially women of the families. The global consensus around micro-credit as a key element of poverty alleviation strategies was evident at the micro-credit summit, which enjoyed the support and patronage of the World Bank, private commercial banks and hundreds of leading NGOs across the globe. The summit discussed the concepts relating to micro- credit. They are:

i. The poor are as good a credit risk as anyone else.

ii. International and national financial institutions should specifically plan for micro-credit.

iii. High repayment is a sign of a well-run micro-credit programme

iv. Beneficiary participation is required to manage micro-credit programmes.

v. Training of staff and beneficiaries is an important factor in successful micro-credit enterprises.

The summit did advocate a networking of NGOs and SHGs federating at appropriate levels and building cross-cultural network, transcending international boundaries. If these micro-credit activities grow into a well coordinated movement, they will have to be integrated with the formal credit structure, in view of the volume of funds required in developing countries. There is no need to build separate structures if the process of bank linkage is coordinated with that of SHG formation.

### *Future Micro-finance Needs*

According to World Bank Estimate, 1995, in most developing countries the formal financial system reaches only the top 25 per cent of the economically active population, leaving bottom 75 per cent with no access to financial services apart from money lenders. In India too, the formal financial institutions have not been able to reach the poor households, particularly women in the unorganized sector. Structural rigidities and overheads lead to high cost of making small loans. Organizational philosophy has not been oriented towards recognizing the poor as credit worthy. The problem has been compounded by low level of influence of the poor either about their credit worthiness or their demand for savings and services. Micro-finance programmes have been implemented by large banks on behalf of the Government.

#### *Empowerment of Women*

Women empowerment is a process, which enables women to have access and control over various factors necessary for their economic independence, political participation and social development. Empowerment of women may normally mean equal access to and control over important productive resources. Women empowerment, therefore, may normally be described as a process by which women would be able to develop their confidence level and increase their inner strength and self-reliance to decide and determine their important choices in life.

The concept of empowerment has been the subject of much intellectual discourse and analysis. Empowerment is defined as the process by which women can take control and ownership of their lives through expansion of their choices. Thus, it is the process of acquiring the ability to make strategic life choices in a context where this ability has previously been denied. The core elements of empowerment have been defined as agency, awareness of gendered power structure, self-esteem and self-confidence.

### Women Empowerment Through Self-help-Groups

The normative structure of Indian society, it cultural ethos, the social taboos and the prevailing stereotype have prevented women from taking equal part in social and economic life. Further women have no control over resources and have no equal property rights over family properties on par with men and hence, there is a male domination. However the most of the women are contributing to their family income by participating in activities like agriculture and allied sectors, business, small industries, crafts, services and many other callings.

The government has passed several acts to protect women and provide reservations in almost in every field of activity to elevate the status of women. Indian's country paper of Beijing called taking counter measures against marginalization of women in the race towards free market economy by expanding social safety needs, gender orientation of social attitude, calling for affirmative discrimination in favour of women. It says there is a need for their empowerment both political and economic. Despite the improvement in health, education, and employment, the paper noted with concern that women still comprise the largest section of population living in absolute poverty.

## *Indian Micro-finance Providers*

### Formal and Informal Sectors in Rural Credit

In the midst of the apparent inadequacies of the formal financial system to cater the financial needs of the rural poor, NABARD sponsored an action Research Project in 1987 through an NGO called MYRADA. For this purpose a grant of Rs. 1 million was provided to MYRADA for an R&D programme related to credit groups. Encouraged the results of field level experiments in group-based approach for lending to the poor, NABARD launched a pilot project in 1991-92 in partnership with non-governmental organizations (NGOs) for promoting and grooming self help groups (SHGs) of homogeneous members and keeping savings with existing banks and within the existing legal framework. Steady progress of the pilot project led to the mainstreaming of the SHG-bank linkage programme in 1996 as a normal banking activity of banks with widespread acceptance. The RBI set right the policy environment by allowing savings bank accounts of informal groups to be opened by the formal banking system. Launched at a time when regulated interest rates were in vogue, the banks were expected to lend to SHGs at prescribed rates, but the RBI advised the banks not to interfere with the management of affairs of SHGs, particularly the terms and conditions at which SHGs disbursed loans to their members. As at the end of March 2006, over 2.24 million SHGs comprising about 32.98 million rural poor, 90 per cent of them women, were accessing financial services in the form of savings and credit from 44,362 bank branches of the formal financial sector in different parts of the country. These 32.98 million rural poor have received loans aggregating Rs 113.98 billion, through SHGs.

The uniqueness of micro-finance through SHGs is that it is a partnership-based approach and has encouraged NGOs to undertake not only social engineering but also financial intermediation, especially in areas where the banking network was inadequate. The rapid progress achieved in SHG formation, which has now turned into an empowerment movement for women across the country laid the foundation for emergence of MFIs, in India. Micro-finance Institutions can be broadly subdivided to four categories of organizational forms viz., NGO-MFIs, Non profit NBFC-MFIs. While there is no published data on private MFIs operating in the country, the number of MFIs is estimated to be around 800. However, not more than 10 MFIs are reported to have an outreach of 100,000 micro-finance clients.

It is estimated that there are around 1600 private MFls operating in the country as at the end of 2007 with varied legal forms. While most are registered under Societies Registration Act, some are functioning as non-bank financial companies. Micro-finance has emerged as an important sector in many countries for providing financial services such as savings, credit, insurance and remittance services to the poor. Micro-finance has become a global phenomenon. Governments, central banks, donors, practitioners, and other development agencies promoting micro-finance are increasingly involved in developing suitable policy initiatives for meeting local needs. In India, a range of institutions offers micro-finance services. These can be broadly categorized into two categories namely, formal institutions, semi-formal and non-formal institutions. The former category comprises apex development financial institutions such as NABARD, SIDBI, commercial banks, Regional Rural Banks (RRBs), and Co-operative Banks (CBs) that provide micro-finance services in addition to their general banking activities and are reoffered to micro-finance providers.

### Micro-finance Service Providers

The micro-finance service providers include apex institutions like National Bank for Agriculture and Rural Development (NABARD), Small Industries Development Bank of India (SIDBI), and Rashtriya Mahila Kosh (RMK) etc. At the retail level, commercial banks, regional rural banks, and co-operative banks provide micro-finance services.

#### *Apex Level Institutions*

##### NABARD

In 1979 the RBI, at the instance of the Government of India, constituted a Committee to Review Arrangements for Agriculture and Rural Development [CRAFICARD] under the Chairmanship of Shri B. Sivaraman. Stressing on the need to provide the rural poor with access to institutional credit, the committee in its report stated the lack of assets coupled with lending policies based on assets leads to reduced opportunities of the rural poor to avail credit facilities for improving their incomes. NABARD was founded in June 1982 on the recommendations of the committee for providing undivided attention, forceful direction and pointed focus to the credit problems arising out of integrated rural development. Since its inception in 1982, National Bank's efforts have been directed towards extending the coverage of weaker sections in other sub-sectors of the rural economy.

NABARD's involvement in promoting micro-finance through the concept of SHGs started in 1987 with, a sanction of Rs. 10 lakh as grant assistance from its R&D fund to MYRADA for providing seed money to the credit management groups (CMGs) promoted by it. The objective of providing grant assistance was to facilitate building up a thrift fund and aiding the members of the CMGs with margin money to borrow from the formal credit system.

The success of this experiment was the precursor to the launching of the pilot project in 1992 for linking 500 SHGs with banks. NABARD is providing refinance at 7.5 per cent to the banks for micro-finance lending. The linkage programme promoted by NABARD is unique as it facilitates "relationship banking" as compared to "parallel banking" practiced in other countries. Under the "relationship banking", improvements in the existing relationship between the poor and the banks are attempted with intermediation by NGOs, who either play the role of promoters of SHGs or financial intermediaries. A separate fund for promotion and development of micro-finance sector in India was established by NABARD in April 2000 with a start-up contribution of Rs.1,000 million. NABARD contributions Rs.400 million, Reserve Bank of India Rs.400 million; and 11 public sector commercial banks Rs.200 million NABARD has further contributed Rs.149 million from its operational surpluses during the last four years to the corpus.

*SIDBI*

The Small Industrial Development Bank of India (SIDBI) was established in 1990 to serve as the principal financial institution for promotion and development of industry in the small scale sector as well as to co-ordinate the functions of other institutions engaged in these aspects in the sector. The bank launched the micro-credit scheme (MCS) in 1994 for extending financial assistance to the rural poor, particularly women, through NGOs for taking up income generating activities at the micro-level.

The scheme envisages provision of soft loan assistance at nine per cent per annum to accredited NGOs for on-lending to the poor women (SHGs/individuals), an amount not exceeding Rs.25, 000 per borrower for promoting micro-enterprises. A salient feature of the scheme is the grant assistance extended by the bank for developing the capacity of the NGOs to run credit programme efficiently and to enhance the credit absorption capacity of the borrowers.

SIDBI in January 1999 launched SIDBI Foundation for Micro-credit (SFMC), a specialized department for micro-credit, with a mission to create a national network of strong, viable and sustainable micro-finance institutions to provide micro-finance services to the poor, especially women. Under its micro-credit scheme the banks have so far sanctioned assistance of over Rs.19,000 crore covering about 21 lakh poor, mainly women.

SIDBI has been making investments in improving the credit absorption and usage capacity of the women's groups and credit delivery skills of the functionaries of MFls /NGOs for training interventions in the area of maintenance of accounts, book-keeping, credit management, identification and selection of income generating activities and management of micro-enterprises. The bank has been supporting orientation programmes for NGOs desirous of undertaking thrift-cum-credit activities. These programmes are being conducted through NGOs and professional institutions having ample exposure/experience in the areas of managing micro-credit programmes.

*Rashtriya Mahila Kosh (RMK)*

The Rasthriya Mahila Kosh (RMK) scheme aims at economic empowerment of poor women by meeting their credit requirements. The economically disadvantaged and illiterate women find it difficult to borrow even small sums of money for their economic activities. Most of their borrowings are met through private money-lenders at exorbitant rates of interest. Keeping in view the shortage of micro-credit facility for poor women and to utilize the income generation skills of millions of such women in the country, the government of India established the RMK (National Credit Fund Women) with a corpus of Rs.31 crore in March, 1993 and is registered as society under the Societies Registration Act, 1860.

*Private Micro-finance Institutions*

The micro-finance Institutions in the private sector can be traced to the initiative undertaken by Ela Bhatt for providing banking services to the poor women employed in the unorganized sector in Ahmedabad and Gujarat. Shri Matula SEWA (Self-employed Women Association) Sahakari Bank was set up in 1974 by registering it as an urban co-operative bank. Since then the bank has been providing services to the poor self employed women working as hawkers, vendors, domestic servants, and so on.

*SEWA*

Self-employed Women's Association (SEWA) established in December 1971, was registered as a trade union in April,

1972. In 1974, the Shri Mahila Sewa Sahakari Bank Ltd., was established by 4,000 members of SEWA, with the specific objective of providing credit to self-employed women so as to empower them and reduce their dependence on money sharks. The intervention methodologies of SEWA interalia in micro-finance include: (a) providing facilities for savings and fixed deposit accounts; and (b) providing credit for income generating activities of poor self-employed women and helping in creating assets of their own.

*MYRADA*

The Mysore Resettlement and Development Agency (MYRADA) an NGO based in Bangalore, was established in 1968 to facilitate the resettlement of Tibetan refugees. Since 1978-79, the NGO has been involved in programmes for the rural poor, whom it defines as "Those who depend on others for basic needs".

Alternative credit system experiment in mid 1980s was geared to achieving a change in banking policy that would enable the banks to relate directly with the credit groups as "bankable institutions". The affinity group strategy of credit management based on group of 15-20 members is an alternative strategy for credit, which is not part of the official delivery system. It is also a decentralized model where decisions are taken at the group level; it is based on alternate institutions, which are free to operate according to their own rules and regulations. MYRADA is a successful NGO in group-based lending programmes.

*BASIX*

BASIX was set up in 1996 by a group of companies as a holding company, which is a non-banking financial company, not for Profit and Local Area Bank. Its mission is to promote a large number of sustainable livelihoods, including for the rural poor and women, through the provision of financial services and technical assistance in an integrated manner. The company also strives to yield a competitive rate of return to its investors so as to enable them to access mainstream capital markets and human resources on a continuous basis. BASIX now has financial operations in 2,200 villages in 18 districts across the states in India.

*SHARE*

SHARE, a micro-finance institution registered as a society in the year 1989 operates with 12 branches in five districts in 502 villages of Andhra Pradesh. It provides financial and support services to the very poor rural women whose per capita income is less than Rs. 250 per month and asset holdings less than Rs. 20,000. A maximum loan amount of Rs. 25,000 is lent at interest rate of 15 per cent on a flat rate basis to an individual.

*Micro-finance Retail Level Institutions*

At the retail level commercial banks, Regional Rural Banks, and Co-operative banks provide micro-finance services. Today there are about 60,000 retail credit outlets of the formal banking sector in the rural areas comprising of 12,000 branches of district level co-operative banks, over 14,000 branches of the Regional Rural banks (RRBs) and over 30,000 rural and semi-urban branches of commercial banks besides over 90,000 co-operative credit societies at the village level. On an average there is at least one retail credit outlet for about 5,000 rural people. This physical reaching out to the far flung areas of the country to provide savings, credit and other banking services to rural society in general is an important unparalleled achievement of the banking system.

## Micro-finance Delivery Models in India

India has been a fertile breeding ground for a large number of models of micro-finance , of which SHG has become hugely popular. In fact, it can be said that India hosts the maximum number of micro-finance models, both in indigenous practices as well as in modern micro-finance . The models range from pure 'home-spun' varieties like the SHGs and co-operatives to the 'adapted' models like the Grameen methodology and for profit corporate models.

Various traditional as well as innovative approaches have been adopted for increasing the credit flow to the unorganized sector. Despite a few disadvantages, the perceived advantages of SHGs have far outweighed its disadvantages and have made the SHG as a popular model for micro-finance in India. So much so that even the Government programmes have SHGs at the core of their strategy. Undoubtedly, the SHG model has emerged as the 'Indian' model of micro-finance . Micro-finance Institutions (NGO-MFIs, Mutual Benefit MFIs and For-Profit MFIs) in India have adopted various traditional as well as innovative approaches for increasing the credit flow to the unorganized sector. The above-mentioned Micro-finance Institutions in India can be re-categorized as:

1) Not-for Profit MFIs: Charitable Society, Trust and Section 25 Companies.
2) Mutual Benefit MFIs: State Cooperatives, National Cooperatives and Mutually Aided Cooperative Societies (MACS);
3) For-Profit MFIs: Non Banking Financial Companies, and
4) Banks.

***Self-help Group (SHG) Model***

SHG has emerged as the "Indian" model of Micro-finance . The SHG model has evolved in the NGO Sector. NGOs primarily have the functions of enabling, educating and networking. This model has emerged as the capacity building of community based institutions. SHGs are small and informal groups having homogeneous socio-economic background. Groups are composed either by male only or by female only. In India 90 per cent of the SHGs are composed of female only. Group members are self-selected. NGO acts as a facilitating agency to build in processes and systems that make the SHGs viable and sustainable institutions. The group members meet regularly at an appointed time and place for carrying out their savings and credit activities and other issues of development. The group mobilizes savings among the members and issues need based loans to the members (only) out of the common funds created. The rules and norms are determined by members themselves and the NGO does not interfere in this matter. After the SHG has been put on the path to sustainability, organizationally and financially, the NGO may decide to withdraw from supporting the SHG and move on to new groups. The main motive of the SHG is to empower poor socio-economically and improve their livelihood pattern.

### *Federated Self Help Group Model (FSHG)*

Federations of SHGs bring together several SHGs. In India FSHGs include those promoted by the Dhan Foundation, PRADAN, Chaitanya and SEWA are famous in India.

Federations usually come under the Societies Registration Act. They have between 1000-3000 members. There is a distinct three-tier structure in federations – the SHG is the basic unit; the cluster is the intermediate unit and an apex body or a federation, represents the entire membership. Each SHG participates directly in the representative body at the cluster level. Two members from each SHG attend the monthly cluster meetings. Information from the groups to the apex body and *vice-versa* is channelled through the cluster level representative body. The cluster leaders are a highly effective part for group monitoring and strengthening. So the operations of the apex body are decentralized through the clusters. The executive body at the apex level is consists of 9 to 15 members. Three common financial activities of Federations are: -

a) Acting as an agent and manager of external credit funds.

b) Assisting SHGs with loan recovery in difficult cases.

c) Strengthening weak SHGs, so that they are able to carry out their savings and credit function smoothly.

***Grameen Bank Model***

The Grameen Bank Model of Bangladesh, developed by Muhammad Yunus, its former chairman was considered as the pioneer micro-finance institution. It has been highly successful in its banking service to the poor as well as in its poverty alleviation programmes. With its well-recognised success, many organizations in India, like SHARE , Microfin Ltd, Activities for Social Alternative (ASA) and CASHPOR Financial and Technical Services Ltd. have adopted this methodology with little variations. The model has the following features;

- ☑ Homogeneous groups of five members are formed at the village level.
- ☑ The field worker of the Grameen Bank facilitates the process of group formation.
- ☑ All the group members undergo a 7-day compulsory training of 1-2 hours per day. Some groups under go the Group Recognition Test (GRT). It is a screening test that can distinguish between serious and non-serious groups. Actually it is an effective tool to overcome the adverse selection problem.

- ☑ Once the preliminary groups have passed GRT, and then the women become members of Grameen Bank by paying a one-time member fee.
- ☑ Eight joint liable groups affiliate together to form a center. Every weak Centre meets at a defined time. Bank Assistant attends the meeting and it is mandatory for the members to attend the weakly meeting and all the loan applications have to be approved by other group members as well as Centre members. The loan is disbursed from the bank fund and it is not linked with the group savings. Loan is given to the individual not to the group or the centre.
- ☑ The loan disbursement is always done in the Centre. The housing loans are disbursed at the Branch to maintain documentation.
- ☑ Various loans are provided by the Grameen Bank such as General Loans, Supplementary Loans, Special General Loans, Sanitation and Housing Loans etc. The size of loan ranges from Rs. 4,000 to Rs. 10,000 for general yearly loans. The first loan is Rs.4,000 and there is an annual increase of Rs.1, 000 in loan size in each year there after.
- ☑ Every members save compulsorily Tk.10 per weak. This saving is deposited with Bank. The bank funds their consumption needs with this deposit. This strategy overcomes the problem of default as it is proved that nobody is likely to default on his or her own money.

***The Co-operative Model***

The leading organization that has been successful in using the co-operative form in rural micro-finance in India has been the Cooperative Development Forum (CDF), Hyderabad. It has built up a network of financial co-operatives based upon women's and men's thrift groups. It has registered under the New Generation Cooperatives Act, 1995.

The dynamics of Co-operative Model includes:

(1) The primary entities of CDF's Micro-finance Cooperative are the Women's / Men's Thrift Cooperative (W (M) TC). Each consists of 300 members. Generally these members reside in the same village.

(2) CDF has started to promote much smaller units and now it has encouraged these units to extend into large unit.

(3) The important factors behind the running of a successful cooperative venture are: a) to justify human resources (staffs); b) to meet statutory / administrative requirements such as audit.

(4) The WTC or MTC are divided into small groups (10 to 50 members) to facilitate better monitoring of thrift and repayment of loans.

(5) The group members nominate a group leader and the leader enjoys the confidence of the group.

(6) CDF encouraged members to identify more strongly with their WTC/MTC rather than with the groups, as WTC/MTC are the primary legal entities and viable units of operation.

(7) Most of the WTC/MTCs decided to register themselves under the New Generation Cooperative Act, which allows for greater flexibility and autonomy in operations.

(8) The General Body constitutes of all the members of the primary cooperatives. It adopts a uniform set of bylaws. The General Body meets once in a year to elect the directors, review and discuss the other issues. The

Board of Directors consists of 12 directors who are elected by the members. Each director is elected for three-year term. The retired directors are eligible for re-election. The directors elect a chairperson and appoint a managing director (MD) among themselves. Chairperson and MD have a one-year term. They are also eligible for re-election. The Chairperson presides the board meetings. He/She represents the cooperatives in other organizations (forums) and ensures that they function in accordance with the Cooperative principles and by-laws. The MD is responsible for ensuring that the operations of Cooperative are properly conducted and that the resolutions of the board are implemented.

(9) A set of geographically contiguous cooperatives forms an Association of WTC/MTCs. The Chairperson and MD of each participating Cooperative are members of the General Body of the Association.

(10) General Body elects a Chairperson and MD to oversee the affairs and

(11) The Association provides training, management of the Loan Insurance Fund and inter-lending. It also plays a support role by helping the member cooperatives in handling accounting, auditing and other administrative matters.

## Review of Research on Micro-finance

The strategies of development bringing credit to the central stage widely employed as a means of accelerating the rate of growth and improving the income generating, social and financial empowerment, and poverty alleviation have undergone a metamorphosis in recent times. The literature on self-help groups (SHGs) is somewhat limited as it is of a recent phenomenon. Such studies tend to focus mostly upon the quantitative dimensions of different types of self-help groups. Some studies have examined the economic aspects of the groups functioning, while some others discuss the psycho-social aspects, in particular the "group dynamics". - The review of literature undertaken is given briefly as under.

A study group of the Government of India (1962) recommended the rationally desirable minimum level of consumer expenditure of Rs. 20 per capita per month at 1960-61 prices. This recommended figure was criticized on the ground that it was an underestimation as it excises the expenditure on he it and education assuming that they are provided free most by the state according constitution.

Chatterjee and others (1963) in their paper "A preliminary study on the Dietary Levels of Households in Rural India" found that about 53 per cent of the rural population fall below the norm of 2400 calories per capita per day. He uses NSS consumption data which does not take into account the non-food expenditure. Thus they have under –estimated the extent of rural poverty in India.

Mukherjee (1969), in his study "Size and Areal Distribution of Level of Living in India" with a different methodology and considering the country's population as a whole (without any bifurcation of rural and urban) has arrived at the conclusion that in terms of the density of the poor, Orissa, Kerala, Bihar, Mysore and Andhra Pradesh are poorest States in 1963-64. But he did not consider the price-variation, type, nature and intensity of activities, cropping pattern and climate factors in different regions of the country. He has used uniform measure for all regions to measure poverty.

Minhas (1970) slightly modified the study groups figure as Rs. 200 per capita per annum relating to rural areas on the ground that urban cost of living tends to be some what higher at 1960-61 prices. Using the norm, he found that between 1956-57 and 1967-68, the rural poor declined by 19 million though the number of poor tends to rise in bad harvest years. Minhas was also subject to criticism by the study groups as he failed to take into consideration the expenditure on clothing, fuel, light, health, education, etc.

Ojha (1970), adopting a different methodology, estimated the poor both in rural and urban areas for two different years. Using caloric – norm of 2250 per capita per day for an average Indian he worked out the minimum required food consumption as 518 grams for rural areas and 432 grams for urban areas. According to his estimates 51.8 per cent of the rural population and 7.6 per cent of urban people fell below poverty line. For the year 1967-68, he concluded that 70 per cent of the rural populations were below the minimum level of food grains consumption. Ojha too has excluded the expenditure on health, education and housing.

Bardhan (1970) used minimum level of income (i.e. Rs. 15 per capita for rural and Rs. 21 per capita for urban areas) as norm and examined the trend of rural poverty over the years 1960-61 to 1968-69. Bardhan estimated that of the total population38 per cent in rural areas and 44 per cent in urban areas during the year 1960-61 at same year prices fell below poverty line. During 1968-69 at 1960-61 prices Bardhan estimated that 54 per cent of the rural population and 41 per cent of the urban population fell below poverty line. Bardhan found that the rural poor have increased at a staggering rate (i.e. by 95 million 1960-61 and 1968-69).

Martin Rein (1970) regarded poverty as subsistence, inequality and externality. Most economically backward people who are unable to maintain the minimum level of sustained, other words; the poor are incapable to maintain a defined level of consumption income at that particular time. The main idea of defining poor or distinguishing between poor and non-poor is to analyze the socio-economic aspect of poverty. The line of draw between poor and non-poor is called poverty line.

Dandekar and Rath (1971) emphasized that poverty is a problem of low national income and its unequal distribution, of the slow pace of development and inequitable distribution of the small gains of development. They used estimates of consumption expenditure and adopted a nutritional norm to define the poverty line.

Vyas (1972) observed that proportion of rural poor fell from 45 per cent in 1954-55 to 38 per cent 1960-61, though there was to agricultural growth and no sectoral changes.

Panikar (1972) in his study of Kerala, without mentioning the figures, examined the reliability of minimum consumer expenditure norm at Dandekar and Rath under Kerala's conditions. His basic conclusions are that by ignoring regional factors, they reached wrong conclusions about the cost of nutritionally adequate diet in Kerala. By using national-minimum norm Dandekar and Rath have over estimated the number of the poor in Kerala. It id found that the diet for Kerala to attain minimum norm at 1970-71 prices would cost Rs. 28.30 per head per month and the total per capita consumption expenditure corresponding to his diet would be Rs. 37.80.

Vidyanathan (1974) in his paper "some Aspects of Inequality in Living Standards in Rural India", by using Rs.21.44 as average per capita consumption per month at 1960-61 prices, found that about 15.65 per cent were living in poverty. With regard to trend, based on NSS data, he observed that rural poverty had gone up from 59.5 per cent in 1960-61 to 67.9 per cent in 1967-68.

Bhatty (1974) estimated the poverty levels for different categories different income levels for 1968-69 by using the techniques of Sen's poverty India and head count ratio. He observed that incidence of poverty was maximum amount agricultural labourers category (89.56%) followed by non-agricultural workers (78.77%) and cultivators (70.28%).

USAID (1972) and the World Bank (1974-75) revealed that the design and implementation of rural credit programmes were very complex and that traditional models were irrelevant. Rural credit is but one of the many inputs necessary for rural regeneration and if it is to be effective, it has to be supported by improved technology, infrastructure, inputs, extension services and markets, i.e., the economic opportunities associated with rural credit. The viability of rural credit agencies could be eroded by interest rates, high administrative costs associated with small loans and shoddy banking practices inappropriate to the needs of small farmers. It must be remembered that the factors that have retarded agricultural development (economic. Social, political etc.) also hinder the development of credit institutions which serve the rural poor.

The growth of non-governmental organizations (NGOs) has assumed gigantic proportions all over the world. Their importance in the development panorama is almost crucial today. The preference shown by many developed countries to NGOs for developmental activities amply testifies this. On the other hand, the spirit of voluntarism is gradually dying out in the social services sector and is replaced by a new breed of professionals who approach the question of development with a completely new perspective.

Planning Commission (1977-78) in its draft plan estimated that 48 per cent of the rural population and 41 per cent of the urban population in India fell below poverty line.

Ahluwalia (1978), in his using the norm of the per capita consumer expenditure of Rs. 15 per month at 1960-61 prices for both country as a whole and different states examined the trends in the incidence of rural poverty for about two decades from 1956-57 to 1973-74. He concluded that the time trend is insignificant but the series shows that the incidence of poverty fluctuates in response to variations in real agricultural output per head. He found that there is an inverse relationship between rural poverty and agricultural performance for the country as whole. The same trend was also noticed in several individual states. There was also evidence that there are processes at work which tend to increase the incidence of poverty independently of variations in agricultural out put per head.

Sen (1979), in his study defined level (poverty line) explains poverty partially. He stated that poor are those people who are living below poverty line. But one cannot isolate the poor and non-poor in real term. Therefore, poverty should include absolute poverty and relative poverty in context of society. Concept of poverty can further be implied as individualized poverty i.e., those individuals who cannot meet the minimum expenditure of essential items (basic necessities) like food, shelter and clothing. Further, collective or mass poverty is the product of social system and can be analyzed at aggregate level. This situation is commonly observed in the developing countries.

Saint (1979) found that voluntary organization continued to play a significant role in the field or rural development and nation building. Great individuals and organizations including missionaries and other religious bodies initiated most of the efforts for rural development. These organizations are at present performing a key role in the field of development. Until the time that genuinely democratic machinery of governance comes into being. There will remain a sense for organizations to perform the mediating role between the state and the people.

Kakwani (1981) suggested alternative measures of intensity of poverty rather than the conceptual problem of poverty and made use of the three poverty indicators, the per centage of poor, the aggregate poverty gap and the distribution of income among the poor. While using NSS data

(16th round, July 1960-61), he observed that 11.2 per cent of the total income must be transferred from the non-poor to the poor to eliminate the poverty.

Food and Agricultural Organization (1982), has reviewed poverty in rural areas in developing countries and the means of poverty alleviation. The study, based on absolute poverty norms has come to the conclusion that one of the origins of this poverty must lie in inadequate access to land and other factors leading to insufficient production. By projecting World Agricultural Perspective and policy issue up to the year A.D. 2000. With particular attention to developing countries, the study found that over the next two decades the developing countries could double their food and agricultural production but it observed the improved food production must go hand in hand with a more equitable distribution of this larger output. The study concludes that sustained effort is needed on many fronts. Limited access to land due to unequal distribution of land or population pressure is undoubtedly a major contributory cause of insufficient production but the inherent quality of the land quantity of labour and capital are also the determinants of the level of farm output. The study has further observed that mere economic growth in general or agricultural growth in particular will not be sufficient to solve the problem of rural poverty. The alleviation of poverty within an acceptable time scale requires a political commitment to the reshaping of the pattern of national economic growth and new distribution of its benefits.

U.V.N. Charyulu (1984) concluded that the voluntary organization has to be assigned the role of a partner of the state in rural development efforts to support its endeavor or compete with it sometimes. Some of the voluntary organizations would not like to 'resign' themselves to this position of playing a secondary role to the state. Most of them profess Gandhian ideology. According to them, a voluntary organization should be a trailblazer, experimenting with new methods and strategies. The state may profit from these experiences and experiment in larger geographical areas with wider resources at its disposal. While these conflicting opinions continue to prevail, it would be appropriate to discuss the role played by these bodies at present. A small numbers of organizations, which function as independent bodies gave experimented successfully, and established new strategies for rural development. A large number of voluntary organizations have played supplementary and complementary roles to the state.

Tendulkar and Sundaram (1985) in their study "Growth Trickle Down Effects and poverty", have concluded that the per centage of population below poverty line has fluctuated without any trend towards increase or decrease both for rural and the urban population. The absolute population of the poor has, however, been rising at an annual average rate of 3.5 million in case of rural areas and 1.45 million in respect of urban areas. Further, they found that there was no relation between growth rate and poverty.

Parthasarathy (1985) in his presidential address at a National Seminar on "Growth, Stability and Equity with in the Agrarian Sector of Andhra Pradesh" held that poverty ratios in Andhra Pradesh are sensitive to growth performance in agricultural although it is not significantly true in the case of bottom classes. Growth lower ness benefited much more the top cultivators group rather than the bottom cultivators group in the State.

Radhakrishna and Sudhakar Reddy (1986) in their paper on "class Composition, poverty and Agricultural Development", using Rs. 50 per capita expenditure per month as poverty-line, have concluded that rural poverty is concentrated among the agricultural labourers in almost all the districts and cultivators and self-employed in back-ward districts.

Perraju Sarma (1987) examined the dimensions of rural poverty with reference to agricultural labourers in Andhra Pradesh. The intergenerational declines in occupational status and access to land have been the important factors explaining poverty among agricultural labourers. But there is no association between income, poverty and generation change.

***Empowerment of Women through SHG***

Charyulu and Reddy (1987) found that there is an increasing awareness of the need for better education, health and hygiene and the explorative and suppressive nature of the system. Women preferred to depend on men in several aspects of home and social life. But also have a strong desire to particular in public activities and gain equal status. The authors concluded that efforts to emancipate women should be directed towards organization, building awareness and collective action, in order to achieve real changes in the status and role.

Vasant Desai (1988) felt that, it has been recognized that voluntary agencies can play a very creative role in motivating the people and supervising the distribution of the resources with a view in ensuring their proper utilization. They can also play a very useful role in matching projects to the local conditions and supplying local know-how about the various factors affecting productivity and marketing.

Sudhakar Reddy (1989) in his paper 'Poverty in Andhra Pradesh' concluded that though there is a declining trend in the incidence of poverty in seventies and eighties the people below poverty line in the year 1986-87 were still higher (41.85 per cent) in rural Andhra Pradesh. The studies which were conducted up to 1992 have concluded more or less on similar lines.

Dhillon and Singh (1990), established the fact that role of voluntary agencies in the rural development could act as pathfinders. Their power and potential to motivate people can be fully utilized in the implementation of Government programmes for rural development. They can serve as a link between the administration and the people and act as a catalyst in the rural areas to bring about change especially in the attitude of people through motivation and awareness.

Williams (1990) examines the status of women with in the family in rural Indonesia from the historical role they have played in Indonesian society to their current status in household decision making. The study shows that martial duration and the education of both spouses' fathers are among the strongest predictors of both husbands' and 'wives' perceptions of their abilities to affect the marriage decision. Moreover, residence in a larger urban community prior to marriage is particularly important for women in terms of improving decision-making power. The more input the spouses perceive themselves to have had in making the marriage decision, the more they are able to influence later decisions as well.

Sultana (1990) in the study 'Participation, Empowerment and Variation in Development for Rural Bangladesh Women' found that women's participation in paid work is not sufficient to increase women's autonomy and voice in the family and the village. On the other hand, women's group formation, regular savings and income, new knowledge, consciousness raising and group mobilization together creates an alternative to women's traditional conditions and thus contributed relatively higher status for women in the family and in the village.

Ponna Wignaraja (1990) suggested that by providing independent sources of income outside home, micro credit tends to reduce economic dependency of the women on husbands and thus help enhance autonomy. Second, the same independent sources of income together with their exposure to new sets of ideas, values and social support could make these women more assertive of their rights. And finally, micro credit programmes - by providing control over material resources should raise women's prestige and status in the eyes of husband and there by promote intersperse consultation.

Trivedi, Neela (1992) studied the non-formal education needs of rural women in the socio-cultural context of a village in India. It was found that women were not aware of many of their needs. Their needs were complex and varied according to their roles and responsibilities, and the different categories of class, caste, age and occupation, in general, interest in learning skills that generate income was high, whereas interest in health, family planning and nutrition education programme was low. There was little 'felt need' for literacy. Literacy was considered to be important but was not perceived relevant for improving their living conditions. It is also concluded that the need in non-formal education for adults is to design programme that will create a consciousness among people to enable them to analyze their situation, recognize their needs, and to develop their skills and abilities to transform their reality. Thus turning the negative cycle into a positive one that leads to greater awareness and participation self –reliance and empowerment.

Sheilds, Laurene Elizabeth (1992) found that women experience empowerment as a multifaceted expansive process in which the development of an internal sense of self, the ability to take action based on the internal sense of self and ethic of interconnectedness are essential elements. The process was initially characterized by feelings of disempowerment associated with minimal choice, feeling acted upon by life and a perception of marginally due to gender, sexuality and sex role. Subsequently, recognition of this felt sense of dissonance occurred and the women entered a process of transformation. The transformation was characterized by the emergency of an internal sense of self, which included claiming, listening, accepting and valuing their identity.

Kurata, Satoko (1994) in 'Empowerment of women in self Employment Programmes: A study to Conceptualize Empowerment' explore the concept of empowerment through a commonly planned intervention scheme-income generation/ small enterprise projects. Empirical data were collected from an equivalent intervention scheme, self employment creation programmes for women in poverty in the mid-Michigan area in the United States. His focus group discussions revealed that empowerment centered on four dimensions: economic, social, psychological and political. The data revealed that empowerment is a process which starts from awareness with individual consciousness, grows into action and broadens to the collective level. Empowerment also is a transformative and bottom-up process in which the beneficiary becomes an agent of change.

**Review of Literature on SHGs**

Harper, M (2001) in his study: "Self-Help Groups Some Issues from India" indicated that the banking community was extending its services to the rural poor through self-help groups. Because of SHGs, the bank's transaction costs were reduced. He reported that over 2000 SHGs had borrowed from the banks in India for lending to their members. The average loan was around Rs. 3,000 per group. Repayment rates were generally over 97 per cent.

Das et al. (2001) in their study "Performance of Self-help Groups in Sonitpur District of Assam" assessed the performance of Self -help Groups in Sonitpur district of Assam and opined that more grants and aids would help to build adequate infrastructure which would eventually streamline the various activities of the SHGs resulting ultimately in economic prosperity and social stability.

Das, M. R. (2004) in his study 'Micro-finance though SHGs: A Boon for the Rural Poor', concluded that micro-finance through SHGs has now become a modem economical weapon for the poor to fight against poverty. Many big and small institutions are taking part in this revolution of micro-finance vigorously. Still it has a long way to become successful. Many programmes from "Garebi Hatao" to IRDP were started by the Government enthusiastically, but they were not able to achieve their objectives.

Kumaran, K.P. (2002) in his empirical study "Role of Self-help Groups in Promoting Micro-Enterprises Through Micro-Credit: An Empirical Study" primarily intended to document the experiences in SHGs in promoting micro-enterprises through micro-finance intervention. For the study conducted in Pune District of Maharashtra state 15 samples of SHGs were selected on a random basis. Among them 10 groups were promoted jointly by NGO and Bank, while the remaining five of them were formed by District Rural Development Agency. The study has been undertaken with the following objectives: To study the structure and function of SHG in terms of mobilization of saving, delivery of credit and recovery of loan; and to examine the role played by SHG promotion agencies and SHGs in promotion and effective management of micro-enterprises.

Kotaiah and Chairman NABARD (1995) in his forward to "Linking SHGs with Banks Indian Experience". The self-help groups (SHGs) have been the social innovations of the poor particularly in the under developed regions. They have a long history and university. "The savings and credit functions of SHGs have a great appeal to the rural financial institutions. They offer an outstanding market opportunity as the poor are concerned with the opportunities for earnings than the cost of capital. I am sure the SHGs with there unique strengths of autonomy, discipline, flexibility and an inherent bias for the poor women will attract greater attention from the development financial institutions and commercial banks. I also forces the SHGs building up their own federal structure which then can offer a package of financial and non-financial services to the poor".

Felix De Sousa and Isabela Cabral (1995) in their study "Can reproduction Health Education empower women? – A Brazilian Qualitative Study" concluded that a non-formal programme designed to each health education and sexuality can be an effective tool to bring about women's empowerment in the psychological, cognitive and physical dimensions. The authors recommended that this programme should add efforts to empower women in the economic and he political dimensions so that women's strategic gender needs can be fully addressed.

Chowdary (1996) in her study stressed the need for sharpening women's empowering strategies to make them effective and result oriented. She pointed out that money earned by poor women is more likely to be spent on the basic needs life than that by men and this realization would bring women as the focus of development efforts. She also examined the advantages of organizing women groups there by creating new sense of dignity and confidence to tackle their problems with a sense of solidarity and to work together for the cause of economic intendances.

Namaea M.C (1995), A World Bank study on "Assault on World Poverty" observed that growth is not equitably reaching the poor and the poor are not significantly contributing to growth. Development strategies, therefore, need to be reshaped in order to help the poor to become more productive. The study suggests that agricultural credit and land reforms are the key elements in helping the rural poor to become more productive. Unfortunately, the flow of credit to poorer has been inadequate due to lack of sufficient collateral and high administrative costs of small loans to them.

Hays, A, Amin. R and Becker. S (1998) analyzed the relationship between poor women's participation in micro credit programmes and their empowerment by taking both SHG and non-SHG members in rural Bangladesh. They have split the concept of Women Empowerment into three components and measured separately in order to arrive at a better understanding of their underlying factors and their relationship to women's empowerment. These separate indices are interspersed consolation index, individual autonomy index and authority index. Over all, it was found that part of the higher autonomy and authority indices in the NGO programme areas in contrast to the comparison areas is accounted for by the contribution of the both NGO credit members and non-members in the NGO programmes areas. Being empowered by their new sources of financial income and related credit group supports, female recipients of NGO credits may have asserted their autonomy and authority *vis-à-vis* their husbands' restrictions and dominance in related households affairs.

It was further found that education, house type, annual income etc., tend to be positively associated with autonomy and authority indices. Also positively associated to duration of NGO membership and non-agricultural occupation. The implications of these findings are that NGO credit programmes in rural Bangladesh are not only likely to bring about rapid economic improvement in the situation of women but also hasten their empowerment. The NGO credit members are reported to be more confident, assertive, intelligent, self-reliant and conscious of their rights. It was suggested that the NGO role alone would not be sufficient. The government has to have a large network of credit programmes for the rural poor women to increase their economic solvency and enhance their empowerment. The complementary role of NGOs and Government can take care of the problem.

Prasad, H (1998) attempted to understand the aptitude of members of DWCRA Groups towards economic enterprises. For these purpose 60 women DWCRA Groups belonging to DWCRA Groups were interviewed. Based on the study results the author was of the view that age, ability, aptitude and awareness were crucial for lunching skill based unit, the author was of he view that. Arbitrary selection of unit is against the spirit of the group activities. The author was also found that women ware not independent in participating the SHG activities. In the absence of proper mechanism for monitoring and guidance of the SHGs desired success cannot be achieved.

Karamakar (1999) in his study "performance of women SHGs (formed with the financial support of MYRADA) in T.N." found that SHGs have been formed with the agricultural labourrers and marginal farmer and found that rotation of leadership has been followed. Further, the group accounts have been prepared by an educated member of the SHG, and the same member was in charge for documenting the proceedings of the weekly meetings of the group. Further, the same member was being appointed as animator by MYRADA. Own savings the amount contributed by MYRADA and the interest occurred forms the main financial sources of the SHG which have been rotated by the members. Group decides the members to whom the loan is to be sanctioned and other terms and conditions. However the purpose wise borrowings show that of the total 24 loans only two were utilized for productive purpose and other loans were utilized to meet urgent family requirements viz. Health, consumption, marriage. As far as bank linkage is concerned Indian bank branch has sanctioned loan for under taking allied activities. The recovery performance of the bank loan was found highly satisfactory with 93 per cent. All this clearly shows that SHG has followed self help and mutual help principle in true spirit.

Singh and Jain (1999) in their working paper 'Evaluation and survival of SHGs: Some theoretical and empirical evidences' explained that there are four stages of group formation: Formatting, norming, and performing. They identified factors, which have an impact on group formation as full participation of all members, quality in leadership, some short homogeneity among the members, and transparency in operations and functioning of the groups.

Muhamme Hussain Bhatti (1999) found that the improvement of women's economic situation is the basic determinant of their empowerment. Women are being extended extension, advice and the financial assistance to generate income in farm and off farm sectors. These efforts of women are being responded significantly, resulting in a start of women's recognition not only as income earning hands but as responsible business partners in joint families as well.

Mohan (2000) in his research paper "role of thrift and micro credit activities in women empowerment" reveals that through participatory approach women child could share their problems. The researcher is of the view that NGOs have adequate capabilities and infrastructure to organize training programmes and may also stand guarantee to the loans accessed from the formal banking institutions. More over NGOs could facilitate resources mobilization for the benefit of the women. Even in facilitating the micro credit the role of NGOs need to emphasis. It only means that micro programme will show fruitful results if the SHGs are supported by reputed NGOs.

Nityananda (2000), made a historical review on the "role of NGOs in rural development". According to the study, immediately after the independence, there was an atmosphere of cooperation and complementarily in the State-NGO relationship. The state was supportive of NGOs, specially the Gandhian ones. The policy makers also believed that the voluntary sector was capable of tackling social problems in far better way than the state itself could resolve. The State welcomed NGOs as their activities were predominantly welfare and modernization oriented and substituted or supplemented the State's effort. Hence, there was hardly any question of conflict. This kind of cordial State-NGO relationship did not last long and started deteriorating as some Action Groups or Empowerment/Advocacy oriented NGOs emerged. The NGO sector also has undergone some changes. Today young professional motivated by job prospects rather than social commitment dominate the NGO Sector. Moreover, the competition within the NGOs has also increased. Thus NGOs are also willing to get involved with government projects even with more control. The Foreign Contribution Regulation Act (FCRA) was enacted in 1976 to keep a watch on foreign funded NGO activities. Many of foreign missionaries and NGO officials were also expelled. The nature of the state also explains this increased control over the NGOs and ability of the state to set the development agenda.

Jha and Kumar (2000) made a case study of Vikas Bharti regarding opportunities of NGOs. According to them, a review of the process of socio-economic development effort of the country indicates that immediately after independence, the First Five-year plan initiated a process of rural development through Community Development Programme (CDP). The second and Third plans also stressed on the need for involvement of people. The Fourth plan stressed that, in ultimate analysis we found very little achievement in respect of people's participation. The Fifth Five-year Plan assigned "a high place to the role of voluntary Organization in social welfare programmes. In the Seventh Five-year Plan inadequacy of people's participation was felt strongly.

Eight Five-year Plan confirms the requirement of people's participation in the preface itself by stating involvement of NGO and other institutions, consequently, since the seventies non-government organizations have been considered as an alternatives means in the implementation of different development programmes for the rural poor. They argued that in the development dynamics, NGOs assume greater importance because of a few unique advantages enjoyed by such organizations. These are: (a) proximity to he target beneficiaries; (b) ability to maintain strong linkage between the programme, workers and the bureaucracy; (c) easier assessment of techno-economic feasibility; (d) technical ability of skills; (e) social system information base; (f) democratic build up with these advantages the NGOs can organize the deprived classes, activise the system, mobilize resources, improve social accountability and finally supplement the government efforts.

Jain (2000) highlighted the greatest potential of NGOs lies in their capacity to generate self-help initiative. It is in this vein that NGOs are viewed as vehicles for development and more specifically as vehicles for "democratic development". NGOs have the potential to be significant vehicles of empowerment because of their ability to reach the grassroots.

Maharana, *Nayak and Sahu* (2000) have found that the loans advanced by formal credit agencies are unsecured and unlinked. There were too much of loans remaining as overdues even after many years. So, these agencies are very reluctant to extend further credit to fishermen. At this juncture, the role of voluntary organizations is essential to uplift the socio-economic conditions of the fishermen in the following respect:

i. To liberate the indebted credit for the purchase of fishing of the money lenders.

ii. To arrange institutional credit for the purchase of fishing equipment.

iii. To make marketing arrangements for the disposal of fish and fish products.

iv. To disseminate latest and appropriate fishing technology to small-scale fishers.

v. To introduce different fishermen welfare schemes; and

vi. To open training and servicing centers for repairing outboard engines.

Ganesh Bhat (2000) has felt that they are involved in a type of social change that does not primarily concentrate on structure, but rather on the conscientisation of individuals, and equipping them to break the customs out, within the socio-cultural matrix of their society. Through a selective approach, NGOs have concentrated their efforts for the development of micro-entrepreneurship in the informal sector rather than the more substantial formal sector business. Yet it is not an easy task to develop micro enterprises when they deal with following type of people.

- Women and men (which is harder than working with men only.)
- The poor (which is harder than working with the rich
- People with limited enterprise cultural (which is harder than working in the context of a strong enterprise culture).
- The rural population (which is harder than working with the urban population).

T.R. Gurumurthy (2000) in his article "SHGs Emperor Rural Women" states that SHGs disburse micro credit to rural women. This makes them enterprising and encouraging them to enter into entrepreneurial activities. Credit needs of rural women are fulfilled totally through SHGs. The author says that SHGs enhance equality of status of women as participations, decision makers, and beneficiaries in the democratic, economic, social and cultural spheres of life. SHGs encourage women to take active part in socio economic progress of our country.

Rai and Tandom (2000) in their study concluded that the financial institutions in our country, whether public or private, have almost excluded poor-men and women. Landless small farmers, artisans, and laborers-form their financial services for various reasons such as opportunity cost and low financial credibility. Providing micro-finance (small deposits, loans and micro-credits) to the poor have been increasingly acclaimed as effective means of reducing poverty and powerlessness, whether in an absolute sense or in relation to others. The poor themselves have a better appreciation of their socio-economic situation, the micro-enterprises that can come-forth and the necessary support required for the same. The voluntary sector has made successful attempts in reaching to the poorest through innovation micro-finance services like savings and credits through self-help groups have been encouraged to practice thrifts and the small savings collected are lent to individual's members to meet consumption needs.

Karmakar (2000), highlighted that micro-enterprises can play an important role in improving the quality of life and poverty alleviation. Ensuring their success is cost-effective and enables the vulnerable sections, such as women and weaker sections of society, to smooth over seasonal fluctuations in households income. The provision of credit and generation of savings have long been recognized as an essential element in any rural development strategy. Credit plays a crucial role in the modernization of agricultural but in role in the fight against rural poverty has seldom been recognized. Financial institutions in developing countries, whether public or private, have shunned rural areas for various reasons such as opportunity costs and low financial creditability. Rich farmers, who are able to use their large endowment base and influence with in the local power structure to secure loans at very advantages terms, have mostly controlled further, rural financial services. Credit policies are also generally concentrated on land-based agricultural production programmes, neglecting off-farm activities in which the poor are mainly engaged.

**Rural Development and Rural Credit**

UNDP (1997), highlighted on the limitation of SHGs with a reference to micro credit. It is shown in that micro credit self-help groups, especially linked to micro-credit schemes, have not been without their critics. They are not panacea for meeting challenges in economic and social develop men. It is widely recognized that such schemes are not universally successful. One promising strategy is the use of market-driven measures to enable the poor to own and operate enterprises to add value to the primary products they usually produce. However, they highlighted on the limitations of SHGs with references to micro credit.

Sood, A (2004), in her article "Sustainable Rural Development - Focus on Women;' said that women's empowerment is the key to socio-economic development of the community. The author says that the Government is providing several opportunities to women led SHGs to market their products without any intermediaries to urban consumers. The exposure is helping in improving their professional skills, promoting entrepreneurship among them.

Das, B.C (2004), his article on "Stakeholders in Rural Development, Concerns, and Challenges" says that in the last few years, there has been a paradigm shift in the strategy for rural development with focus on decentralization through speedy and effective devolution of financial and administrative power to Panchayati Raj institutions. A strategic pro - poor policy has been adopted in terms of which the rural poor are treated as a resource rather than as a burden.

Murali, P. and S. Trilochan (2004) in their article "Capitalism and Cooperation - Cooperative Institutions in a Developing Economy" talk about cooperatives as organizational arrangements of collective economic activity. These cooperatives can break up interlocked capital, labour, output markets in rural areas, and alleviate poverty. The recent parallel law on cooperatives provides an opportunity to take a fresh look at the issue. Some basic concepts have been discusses in this article, while comparing different types of economic organizations with a few empirical examples to bring out the conditions under which cooperative arrangements can generate economic surplus and alleviate poverty. Another interesting feature of the cooperatives stressed in the article is that they benefit only the poor and not those who are better off and have access to mainstream credit and markets.

Nair, Tar S. (2001) in his article 'Institutionalizing Micro-finance in India: Strategic Issues' studied the rural financial intermediation and commercial banks, and the role of banks in the newly emerging institutional forms with a thrust on micro-finance . He felt that healthy rural financial sector must be developed to meet the needs of agriculture, infrastructure, the rural poor such as agricultural laborers, artisans and self - employed persons.

Dubhashi, Dr. Medha (2004) in her report "Expert Committee on Rural Credit: Findings and Recommendations" observes that the rural financial institutions were not accessible to the poorest of the poor, including women. It has suggested that newer financial agencies or SHGs and non banking financial companies should fill this gap. Also, since the Government's target oriented programmes had a limited impact, the thrust must be on financing through groups. Successful experiences of forming SHGs of the poorest especially rural women have proved that the poor are bankable.

Satish, P. (2004) in his article "Rural Finance: Role of State and State – owned Institutions" says that Governments have a critical role to play in the rural financial institutions. However, state implementation of rural financial system has proven expensive and inefficient. Subsidized credit programmes, which are part of state intervention in rural financial markets, undermine the institutional sustainability of financial institutions, distort finance markets and discourage savings mobilization and fail to develop market - driven sources of funding. The author feels that revitalization of the state owned rural financial institutions is possible without a wholesale structural and ownership change.

Kanthimathinathan, S. (2004) in "Rural Credit at Cross Roads" says that the rural credit delivery system is a facilitator but rural credit by itself cannot bring about development in the rural poor if they are not involved in their transformation with credit and infrastructure being necessary inputs along with technology. The rural credit delivery system in India is now over nine decades old. However, a large number of changes that have been initiated in it without taking into account issues like willful non-payment of over dues have adversely affected the credibility of the- system.

Sivaloganathan, Dr. K. (2004) in 'Problems in the Recovery of rural Credit' says that the problem of recovery of agricultural credit has become a constant source of anxiety for the financing institutions and a large chunk of banks' funds remains unloaded. The author feels that the basic causes for this problem include weather conditions, drought and floods' as well as the socio political involvement in which the rural credit institutions function.

Gogoi, J. (2004) in his document 'Rural Credit Scenario in North East India' gives an analytical account of the rural credit in the North Eastern Region. The author points out that the credit deposit ratio in almost all the states of North East lags far behind the National ratio, which is an alarming situation. Also due to high cost of operation of banks and very high transaction costs, for both borrowers and the banks, it is not perhaps feasible for the commercial banks to provide micro credit in the rural areas of the region. The author points out that the Government sponsored SGSY with subsidy element is also proving to be a hurdle in achieving the basic objective of SHG movement in the North Eastern India.

Indra, D. (2004) edited book, Strategies for the sustainability of Self Help Groups, examines the concept of sustainability of SHGs and various related issues. It also throws light on the experiences of SHGs in Southern India, the various problems faced by them, finally suggesting suitable strategies for their sustainability. The book is divided into four segments. The first segment deals with the concept and sustainability of SHGs and related issues. The second segment covers the experiments and experiences of SHGs in various districts of Andhra Pradesh. The third segment focuses on the obstacles encountered by SHGs on the way to sustainability. The final segment deals with strategies for sustainability.

Purushottam, P. ( 2004) in his study 'Marketing Support to the SHGs' says that most of the SHG members living in regions of high poverty, low levels of agricultural surpluses, scanty resources and underdeveloped infrastructure find it difficult to identify and promote viable micro enterprises because of several constraints. Of these, poor resource base, infrastructural backwardness, illiteracy, and low level of entrepreneurial profile of the working poor are predominant. Yet, in several villages and rural towns, the working poor have evolved and built different survival mechanisms. To be effective, any development support to these people has to be based on reckoning of these mechanisms. In this backdrop, the author proposes market development strategies for SHG members. These are based on action research experience with working poor, particularly members of SHGs, in some parts of the country. These strategies are invariably location specific, dynamic, and illustrative.

Tripathy, K.K. (2004) in his article 'Self-Help Groups - A Catalyst for Rural Development' says that SHGs are formed and developed under various programmes provide a great opportunity for convergence of various activities of various ministries and organizations. He says that the groups, while aiming at promotion of savings and credit, should work as pressure groups to address social issues like education, health, lack of access to natural resources etc. He also mentions that the necessary training could be given to the SHG members to create awareness on community health, traditional and modem agricultural practices, micro credit, veterinary practices, and water resource management.

Ueshmukh, J and Kanadlve (2004) in their study 'Women's Self-help Groups in Andhra Pradesh - A Participatory Poverty Alleviation in Action' say that capacity building has been an important component in scaling up of Andhra Pradesh's poverty alleviation initiatives. The authors also say that the primary aim of SHG Bank Linkage is to integrate informal savings and credit groups with mainstream banking, to provide them with credit to enhance their fund base.

Shylendra, H.S. (2004) article on 'The SHG-Bank Linkage Programme: An Assessment and Future Strategies' makes an attempt to critically assess the SHG -Bank Linkage Programme focusing on its approach and the strategy and arrive at possible ways to take it forward. The author says that the main aim of the programme being implemented since 1992 is to tap the potential of the SHG concept to bring banking services to the doorsteps of the poor. In terms of reaching physical targets, the programme seems to have done quite impressively in the last one decade. It has all the potential to unfold new avenues for banking with the poor.

Chowdhary, S (2005), in his article 'Self-help Groups Formation through Frequently Asked Questions' says that real participation of the poor and the marginalized can only be achieved by adding value to the individual need of the poor. This article describes an experiment undertaken to form SHGs through certain specific questions asked of the people in the SHG formation process. The way in which the questions are answered forms the basis of SHG formation. It was found that a big difference existed between the qualities of groups formed through this process.

Rao, R (2005), in his article 'Women's Groups Herald a Wind of Change in Rural Uttaranchal' talks about the forces of community awareness and social mobilization for development unleashed by the United Nations development Programme. (UNDP) sponsored project which motivated the rural community of Garhwal to move ahead on the already created path of development. The all women SHGs took upon themselves the task of giving a fresh thrust to developmental activities and community empowerment.

Rajeev, M. (2007), in his article in the *Hindu* "World Bank floored by SHGs" (March 14), says that the World Bank has plans of utilizing the women members of SHGs of Andhra Pradesh to train, educate and help their counterparts in other countries. According to the World Bank, several countries like Cambodia, Vietnam and china have expressed interest in the SHG project of Andhra Pradesh. The World Bank is also planning to rope in SHG women from Andhra Pradesh to train their counterparts in Bihar, the poorest state in the country.

Kumar, Surendra and Singh, A. K (2005) in their article 'Role of Special Employment Programmes for Poverty Eradication in Rural India' says that their experience with the implementation of poverty alleviation programmes has not been encouraging. Leakages, corruption, lack of sectoral integration and absence of people's participation have contributed to their limited impact. An effective delivery system is an essential prerequisite for the success of such programmes. Further policies will have to emphasize higher growth rate since they are essential for poverty reduction. Besides it has to be simultaneously ensured that higher growth is accompanied by job creation at a higher rate than the rate of growth of labour force. This would require encouragement to labour intensive sectors of the economy. For this purpose the reform process will have to encourage micro enterprises and small and medium entrepreneurs to expand their business. Employment in small-scale sector can be encouraged by providing credit and other support measure to this sector. Finally the poverty alleviation programmes have a chance of success only when the nexus between corrupt bureaucrats, politicians and village landlords is broken and real beneficiaries are put in-charge of these programmes.

Sidhu, *et al.* (2006) in their article on 'Urban Poverty in India Some Issues' observed that rapid urbanization has taken place in India. The challenge of urbanization became even more serious in the context of urban poverty, which is largely an extension of rural poverty. The Government has also taken a number of welfare measures regarding reduction of poverty in the rural and urban areas. The urban poor did not enjoy modem facilities of life. This happened mainly due to their poor economic condition. It is suggested that additional financial resources should be mobilized by the Government for the up-liftment of the poor. The 21st century is an era of development with a human face otherwise the poor will not forgive all of us.

Rajan (2006) in his paper 'Post-Reform Poverty Trends: An Analysis' have concluded that the structural adjustment programme (Reforms) initiated in 1991 is concentrated on Liberalization, Privatization and Globalization (LPG). The reforms have serious implications for the country's economic growth in general and for the poverty in particular. Thus the study concludes that economic reforms in India has resulted in accelerating very low economic growth of the pre-reform India that has resulted in significant reduction in the incidence of poverty during the post-reform period. The analysis also shows that inequality in income and consumption expenditure has declined during the post-reform period. Thus there are ample evidences to show that the economic reforms initiated in India are pro-poor and not anti-poor.

*Micro-finance*

*Bouman, F.A.J. (1989)* in his book *Small Short, and Unsecured Informal Rural Finance in India* thoroughly described the concept of Micro-finance . The author described micro-finance as the provision of providing very small loans that are repaid within short periods of time and is essentially used by low income individuals and households. The author says that micro-finance is an enabling, empowering, bottom up tool to poverty alleviation that has provided considerable economic and non-economic externalities to low income households in developing countries. Micro-finance as stated by the author is being hailed as a sustainable tool to combat poverty, combining profit-oriented approach that is self sustaining and a poverty alleviation focus that empowers low-income households. Micro-finance is increasingly becoming a tool to exercise developmental priorities for governments in developing countries. However, there has been a gradual realization that micro-finance alone is not enough. The main objective of micro-finance institutions - poverty alleviation - requires a holistic and in depth understanding of the interplay between economic, social, cultural extract of the developmental process.

Karmakar, K.G. (1999) in the book *Rural Credit and Self-help Groups; Micro-finance Needs and Concepts in India* says the India pioneered the involvement of the banking system in the assault on rural poverty and in the channellisation of adequate financial resources to the agricultural sector. However, wrong priorities, narrow bureaucratic and political interests, abysmal recoveries, and decisions forced by the economic liberalization have led to the creation of a vast and complex multi-agency credit stem beset with many problems. This book also talks about the existing rural credit system in India, analysis its strengths, weaknesses, and prescribes various strategies and innovations, which will enable the existing rural credit delivery system to emerge stronger and more viable.

Eichfeld, R and Wendt, H. (2006) in their paper 'Building on Success – The Next Challenges for Micro-finance ' the authors talked about the growth of the micro-finance sector and its astonishing success in harnessing capital markets to alleviate global poverty. They feel that expansion of micro-finance and its integration with the global banking system can create the economic opportunity for many and unite communities. Micro-insurance, covering health, life, agricultural, and livestock risks is also coming up. The authors also say that technology companies are entering the field by designing data processing and telecommunication system serving micro-finance units and small business at the village level and micro-finance are now being integrated with the capital markets.

UNCDF *Annual Report (2002)* says that as women's labour participation rate continues to grow and so will their need for support services such as micro-finance . Micro-finance programmes are particularly useful in increasing women's economic options, because women tend to have less access to sources of informal credit than men. Participation in savings and credit programmers has been shown to help empower women by increasing their contribution to household income and by exposing them to contexts outside the domestic realm. The women derived income from these business often acts as the economic safety net that government in poor countries cannot provide. According to the report, micro-finance has a role to play both in supporting women's productive role and as a strategy for mitigate.

Micro-finance can also reduce gender-specific risks for women by helping them increase decision-making power and control over assets. Women's use in financial services can increase income and economic security, enhance their independence, reduce the vulnerability of their families, and stimulate local economics. However, neither women's access to financial services nor the benefits of those services are guaranteed. Although micro-finance is seen by some as synonymous with women's finance", in come parts of the world women remain marginalized as micro-finance clients. And even where women's access to micro-finance has been established, the virtuous spiral of access and empowerment for women is not automatic. Making financial services available to women clients, without adopting those services to the special constraints and coping strategies that arise from women's multiple social roles, misses the opportunity to achieve both significant outreach and economic and social empowerment.

Bhatia, N and Bhatia, A (2004) in their article 'Micro-finance Institutions of Bangladesh: lessons for India' say that the micro-finance movement of India has now come of age and is it at a take off stage. At the present juncture, few lessons can be drawn from the experiences of micro-finance institutions of Bangladesh. In this article, an attempt has been made to examine the micro-finance products and practices of four major Micro-finance s Institutions of Bangladesh as against the prevailing position in India, with a view to draw lessons for strengthening the movement in India.

Mishra, J and Thanvi, R (2004) in their article 'Indian Banking System and Micro-finance' suggests that micro-finance has emerged as one of the most suitable and effective tools for enabling the poor and disadvantages sections of the society to access institutional credit. The authors feel that the Indian banking system has shown a willingness and resilience to experiment and join the micro-finance movement in a way that has no parallel any where in the world. With 504 banks providing access to credit to 116 lakh poor families through 30,942 participating branches supporting over 7 lakh SHGs, the micro-finance movement in the country has come to be recognized as the largest in terms of its outreach.

Das, R.M. (2004) in her article 'Micro-finance through SHGs, A Boon for the Rural Poor' points out that easy access of poor to credit is the biggest need of the hour rather than cheaper rate of interest. Micro-finance provides opportunity to the poor for getting sufficient amount of credit easily to start any income generating activity. According to the author, micro-finance not only deals with the credit part, but also deals with the savings and insurance part. It ensures the right to save and is one of the most powerful weapons, which workers for beginning the poor rural people into the main stream.

**Micro Credit**

Patel, A. (2004) in his article 'Micro-credit and the Role of Banks; Need for Initiative and Commitment' talks about the latest figure that reveal the number of poor people who benefited from micro credit programmes has grown more than four times from 1997 till the end of 2001. The author says that it has been a cause of dismay that India's performance most unsatisfactory despite the fact that India has a large number of poor people and rural financial intermediaries re quite capable if they demonstrate their willingness and commitment in this area. The author also feels that while there is no dearth of financial resources as well as the problem of repayments under the micro-credit programme, there is a need for well organized and committed micro-finance institution for channelising credit and making it available to the poor households individually or in groups in India.

Mohanan, N. and Kulandaiswany, V. (2004) in their paper entitled 'Instructional Linkages for Micro-enterprises Development' comment that sustainability and viability of group enterprises are very much at stake in the context of the ongoing economic reforms. Institutional linkages are the means of economic empowerment, greater access to technology and expended market opportunities. Group enterprises of tiny producers can gain economic empowerment and control over their environment only through appropriate institutional linkages.

Ahmad, R. (2004) in his article 'Role of Micro-financing in Alleviation of Poverty' evaluate the progress of micro-financing programme in India and its impact on rural poverty. It is found that the micro financing through SHG-Bank Linkage programme of NABARD is working very effectively and the credit needs of the poorest of the poor of rural society is catered by the rural financial institutions through SHGs. Because of this, the socio-economic status of rural folk, especially of rural women is improving and poverty is reducing.

Yunus, M. (2004) in his article on 'Grameen Bank, Micro-credit and Millennium Goals' traces the evolution of the ideas and practice of micro credit as pioneered by the Grameen Bank of Bangladesh. The author says that over the years, the micro credit programmes have grown providing a wide range of services to meet the economic and social needs of citizen mostly poor women. It comes up with suggestions regarding emerging issues of financial self-reliance and institutional sustainability of micro credit programmes.

Ghosh, G.N. (2005) in his article 'A Policy Approach for Agricultural Lending' states that it is unrealistic to think that

Public Sector banks can revitalize agricultural credit delivery system without a completely revamped extension services system. The author also says that it is time to consider supporting micro-finance organizations to take on larger responsibility in livelihood development, as the banks alone cannot carry out the full range of rural credit lending services. But the question that needs to be squarely needs to be faced today is that can the commercial banks deliver what is being expected of them in several other areas of rural lending such as livelihood support, and easing the burden of rural indebtedness.

*Sahara Times,* (Feb 12,2005) The article, "Micro-credit can deliver reforms at the Poor's doorstep' states the story of Erranna F Hombalimath, an auto-rickshaw driver who started manufacturing of packaged food and household items in Hubli, Karnataka along with his wife under the banner Swadeshi Foods. After four years of hard work, his efforts paid off and he was rewarded the Citigroup's Socially Responsible Micro Entrepreneur Award and a cheque of Rs.1,00,000 by the Union Finance Minister, P. Chidambaram. The article also talks about micro-finance as a major tool for removing hindrances in the availability of credit in rural areas, where the poor still depend on moneylenders for loans at exorbitant interest rates. The article concludes by saying that micro-finance I more popular in poor counties like Bolivia, Mozambique, Uganda, Cambodia, and Philippines; the United Nations had declared 2005 as the International Year of Micro Credit.

*The Hindu* (March 14, 2005), The article 'Self-help Groups and Micro-finance' talks about the RBI giving priority sector status to the loans provided by banks to MFIs, thus mainstreaming the activity. The Government also hopes to enhance the beneficial role of the MFIs as intermediaries between banks and rural borrowers, in order to make micro credit not just a dispenser of credit but also a variety of social goods and services to the poor.

*Business Line* (July 25, 2005) in an article 'Commercial Banks urged to step up lending to SHGs' says that commercial banks in Andhra Pradesh have lent only Rs. 225 crores by mid-July as against the State Government specified target of Rs. 2,200 crores. The bankers were urged to meet their targets. The discussion was a part of a workshop on Micro-finance and SHGs by the Hyderabad Chapter of the Indian Bank's Association.

Jindal, A. (2005) in his article 'Micro-finance and SHGs – Role of Government Institutions' states that the main foundation of the Government's self employment programmes in the rural areas in the last two decades was erstwhile Integrated Rural Development Programme (IRDP) which concentrated predominantly on providing credit and/or subsidy to individuals for their self employment activities. The Government decided to shift focus from individuals to groups by starting a new programme, Swarnajayanthi Gram Swarozagar Yojana (SJGSY) based on the success of the SHG approach in Indian and outside, the government decided to shift focus from individuals to groups by starting a new programme, (SJGSY). This programme focused mainly on SHGs as an instrument of self-employment and consequently poverty alleviation in the rural areas of the country.

Mayoux, L (2005) in her paper 'the women's Empowerment through Sustainable Micro-finance: rethinking 'best practice' is divided into four segments. They focus on an overview of the contrasting paradigms of 'Best Practice', overview of evidence of gender impact, some of the now considerable experience of 'good gender practice' and a number of critical elements of a gender strategy for equality and empowerment. The responsibilities for donors in promoting a diversity of micro-finance provision to all of which women have equal access and some of which builds on the organizational base of micro-finance as a significant foundation for grassroots based change in gender relations, respectively.

Padma Narayan, B (2006) in her Ph.D. dissertation titled 'Micro-credit for Rural Poor (A study of SHG and SHG Households in Visakhapatnam District, Andhra Pradesh)' discusses a presumption that encourages the poor to organize themselves into social groups. These groups consist of not only men but also women in order to increase their participation in borrowings, so that they can meet their credit needs. Micro credit as an alternative source of credit for the poor has received widespread attention in recent years and it supplements the role of banks and other financial institutions in helping solve the problems of poverty and unemployment in the country. The study analyses the growth of SHGs in India and found that there is a leap and bound growth of SHGs linked with banks, spread all over the country. Commercial banks are the major partners followed by RRBs leaving a limited role for cooperatives. SHGs formed by NGOs and formal agencies, but directly financed by banks continued to have a major share. Southern region occupied the first place and Andhra Pradesh played a leading role. The study brings to fore, the fact that the SHG experiment has increased employment levels, income levels, and has reduced the extent of poverty. The study has found that it is the personal characteristics of the individuals like age, position in the family and in the society, occupation etc. influence their participation in borrowings rather than the household characteristics like value of assets owned by the family, family income and dependency ration etc.It was also found that the presence of micro credit programme increased the about of borrowings from formal sources, thereby reducing the dependence on informal sources.

*Business Line - Life,* (Dec 22, 2006) Bhagat Rasheed in his article 'Grameen Ticks To The Rescue' tells the story of a Bangladeshi women, Jannat E Quanine, Deputy General Manager, and Chief of the International Programme,

Grameen Bank, went to Kosovo in 1999 and seeded the micro-credit programme among women living in the was ravaged area. During those times, there was no bank, and any law and order machinery in Kosovo. Jannat set out with an aim of setting up a Grameen model of micro credit. Her labor was rewarded and the micro credit programme of Kosovo was a great success, working in four of its five regions. Over 25 million euros have been disbursed to 5000 women in 45 villages and the repayment rate has been 100 per cent

*The Hindu* (Jan 19, 2007), an article on 'Micro-finance bill on the anvil' says that the Indian government was working on special bill to create a friendly policy environment for micro-finance services enabling greater availability of credit to the poor. According to the present prime minister, more micro credit must reach the poor in order to build their capacity to absorb more credit.

*Sunday Magazine of the Hindu,* (March 4, 2007), in an article "True Heroes of Rural Development' talks about micro credit as a precious tool in the empowerment of rural women. The article also speaks about Muhammad Yunus and the Grameen Bank, and the replication, the Grameen model all over the Globe, especially in India and in Kerala's Palakkad district.

## Research Methodology

### *Need for the Study*

Despite phenomenal growth of commercial banking in India since late 1960s, the outreach of scheduled commercial banks falls short of expectations. The poor in rural and urban areas have little access to formal banking system in India. In the background of this situation, SHGs have appeared in the horizon as new institution for effective delivery or micro-credit to those un-banked and under- banked weaker sections. Keeping in view the vast scope for the expansion of micro-credit through SHG-bank linkage, this study is undertaken covering various districts in three regions i e., Coastal Region: *Visakhapatnam, East Godavari, and Nellore,* Telengana Region: *Ranga Reddy, Karimnagar and Warangal,* Rayalaseema Region: *Kurnool* and *Chittoor* were selected so as to cover various dimensions of micro-finance.

### *Objectives of the Present Study*

The study is aiming to study the following objectives:

1. To examine the micro-finance scenario at the national level
2. To study micro-finance delivery systems in three regions of Andhra Pradesh covering Coastal, Telengana and Rayalaseema.
3. To examine the nature of SHG-bank linkages in the study area and analyze its role in the flow of micro-finance.
4. To evaluate the performance of SHGs with bank linkage programme;
5. To measure the impact of micro-finance activities of Andhra Bank through SHG route in the three selected regions of Andhra Pradesh

### *Scope of the Study*

The study mainly intends to focus on SHGs as new institutions to bring the disadvantaged group, rural poor women, into formal banking fold. Primary goal of SHGs is to have sustainable economic development through empowerment of rural women with the provision of credit support through SHG-bank linkage programme. Hence linkage is core aspect of SHGs. Bankers are principal actors in the linkage programme, who are also covered in the study. Ultimate beneficiaries of SHG-bank linkage programme are members of SHGs. The economic impact of SHG operations is deeply probed in the study. The impact on SHG members covering various districts in three regions i.e., in Coastal Region: Visakhapatnam, East Godavari, and Nellore, in Telengana Region: Ranga Reddy, Karimnagar and Warangal, in Rayalaseema Region: Kurnool and Chittoor were selected for study in particular with Andhra Bank.

### *Hypotheses*

The following hypotheses are formulated and tested in the study:

1. There is no regional difference to the number of SHGs linked and sanction of SHG-BL at national level
2. There are no differences between the Government, and NGO promoted SHGs, as to agencies and individual SHG promotion, strategies adopted in SHG promotion and assessing agencies and individuals in SHG-bank linkage programme.
3. There are no differences across SHG-caste categories as to savings stagnating and savings growing SHGs.
4. There are no differences between SHG-caste categories promoter-wise as to continuously and intermittently by SHG-members.

### *Sample Design*

Main focus of the study is SHGs and its members as primary unit of analysis. Sample of SHGs are chosen cutting across three geographical regions of Andhra Pradesh namely, Coastal, Telengana and Rayalseema and eight districts are being covered under the study. The data is collected from SHG beneficiaries of Andhra Bank only through personal interview. There are 1567 number of beneficiaries across all caste groups have been selected and interviewed over the three regions. In fact, the study has purposively selected 11% of Minority, 32% of OCs, 27% of BCs, 25% of SCs and 5% of ST from the available beneficiaries' figures of Andhra Bank SHG-BL programme.

The sample selected also represents the basket of activities supported under the SHG-BL initiative of Andhra Bank. Adequate attention has been made on selecting beneficiaries from government supported programmes *vis-à-vis* MCP based programme, Govt promoted self-help groups *vis-à-vis* NGO promoted self-help groups and exclusive Bank-linked SHGs *vis-à-vis* Pvt. Linked SHGs to give justice to the evaluation study of Andhra Bank.

### *Data Sources*

Both primary and secondary data are used in the present study. Secondary data is extensively collected and compiled from wide ranging sources. Primary data for the study are being collected using a structured questionnaire.

### *Data Analysis and Statistical Tools*

The data collected are being process and analyzed using simple statistical analysis as well as advanced statistical tool. The study has exclusively used Chi-square ($\chi^2$) analysis, ANNOVA and coefficient of correlation to prove the hypothesis selected for the study. Besides, the study has adopted a graphical mode of data analysis and presentation to give more insight into the study.

### *Limitations of the Study*

This is a focused study on SHGs as micro-finance institutions and SHG-bank linkage programme as community-based lending of Andhra Bank. Those SHG operations other than micro-credit linkages are outside the purview of the study. Subsidized governmental development programmes routed through SHGs are also not covered in the study. The findings of the study are basically from the beneficiaries of the SHG-BL programme of Andhra Bank and hence, the study limits itself to data analysis of Andhra Bank only. Other banks and financial institutions in micro-finance activities are not in the purview of the study.

***Organization of the Thesis***

The thesis is divided into well delineated and self-contained six chapters with sub sections as mentioned below:

**Chapter 1: Introduction and Design of the Study**

It deals with rural credit, concepts of micro-finance, micro-credit financial institutions and their functions, select review of literature, need for the study, objectives and research methodology of the thesis.

**Chapter 2: Development of Micro-finance: An Over View**

It presents micro-finance overview in International and Indian perspectives. It also presents Micro-finance and SHGs Origin, growth and development which includes rural credit scenario in India prior to and after independence, multi-agency approach to rural credit, priority sector lending, micro-finance structure in India, and evolutionary aspects of SHGs in India.

**Chapter 3: Micro-finance: Experience of Andra Pradesh**

It describes micro-finance Andhra Pradesh Experience. It covers like SHG bank linkage, urban SHGs which unique feature of the State, Velugu project, SHG Federations and financial inclusion in the State.

**Chapter 4: SHG Financing: Role of Andhra Bank**

The chapter is segregated in two sections. The first section discusses the role of Andhra Bank in SHG Lending which includes SHG Financing by Andhra Bank, Innovative Schemes, IT enabled Schemes / Programme, Savings, Loans, Insurance Products, Training of SHGs in livelihood programmes etc. The second section gives a through analysis of SHG-BL programme across the three regions.

### Chapter 5: Performance Evaluation of SHGS-BL of Andhra Bank: Problems and Challenges

The chapter thoroughly presents the different function of Andhra Bank in relation to SHGs, and its impact on the people in the first segment, while the problems associated with the SHG-BL programmes and the challenges ahead is analyzed in the subsequent sections.

### Chapter 6: Summary of Findings, Conclusions and Suggestions

Findings of each chapter is summarized precisely in the first segment, while a broad conclusion on the study objective and hypothesis, suggestions and the road ahead is systematically discussed in the subsequent sections of the chapter.

# 2

# Development of Micro-finance: An Overview

## SECTION 1: INTERNATIONAL PERSPECTIVE

### A Brief History of Micro-finance

Over the past 10 years or so, micro-finance has rapidly evolved and expanded from the relatively narrow field of micro enterprise credit to the more compre-hensive concept of micro-finance (which includes a range of financial services for poor people, including savings, money transfers, and insurance) to the enormous challenge of building inclusive financial systems over a period of time.

The ideas and aspirations behind micro-finance are not new, small, informal savings and credit groups have operated for centuries across the world, from Ghana to Mexico to India and beyond. In Europe, as early as the 15th century, the Catholic Church funded pawn shops as an alternative to usurious money-lenders. These pawn shops spread throughout the urban areas in Europe throughout the 15th century Formal credit and savings institutions for the poor have also been around for generations, offering financial services for cus-tomers who were traditionally neglected by commercial banks. The Irish Loan Fund system, started in the early 1700s, is an early (and long-lived) example. By the 1840s, this system had about 300 funds throughout Ireland.

In the 1800s, Europe saw the emergence of larger and more formal savings and credit institutions that focused primarily on the rural and urban poor. The financial cooperative was developed in Germany. It aimed to help the rural population break from their dependence on moneylenders and to improve their Welfare. The movement emerged in France in 1865 and Quebec in 1900. Many of today's financial cooperatives in Africa, Latin America, and Asia find their roots in this European movement. Another early example is the Indonesian People's Credit Banks (IPCBs) that opened in 1895 and became the largest micro-finance system in Indonesia, with close to 9000 branches.

In the early 1900s, variations on the savings and credit theme began to appear in rural Latin America and elsewhere. These rural finance interventions aimed to modernize the agricultural sector, mobilize "idle" savings, increase investment through credit, and reduce oppressive feudal relations that were enforced through indebtedness.

Between the 1950s and 1970s, governments and donors focused on providing agricultural credit to small and marginalized farmers in hopes of raising productivity and incomes. These efforts to expand access to agricultural credit used State-owned development finance institutions, or farmers' cooperatives in some cases, to make loans to customers at below-market interest rates. These subsidized schemes were rarely successful. Rural development banks were unable to cover their costs with subsidized interest rates. Customers had poor re-payment discipline, because they saw their loans as gifts from the government. Consequently, these institutions' capital base eroded and, in some cases, disappeared. Worst of all, these funds did not always reach the poor. Instead, they of-ten ended up in the hands of more influential and better-off farmers.

Meanwhile, the 1970s saw the birth of micro-credit programs in Bangladesh, Brazil, and a few other countries began lending to poor women entrepreneurs. Early micro-enterprise credit was based on solidarity group lending in which every member of a group guaranteed the repayment of all members. Examples of early, pioneers include Grameen Bank in Bangladesh, which started out as an experiment by Prof. Muhammad Yunus; ACCION International, which began in Latin America and then spread to the United States and Africa; and the Self-Employed Women's Association Bank in India, which is a bank owned by a women's trade union. These institutions continue to thrive today and have in-spired countless others to replicate their success.

In the 1980s, micro-credit programs throughout the world improved on the original methodologies and defied conventional wisdom about financing for the poor. First, well-managed programs showed that poor people, especially women, paid their loans more reliably than better-off people with loans from commercial banks. Second, they demonstrated that poor people are willing and able to pay interest rates that allow micro finance institutions (MFIs) to cov-er their costs. MFIs that cover their costs can become viable businesses that attract deposits, commercial loans, and investment capital. They can reach huge numbers of poor clients without being limited by a scarce and uncertain supply of subsidized funds from governments and donor agencies. Bank Rakayat Indonesia (BRI) is a dramatic example of what can happen when MFIs focus on collecting loans and covering costs. BRI's village-level branch system now serves more than 30 million low-income savers and borrowers.

The 1990s saw growing enthusiasm among international development agencies and networks for promoting micro-finance as a strategy to alleviate poverty. Micro-finance blossomed in many countries where multiple MFIs serve the needs of micro-entrepreneurs and poor households. These gains, however, tended to concentrate in urban and densely populated rural areas.

In the early 1990s, the term "micro-finance" rather than "micro-credit" began to be used to refer to a range of financial services for the poor, including credit, savings, insurance, and money transfers.

To reach ever larger numbers of poor clients, MFIs and their networks increasingly began to pursue a strategy of commercialization, thus transforming themselves into for profit corporations that could attract more capital and become more permanent features of the financial system. An emphasis on creating and growing strong institutions (as opposed to channeling credit to specific groups) is a core element of this recent history.

### *Micro-finance Today*

Micro-finance has achieved astonishing accomplishments over the past 30 years. It has demonstrated that poor people are viable customers, created a number of strong institutions focusing on poor people's finance, and begun to attract the interest of private investors. But despite these achievements, there is still a long way to go to extend access to all who need financial services. Specifically, three major challenges define the frontier of financial services for the poor:

1. Scaling up quality financial services to serve large numbers of people (scale);
2. Reaching increasingly poorer and more remote people (depth); and
3. Lowering costs to both clients and financial service providers (cost).

The question is: How do we overcome these challenges? The answer: By making financial services for the poor a part of every country's mainstream fi-nancial system.

Just as the term micro-credit gave way to micro-finance in the 1990s, many people now advocate moving away from the term micro-finance. These people argue that meeting the frontier challenges means many different kinds of finan-cial service providers-not just specialized ones-should recognize that poor and low-income clients are a viable business proposition. They believe the pre-fix "micro" conjures up an image of something small or marginal. But today's micro-finance should not be marginalized or relegated to a narrow space within the financial system. The potential market is simply too enormous.

The good news is that this integration into the larger financial system is beginning (although progress is uneven across regions and countries). The borders between traditional micro-finance and the larger financial' system are starting to blur. Many specialized MFIs are working at the grassroots level and continue to achieve greater scale. Commercial banks and other formal financial institutions increasingly move down-market to reach larger numbers of ever poorer and more remote clients. As these different institutions start to meet in the middle, they hold out the promise of serving more and more people.

Unfortunately, no comprehensive database tracks the size of the current or potential market for financial services among poor and low-income clients. To begin to grasp the extent of the market, CGAP surveyed a broad range of financial institutions that aim to reach clients below the radar screen of traditional commercial banks. These institutions-State-owned agricultural, development, and postal banks; member-owned savings and loan institutions; other savings banks; low-capital community and/ or rural banks; and specialized MFIs of all kinds-share the common characteristic of a "double bottom line". They aim to serve poorer markets, but they also aim to cover their costs and even turn a profit. The CGAP research revealed a surprising 750 million savings and loan accounts collectively.

The seemingly large number of existing accounts does not indicate that the job is done and that financial systems already work for the poor. On the contrary, adjusted for inactive accounts and for people with multiple accounts, the 750 million accounts may translate into (at most) 500 million active clients, who constitute only a fraction of the potential market of three billion poor people. Also, the quality of services in some of these institutions is not high when it comes to truly meeting the needs of poor and low-income clients. Access is not only about having a bank account. It is also about the convenience and safety of the account and whether these services are fairly priced, meet the needs of customers, and are offered by a solid institution that will be around over the long haul to help its customers manage their financial lives. Many of these institu-tions fall short of providing quality financial access for all, but they represent a huge potential opportunity to reach large numbers of poor clients.

As shown in Fig. 2.1, a large number of accounts are highly concentrated, both geographically and in the types of financial institutions that offer them. State-owned banks, including postal banks, account for nearly three-quarters of all accounts. Meanwhile, 84 percent of all accounts are in Asia and more than half of these are in two countries alone-China and India.

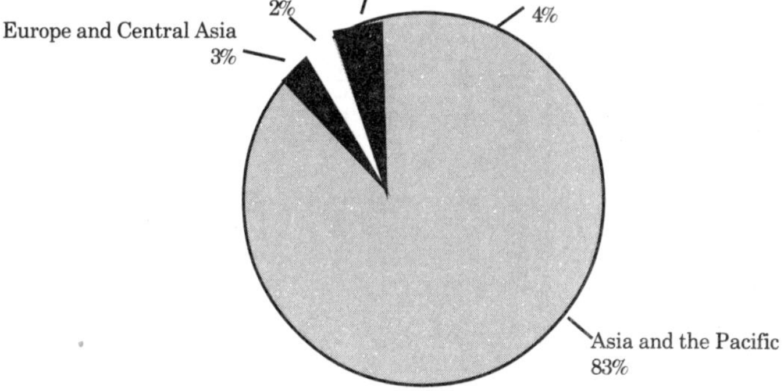


**Figure 2.1: Global accounts by Region**

Generally, MFIs, financial cooperatives, and rural banks are the institutions that have been most deliberate about serving poor and low-income clients with high-quality, accessible financial services. Table 2.1, 2.2, 2.3, 2.4, 2.5 reviews the global land-scape, with an emphasis on these more specialized institutions.

**Table 2.1**
**Global Combined Loans and Savings Accounts**

| | *MFIs* | *Co-ops and credit unions* | *Rural Banks* | *State / agricultural / develop-ment banks* | *Postal Banks* | *Total* | *Percent of Total* | *Account per hundred people* |
|---|---|---|---|---|---|---|---|---|
| Asia and the Pacific | 107,255 | 14,579 | 17,677 | 140,752 | 277,388 | 557,651 | 83 | 17 |
| Middle East and North Africa | 1,422 | 11 | Not available | 30,712 | 16,525 | 48,670 | 8 | 13 |
| Sub-Saharan Africa | 6,246 | 5,940 | 1,117 | 634 | 12,854 | 26,791 | 4 | 4 |
| Europe and Central Asia | 495 | 5,692 | Not available | 28 | 11,503 | 17,718 | 3 | 5 |
| Latin America and Caribbean | 5,156 | 8,620 | 162 | 81 | 179 | 14,198 | 2 | 3 |
| Total | 120,574 | 34,842 | 18,956 | 172,207 | 318,449 | 665,028 | 100 | 13 |

*Source:* Christen, Rosenberg, and Jayadeve, "Financial institutions with a 'Double Bottom Line', *Occasional Paper* No.8 CGAP, July, 2004

- These figures do not include (non-postal) savings banks because the number of accounts was not available. The researchers assume that non-postal savings banks would add 150 millions, brining the total numbers of all alternate finance institutions accounts to well over 750 million.
- China and India are included: China = 156,924; India =187,812.

**Table 2.2**
**The Global Landscape of Micro-finance - Asia**

| *General Characteristics of the Micro-finance Sector* | *Trends* |
|---|---|
| • The micro-finance sector in Asia has a strong social orientation.<br>• There is more emphasis on finance in densely populated rural areas.<br>• Except for a few institutions, there is a focus on enterprise credit (as opposed to multiple financial services)·<br>• The two Asian giants, china and India, have little sustainable micro-finance relative to their population sizes – mostly because of extensive historic government involvement in the financial sector.<br>• Bangladesh and Indonesia are the giants from the micro-finance perspective. But each has taken a completely different approach:<br>• Bangladesh's 24.6 million micro-finance clients generally receive micro-credit from large NGOs and other traditional MFIs that prioritize their social mission.<br>• Indonesia's micro-finance sector is led by BRI, the largest MFI in world history. BRI is an affiliate of a reformed state bank, recently partially privatized, that operates on a more commercial basis. | • Recently, India has started to take off, with a few commercial banks joining traditional community- based self-help groups to offer financial services to poor clients. |

| | *Asia in Numbers* | | | |
|---|---|---|---|---|
| | *Financial Cooperatives* | *NGOs* | *Banks and NBFIs* | *All Institutions* |
| No. of borrowers (thousands) | 11.2 | 96.0 | 248.3 | 119.3 |
| Gross loan portfolio (million $) | 2.3 | 12.7 | 59.0 | 29.9 |
| Loan balance per borrowers as % GNI per capita | 28.9 | 17.1 | 91.6 | 48.5 |
| Deposit per saver as % GNI per capita | 6.1 | 25.0 | 34.0 | 25.6 |
| Return on assets | 8.9 | -4.5 | 1.0 | -0.7 |
| Costs per borrowers ($) | 37.9 | 32.0 | 75.0 | 50.0 |

*Note:* All figures in tables are average; BRI=Bank Rakayat Indonesia; ECA=Eastern Europe and Central Asia; GNI = gross national income; MFI=Micro-finance institutions; NBFIs = nonblank financial institutions; NGO=non-government organization. These tables are based on available data from a subset of institutions that have reported their information to one or more of several existing databases and do not represent the performance of the entire micro-finance sector in each region. The tables include data on institutional averages in developing countries. Data also come from an interview with Adrian Gonzalez, research analyst, CGAP / The MIX, based on MFIs reporting data for 2003 to Micro-banking Bulletin (MBB)-11, Micro credit Summit Campaign Report 2004 (for number if borrowers only), and Mix market.

- Credit and Development Forum, 19, 23,248; email interview with lftekhar Hossian, consultant.
- Robinson, "The Future of Commercial Micro-finance Industry in Asia.

## Table 2.3
## The Global Landscape of Micro-finance - Latin America

| *General Characteristics of the Micro-finance Sector* | *Trends* |
|---|---|
| • Of all regions, Latin America has the longest tradition of commercially viable micro-finance<br>• Most micro-finance clients in the region obtain services from regulated financial institutions. | • While most financial institutions focus more on micro-credit, leading i nstitutions are increasingly offering a variety of financial services to their clients, |

- In some countries, interest rates have declined dramatically as a result of that competition, in Bolivia interest rates plummeted from an average of 50 percent in the mid 1990s to around 21 percent in 2004.

including savings and management of international and domestic funds transfers.

- Despite market penetration and a variety of services offered in some countries, there are enormous opportunities in large countries where little micro-finance is happening (for example, Mexico and Brazil), in secondary cities and in rural areas.

*Latin America in Numbers*

| | *Financial Cooperatives* | *NGOs* | *Banks and NBFIs* | *All Institutions* |
|---|---|---|---|---|
| No. of borrowers (thousands) | 12.6 | 17.0 | 36.0 | 21.0 |
| Gross loan portfolio (million $) | 35.2 | 10.1 | 36.9 | 22.1 |
| Loan balance per borrowers as % GNI per capita | 72.2 | 47.3 | 71.7 | 58.4 |
| Deposit per saver as % GNI per capita | 30.9 | 55.3 | 213.4 | 129.3 |
| Return on assets | -0.3 | -1.0 | 1.4 | -0.1 |
| Costs per borrowers ($) | 156.2 | 150.3 | 224.7 | 176.1 |

*Note:* All figures in tables are average; BRI=Bank Rakayat Indonesia; ECA=Eastern Europe and Central Asia; GNI = gross national income; MFI=Micro-finance institutions; NBFIs = nonblank financial institutions; NGO=non-government organization. These tables are based on available data from a subset of institutions that have reported their information to one or more of several existing databases and do not represent the performance of the entire micro-finance sector in each region. The tables include data on institutional averages in developing countries. Data also come from an interview with Adrian Gonzalez, research analyst, CGAP / The MIX, based on MFIs reporting data for 2003 to Micro-banking Bulletin (MBB)-11, Micro credit Summit Campaign Report 2004 (for number if borrowers only), and Mix market.

- Gonzalez-Vega and lbarnegaray, *Las Microfinanzas en el Desarrollo del Sistema* Financiero de Bolivia, 92.

**Table 2.4**
**The Global Landscape of Micro-finance - Africa**

| *General Characteristics of the Micro-finance Sector* | *Trends* |
|---|---|
| • Overall, micro-finance in Africa is under-developed and faces higher operating costs than in other regions. In most African countries, a very small minority of the copulation have bank accounts. Even in the most developed economy, South Africa, half the adult population is still "unbanked," and the vast majority of the self-employed are unbanked in two of the other leading economies, Kenya and Nigeria, where only 11 percent and 10 percent, respectively, have bank accounts. | • Recently, banks have begun to enter the market. Examples include Equity Bank in Kenya and Teba Bank in South Africa. |
| • Financial cooperatives are the dominos model in French speaking Africa, reaching several hundred thousand clients. | |
| • English-speaking Africa (outside South Africa) and Portuguese speaking countries also have large numbers of financial cooperatives, but specialized micro-finance NGOs are more prominent in those parts of the continent than in others. | |

| | *Africa in Numbers* | | | |
|---|---|---|---|---|
| | *Financial Cooperatives* | *NGOs* | *Banks and NBFIs* | *All Institutions* |
| No. of borrowers (thousands) | 11.6 | 17.9 | 24.3 | 17.4 |
| Gross loan portfolio (million $) | 4.3 | 2.3 | 4.5 | 3.7 |
| Loan balance per borrowers as % GNI per capita | 144.6 | 59.9 | 140.1 | 115.9 |
| Deposit per saver as % GNI | 32.7 | 25.0 | 85.6 | 49.8 |

| | | | | |
|---|---|---|---|---|
| per capita | | | | |
| Return on assets | -1.6 | -16.8 | -3.9 | -7.3 |
| Costs per borrowers ($) | 136.9 | 256.1 | 346.3 | 237.7 |

*Note:* All figures in tables are average; BRI=Bank Rakayat Indonesia; ECA=Eastern Europe and Central Asia; GNI = gross national income; MFI=Micro-finance institutions; NBFIs = nonblank financial institutions; NGO=non-government organization. These tables are based on available data from a subset of institutions that have reported their information to one or more of several existing databases and do not represent the performance of the entire micro-finance sector in each region. The tables include data on institutional averages in developing countries. Data also come from an interview with Adrian Gonzalez, research analyst, CGAP / The MIX, based on MFIs reporting data for 2003 to Micro-banking Bulletin (MBB)-11, Micro credit Summit Campaign Report 2004 (for number if borrowers only), and Mix market.

- Oxford Analytica, "South Africa: Banking the proves viable" and "Africa: Low banking penetration const4rains growth.

## Table 2.5
## The Global Landscape of Micro-finance - Eastern Europe and Central Asia

| *General Characteristics of the Micro-finance Sector* | *Trends* |
|---|---|
| • Eastern Europe and Central Asia is a newcomer to micro-finance and is dominated by NGOs and other institutions that focus primarily on loans (although there are a few notable exceptions, such as the Pro Credit Banks in several countries, which offer a variety of services). | • The main threats to future viability are high costs and moving from donor dependence to linking to financial systems. • Micro-finance in the region still has a significant opportunity to expand to reach poorer and more remote clients. |
| • Micro-finance has developed differently in this region than in the rest of the world. For instance, higher income and education levels partly explain the larger loans offered in the region. And interestingly, institutions have rapidly achieved financial self-sufficiency when compared with other regions. | |

| | *Eastern Europe and Central Asia in Numbers* | | | |
|---|---|---|---|---|
| | *Financial Cooperatives* | *NGOs* | *Banks and NBFIs* | *All Institutions* |
| No. of borrowers (thousands) | 0.7 | 5.2 | 5.1 | 4.8 |
| Gross loan portfolio (million $) | 1.3 | 4.2 | 12.4 | 7.0 |
| Loan balance per borrowers as % GNI per capita | 52.8 | 77.6 | 264.6 | 144.3 |
| Deposit per saver as % GNI per capita | 87.2 | Not available | 92.9 | 89.6 |
| Return on assets | -0.2 | -0.1 | 1.9 | 0.6 |
| Costs per borrowers ($) | 392.6 | 263.7 | 362.0 | 309.8 |

*Note:* All figures in tables are average; BRI=Bank Rakayat Indonesia; ECA=Eastern Europe and Central Asia; GNI = gross national income; MFI=Micro-finance institutions; NBFIs = nonblank financial institutions; NGO=non-government organization. These tables are based on available data from a subset of institutions that have reported their information to one or more of several existing databases and do not represent the performance of the entire micro-finance sector in each region. The tables include data on institutional averages in developing countries. Data also come from an interview with Adrian Gonzalez, research analyst, CGAP / The MIX, based on MFIs reporting data for 2003 to Micro-banking Bulletin (MBB)-11, Micro credit Summit Campaign Report 2004 (for number if borrowers only), and Mix market.

- MIX, "Benchmarking Micro-finance in Eastern Europe and Central Asia".

## Table 2.6
## The Global Landscape of Micro-finance - Middle East and North America

| *General Characteristics of the Micro-finance Sector* | *Trends* |
|---|---|
| • 70 percent of MFIs in the Middle East and North Africa are NGOs and donor dependent.<br>• Micro-finance is largely perceived as charity and not part of an inclusive financial system.<br>• Nonetheless, commercial banks from the region (especially Egypt) are starting to move down-market and develop services for the poor. | • Micro-finance is growing fast, with an annual average growth rate of 50 percent, although much of that growth is happening in two countries – Morocco, where two MFIs reach more than 300,000 clients, and Egypt where commercial banks are downscaling. |

| | *Eastern Europe and Central Asia in Numbers* | | | |
|---|---|---|---|---|
| | *Financial Cooperatives* | *NGOs* | *Banks and NBFIs* | *All Institutions* |
| No. of borrowers (thousands) | 1.6 | 29.6 | 4.7 | 22.7 |
| Gross loan portfolio (million $) | Not available | 6.9 | 2.1 | 6.1 |
| Loan balance per borrowers as % GNI per capita | Not available | 17.4 | 35.7 | 20.6 |
| Deposit per saver as % GNI per capita | Not available | 2.4 | 0.8 | 2.1 |
| Return on assets | Not available | 85.9 | 258.4 | 116.4 |

*Note:* All figures in tables are average; BRI=Bank Rakayat Indonesia; ECA=Eastern Europe and Central Asia; GNI = gross national income; MFI=Micro-finance institutions; NBFIs = nonblank financial institutions; NGO=non-government organization. These tables are based on available data from a subset of institutions that have reported their information to one or more of several existing databases and do not represent the performance of the entire micro-finance sector in each region. The tables include data on institutional averages in developing countries. Data also come from an interview with Adrian Gonzalez, research analyst, CGAP / The MIX, based on MFIs reporting data for 2003 to Micro-banking Bulletin (MBB)-11, Micro credit Summit Campaign Report 2004 (for number if borrowers only), and Mix market.

## Comparative Performance of some countries

It is praiseworthy that at the global level Micro-finance Information Exchange (MIX), for the purpose of benchmarking, collects data from MFIs around the globe, processes it into standardized reporting formats and crosschecks with audited financial statements, ratings and through third party due diligence reports, if available. Performance results are then adjusted using industry standard adjustments, to eliminate subsidy, guarantee minimal provision for risk and reflect the impact of inflation on institutional performance. This process increase comparability of performance results across institutions along a range of industry standard indicators MIX benchmarks. Year 2006 provides comparable data/ratios on 37 MFIs covering their 9 years of operation in India along with 83 MFIs with 8 years operations in South Asian region, 184 MFIs with 10 years of operations in Asian continent and 704 MFIs with 9 years of operations around the globe. Analysis of data/ratios relate to institutional characteristics [Table 2.7], financial structure [Table 2.8], outreach indicators [Table 2.9], overall financial performance, revenues, expenses [Table 2.10], efficiency, productivity, and risk and liquidity [Table 2.11]. Of these 37 MFIs in India, 24 were From Southern India followed by 10, 2 and 1 from Eastern, Northern & Western India respectively. While 11 each belonged to SHG- bank linkage and Grameen models, 15 belonged to individual banking model.

**Table 2.7**

**MIX Benchmarks 2007 – Institutional Characteristics**

| | *India* | *South Asia* | *Asia* | *Global* |
|---|---|---|---|---|
| Number of MFIs | 37 | 83 | 184 | 704 |
| Age | 9 | 8 | 10 | 9 |
| Total Assets | 9,635,690 | 8,610,183 | 5,468,125 | 6,169,918 |
| Offices | 45 | 38 | 15 | 11 |
| Personal | 303 | 248 | 135 | 94 |

*Sources: India Micro-finance Review*, 2007 by Micro-Credit Ratings International ltd India.

**Table 2.8**

**MIX Benchmarks 2007 – Financial Structure**

| | *India* | *South Asia* | *Asia* | *Global* |
|---|---|---|---|---|
| Capital /Asset Ratio | 4.3% | 9.1% | 17.5% | 25.4% |
| Commercial Funding Liability Ratio | 81.1% | 63.4% | 71.0% | 61.0% |
| Debt / Equity Ratio | 11.9% | 6.0% | 4.0% | 2.6% |
| Gross Loan Portfolio/ Total Assets | 83.4% | 78.5% | 73.6% | 77.9% |

*Source: India Micro-finance Review*, 2007 by Micro-credit Ratings International Ltd India.

An attempt is made here to compare the performance of MFIs in India with that of MFIs in South Asian Region, Asian continent and around the globe. Recommendations are made on the need for creating enabling environment for healthy & conducive growth of MFIs in India so that poor households can have easy access to financial services [and not only Credit] and can reasonability improve their standard of living during the recently launched 11th Five-year Plan [2007-12] and subsequent 12th Five-year Plan.

India MFIs have demonstrated their proven capabilities through efficiency and productivity to serve the largest number of borrowers at the lowest cost per borrower. Enabling environment has, therefore, its own significance, since many a time's genuine claimants for credit are denied the same on the grounds of lack of creditworthiness or financial viability of the credit proposal. In this context, it is necessary for the MFIs to dwell upon what could be done to make the claimants of institutional credit bankable or creditworthy. This would require re-engineering of existing financial products or delivery systems and making them more in tune with the expectations and absorptive capacity of the intended clientele. MFIs may need to redeem poor households form private indebtedness as a good number of poor families are indebted to private moneylenders and this debt has become a grinding mill around their neck. A number of families are born in debt, live in debt, commit suicides or die in debt. MFIs may empower poor families socially, economically and politically such that they can demand as a matter of right, form services provides timely, hassle – free and better services of health, drinking water, sanitation, road transport, communication, fuel, electricity, libraries, etc.

The study of comparative performance of India MFIs with that of other MFIs in south Asia, Asia and around the globe revealed that MFIs in India were cost effective, efficient, productive and managing risk well. These factors contributed

**Table 2.9**
**MIX Benchmarks 2007 – Outreach Indicators**

| | *India* | *South Asia* | *Asia* | *Global* |
|---|---|---|---|---|
| Number of Active Clients | 82,562 | 44,647 | 17,583 | 10,102 |
| Percent of Women Borrowers | 100% | 100% | 99.0% | 66% |
| Gross Loan portfolio | 8,648,133 | 6,478,902 | 3,e434,180 | 4,438,677 |
| Average Loan Balance per Borrower | 106 | 120 | 149 | 456 |
| Average Loan Balance per Borrower/GNI per Capita | 14.5% | 18.1% | 20.8% | 40.3% |

*Source: India Micro-finance Review,* 2007 by Micro-credit Ratings International Ltd India

to wider outreach [82,562 active borrowers per MFI], significantly minimizing cost per borrower [$11] and Portfolio at Risk (PAR) > 30 DAYS [0.8%] and PAR >90 days [0.2%]. MFIs paid considerable attention to developing human resources management and training policy as well as selection of geographical area for establishing offices. The staff of MFIs were by and large from local area, adequately qualified having affinity to serve rural areas, trained and periodically exposed to real field situation through cross country exposure for learning and sharing experiences [ study tours, seminars, workshops, conferences, etc ]. Loan policy focusing on proper identification and selection of eligible borrowers, pre-sanction appraisal of client and credit proposal, post disbursements supervision and follow-up on the end use of credit till it is fully repaid was scrupulously implemented. MFIs were able to project to project better image through their staff and clients to establish credibility before commercial banks that have facilitated MFIs to borrow quite sizeable funds for lending.

The financial indicators and ratios, embodied in the MIX Benchmarks 2006 of 37 MFIs in India, 83 MFIs in South

Asian region, 184 MFIs in Asian continent and 704 MFIs around the globe revealed that performance of Indian MFIs was better than that of MFIs in the region, the continent and around the globe in respect of the following parameters:

1. Number of offices [45], personal employed [303] and total assets [$96,35,690]

2. Commercial funding liability ratio [81.1%] and gross loan portfolio to total assets[83.4%]

3. Number of active borrowers [82,562] and gross loan portfolio [$86,48,133]

4. Return on assets [0.2%] which was of course much lower than 0.9% at global level and returns on equity [18.4%]

5. Financial self sufficiency [104.1%] being marginally lower than 105.7% at global level

6. Total expense ratio [18.3%], operating expense ratio [8.8%], personnel expense ratio [4.6%], administrative expense ratio [4.1%] and loan loss provision expense ratio [0.9%]

7. Operating expense to loan portfolio [10.4%], personnel expense to loan portfolio [5.3%] and cost per borrower [$11]

8. Borrowers per staff member [255] and borrowers per loan officer [350]

9. PAR>30 days [0.8%], PAR > 90 days [0.2%], write – off ratio [0.1%], loan loss rate [0.%] and risk coverage [61.7%].

**Table 2.10**
**MIX Benchmarks 2006 – Revenues, Expenses, Overall Financial Performance**

| | *India* | *South Asia* | *Asia* | *Global* |
|---|---|---|---|---|
| **Revenues** | | | | |
| Financial Revenue Ratio | 17.7% | 17.5% | 20.8% | 24.7% |
| Profit Margin | 4.0% | 1.0% | 1.8% | 5.4% |
| Yield on Gross Portfolio [nominal] | 21.7% | 23.3% | 26.5% | 30.2% |
| Yield on Gross Portfolio [real] | 15.0% | 15.7% | 19.1% | 22.3% |
| **Expenses** | | | | |
| Total Expenses Ratio | 18.3% | 19.6% | 22.0% | 24.6% |
| Financial Expense Ratio | 6.7% | 6.4% | 6.3% | 6.3% |
| Loan Loss Provision Expense Ratio | 0.9% | 1.0% | 1.2% | 1.4% |
| Operating Expense Ratio | 8.8% | 10.4% | 12.4% | 15.3% |
| Personal Expense Ratio | 4.6% | 5.9% | 6.9% | 8.3% |
| Administrative Expense Ratio | 4.1% | 4.5% | 6.0% | 7.0% |
| **Overall Financial Performance** | | | | |
| Return on Assets | 0.2% | 0.3% | 0.1% | 0.95 |
| Return on Equity | 18.4% | 0.6% | 2.1% | 4.0% |
| Operational Self-Sufficiency | 109.8% | 107.0% | 113.3% | 115.4% |
| Financial Self-Sufficiency | 104.1% | 101.0% | 101.8% | 105.7% |

*Source:* *India Micro-finance Review,* 2007 by Micro-credit Ratings International Ltd India

However, in case of the following parameters, the performance of Indian MFIs was poor as compared to that of MFIs in the region, the continent and the global level.

1. Capital assets ratio [4.3%] and debt to equity ratio [11.9%]

2. Average loan per borrower [$106] and average loan balance per borrower/ GNI per capita [14.5%]
3. Operational self - sufficiency [109.8%] being marginally higher than 107% in the region
4. Yield on gross portfolio [nominal 21.7% and real 15%] and financial revenue ratio [17.7%]
5. Financial expense ratio [6.7%]
6. Average salary / GNI per capita [2.3%].

**Table 2.11**
**MIX Benchmarks 2006 – Efficiency, Productivity, and Risk and Liquidity**

| | *India* | *South Asia* | *Asia* | *Global* |
|---|---|---|---|---|
| **Efficiency** | | | | |
| Operating Expense / Loan Portfolio | 10.4% | 14.3% | 17.2% | 20.1% |
| Personnel Expense/ Loan Portfolio | 5.3% | 8.6% | 9.8% | 11.0% |
| Average Salary / GNI per Capita | 2.3% | 3.3% | 2.8% | 4.2% |
| Cost per Borrower | 11 | 16 | 39 | 108 |
| **Productivity** | | | | |
| Borrowers per Staff Member | 255 | 160 | 125 | 112 |
| Borrower per Loan Officer | 350 | 241 | 208 | 216 |
| **Risk and Liquidity** | | | | |
| Portfolio at Risk >30 days | 0.8% | 1.2% | 2.1% | 2.8% |
| Portfolio at Risk >90 days | 0.2% | 0.6% | 1.2% | 1.4% |
| Write-off Ratio | 0.1% | 0.6% | 0.7% | 1.1% |
| Loan Loss Rate | 0.1% | 0.5% | 0.7% | 1.1% |
| Risk Coverage | 61% | 80.4% | 86.7% | 90.1% |
| Non-Earning Liquid Assets As % to Total Assets | 5.1% | 5.1% | 6.1% | 6.5% |

*Source: India Micro-finance Review*, 2007 by Micro-credit Ratings International Ltd India.

A report from MIX says of all countries in the survey, India claimed the most leading spot (14, more than double the number held by any other country) due to high scores in both efficiency and outreach. Several factors boosted India's position in the rankings. India is home to the greatest number of fastest growing MFIs, many of which served large client bases. ten out of the 14 top ranked institutions served more than 1,00,000 borrowers. Low transaction cost and small margins also improved the efficiency profile of these MFIs and India leads the global industry in efficient transactions. Relatively low personnel costs and high productivity through group based approaches brought the cost of serving each borrower to less than 3 per cent of GNI per capita. Clients also benefited from thin MFI returns. Prevailing interest rates charged by these institutions include narrow profit margins, keeping client cost stop some of the lowest in the global industry. On an average, Indian MFIs in the top 100 counted just 1.9 per cent net income relative to their loan portfolio, less than half the average of all leading MFIs'.

## SECTION II : ORIGIN, GROWTH AND DEVELOPMENT OF MICRO-fINANCE IN INDIA

### Origin of Micro-finance in India

The post-nationalization period in the banking sector, circa 1969, witnessed a substantial amount of resources being earmarked towards meeting the credit needs of the poor. There were several objectives for the bank nationalization strategy including expanding the outreach of financial services to neglected sectors. As a result of this strategy, the banking network underwent an expansion phase without comparables in the world. Credit came to be recognized as a remedy for many of the ills of the poverty. There spawned several pro-poor financial services, support by both the State and Central Governments, which included credit packages and programs customized to the perceived needs of the poor.

While the objectives were laudable and substantial progress was achieved, credit flow to the poor, and especially to poor women, remained low. This led to initiatives that were institution driven that attempted to converge the existing strengths of rural banking infrastructure and leverage this to better serve the poor. The pioneering efforts at this stage were made by National Bank for Agriculture and Rural Development (NABARD), which was given the tasks of framing appropriate policy for rural credit, provision of technical assistance backed liquidity support to banks, supervision of rural credit institutions and other development initiatives.

In the early 1980s, the Government of India (GoI) launched the Integrated Rural Development Programme (IRDP), a large poverty alleviation credit programme, which provided government subsidized credit through banks to the poor. It was aimed that the poor would be able to use the inexpensive credit to finance themselves over the poverty line. Also during this time, NABARD conducted a series of research studies independently and in association with MYRADA, a leading non-governmental organization (NGO) from Southern India, which showed that despite having a wide network of rural bank branches servicing the rural poor, a very large number of the poorest of the poor continued to remain outside the fold of the formal banking system. These studies also showed that the existing banking policies, systems and procedures, and deposit and loan products were perhaps not well suited to meet the most immediate needs of the poor. It also appeared that what the poor really needed was better access to these services and products, rather than cheap subsidized credit. Against this background, a need was felt for alternative policies, systems and procedures, savings and loan products, other complementary services, and new delivery mechanisms, which would fulfill the requirements of the poorest, especially of the women members of such households. The emphasis therefore was on improving the access of the poor to micro-finance rather than just micro-credit.

To answer the need for micro-finance from the poor, the past 25 years has seen a variety of micro-finance programs promoted by the government and NGOs. Some of these programs have failed and the learning experiences from them have been used to develop more effective ways of providing financial services. These programs vary from regional rural banks with a social mandate to MFIs. In 1999, the Government of India (GOI) merged various credit programs together, refined them and launched a new programme called Swaranjayanti Gram Swarazagar Yojana (SGSY). The mandate of SGSY is to continue to provide subsidized credit to the poor through the banking sector to generate self-employment through a self-help group approach and the program has grown to an enormous size.

Self-Help Groups: A Keystone of Micro-finance in India: Women empowerment and social security MFIs have also become popular throughout India as one form of financial intermediary to the poor. MFIs exist in many forms including co-operatives, Grameen-like initiatives and private sector MFIs. Thrift co-operatives have formed organically and have also been promoted by regional state organizations like the Cooperative Development Foundation (CDF) in Andhra Pradesh. The Grameen-like initiatives following a business model like the Grameen Bank. Private sector MFIs include NGOs that act as financial services providers for the poor and include other support services but are not technically a bank as they do not take deposits.

It is clear from the previous that the objectives of the bank sector nationalization strategy have resulted into several offshoots, some of which have succeeded and some have failed. Today, Self-help Groups and MFIs are the two dominant forms of micro-finance in India.

### *Evolution of Credit Delivery System*

The evolution in relation to credit delivery system has some parallel to the evolution of thought on economic growth and development.

In the first stage, the major concern as simply to accelerate economic growth. Growth was identified with the increase in the availability of material goods and services. Eradication of poverty was to be achieved through faster economic growth.

In the second stage, a greater concern with the distribution, of income emerged. Development was seen as going beyond economic growth and bringing out changes in the structure of economy. Equitable distribution of the benefits of economic growth became an independent goal.

In the third stage, the concept of equity was translated into the provision to everyone of what came to be described as 'basic needs", which included the fundamental requirements of life, such as education, safe water and health services. In the current stage of discussion, the concept of basic needs has been widened and the objective of growth is set as human development which means an improvement in the quality of the life of the people. Enhancement of human development implies on the one hand to the creation of human capabilities through improved health, knowledge and skills and on the other, the opportunities for the people to make use of these capabilities.

In the case of credit delivery system, one can set: a similar evolution of thought. While in the early stages, the emphasis was on providing more credit in later stages the emphasis shifted to ensure that credit went to all segment of society. Even the prescription of a proportion of total credit for priority sectors was not considered to be adequate. Despite the expansion of the organized banking system deep into the rural areas, a very large number of the poor continued to remain outside the fold of the formal banking system. The formal banking system with its systems and procedures was found to be inaccessible to the poor. This led to a search for an alternative delivery mechanism, which would meet the requirements of the poor and particularly the women among them.

### *Emergence of the SHG Movement*

While no definitive date has been determined for the actual conception and propagation of SHGs, the practice of small groups of rural and urban people banding together to form a savings and credit organization is well established in India. In the early stages, NGOs played a pivotal role in innovation of the SHG model and in implementing the model to develop the process fully. In the 1980s, policy makers took notice and worked with development organizations and bankers to discuss the possibility of promoting these savings and credit groups. Their efforts and the simplicity of SHGs helped to spread the movement across the country. State governments established revolving loan funds which were used to fund SHGs.

By the 1990s, SHGs were viewed by state governments and NGOs to be more than just a financial intermediation but as a common interest group, working on other concerns as well. The agenda of SHGs included social and political issues as well

### *Origin of SHGs and MFIs*

It is in this background that the idea of organizing self-help groups began to take shape. A self-help group is a group of about 10 to 20 persons from a homogeneous background who come together for addressing the common problems. They collect voluntary savings on a regular basis and use the pooled resources to make small interest bearing loans to their members. At a later stage, these groups are able to obtain credit from outside sources to support income-generating activities. Very often there is a self-help promoting institution (SHPI), which enables the self-help group to function effectively. A stimulus to the rapid growth of self-help groups was provided when the SHG-bank linkage programme was initiated in 1992. It was a pilot project for promoting 500 SHGs. As the idea gained acceptance from the banking system and the results were promising, the Reserve Bank of India encouraged this positive initiative by issuing instructions to banks in 1996 to cover SHG financing as a main stream activity under the priority sector lending portfolio. A working group set up by the RBI in 1994 came up with wide ranging recommendations on SHG and bank linkage as a potential innovation in the area of banking with the poor.

Another approach to providing micro-finance has been through the micro-finance institutions. Even before the SHG method was perfected, many NGOs were using a variety of delivery mechanisms for providing credit services to the poor with financial support from external donors and later by apex institutions including the Rashtriya Mahila Kosh set up by the government, the SIDBI Foundation for Micro Credit and NABARD.

Since 2000, commercial banks including regional rural banks are providing funds to MFls for on-lending to poor clients. The exact number of MFls functioning in the country is not available. However, it is estimated that there are around 800 private MFls operating in the country with varied legal forms. While most are registered under Societies Registration Act, some are functioning as non-bank financial companies.

SHGs go through various stages of evolution, which are explained as:

**Group formation:** At this stage, groups are formed, developed and strengthened to evolve into self-managed people's organizations at the grassroots level.

**Group stabilization** through thrift and credit activity among the members and building their group corpus — the group takes up internal loaning to the members from the corpus.

**Micro-credit:** The group corpus is supplemented with Revolving Fund sanctioned as cash credit limit by the banks to take livelihood.

*The Evolution of Self-help Groups at Three Levels*

At the first level households use micro-finance to meet 'survival' requirements where small savings and loans serve as a buffer in the event of an emergency or to smoothen consumption or even service previous debt to give itself more liquidity during lean times.

At the second level, 'subsistence' needs are met through micro-finance, where a household begins to utilize micro-finance to diversify its basket of income-generating activities, or to meet working capital requirements in traditional activities.

At the third level as households reach a stage where they can assume a higher degree of risk, micro-finance would be used to invest in setting up an enterprise or facilitating entry into employment in one way or the other in order that the household becomes 'sustainable'.

In relation to the MFI model, it is quite clear that many micro-finance institutions have played a pioneering role in organizing the poor to obtain credit. They have played an excellent role in guiding the poor in undertaking appropriate productive activities. As indicated earlier, there are around 800 private MFIs operating in the country with varied legal forms. The overwhelming majority of MFls have 500-1500 clients and a few MFls have reached an outreach of 100,000 micro finance clients. A multi agency approach even with respect to micro-finance is useful. However, some thinking has to go into determining the appropriate legal form of micro-finance institutions.

### *Growth of SHGs*

The conceptual thinking behind the SHG initiative is that self-help supplemented by mutual help can be a powerful vehicle in the upward socio-economic transition of the poor. Poor can save and are bankable. Collective wisdom of the poor and peer pressure are valuable collateral substitutes.

NABARD has played a key role not only in promoting SHGs but also in standing behind the SHG-bank linkage programme. The performance of the SHGs has been extremely encouraging. Repayments by members to SHGs have been exceedingly high and on-time payments have hovered around 98 per cent. Many of the expectations behind the basic philosophy underlying the formation of SHGs seem to have been fulfilled. It has, however, to be noted that there is a concentration of SHGs in southern states. The experience so far has shown that the poor can organize themselves and do things to promote the well being. It has also had a tremendous social impact. It has made women more self-confident.

This impression is largely derived from - Andhra Pradesh. Despite this encouraging picture, as of now the total disbursement of credit is very limited and per household credit made available is very small. If a serious impact on the economic conditions of the rural poor has to be made, a much larger flow of credit to support a much broader production base is required. It is in this direction the movement has to travel.

## Scenario of Rural Credit Before and After Independence

The need for rural credit in India had been recognized even before Independence by the erstwhile British Government as early as 1793 when it issued regulations for *Taccavi* loans to farmers and subordinate tenants for various purposes. The measures initiated to reduce rural indebtedness and regulating money lending activities for agricultural purposes failed to provide a long-term solution. The Co-operative Societies Act passed in 1904 to provide necessary legislative support to the financing of agriculture and regulating credit in the interest of cultivators signaled the entry of credit for agriculture from the institutional sector. Since then, and till the late fifties, co-operatives had been the major institutional source for all agricultural loans. In the early days of independence, that is, during 1950s, banking activities were restricted to certain select towns and metropolis. Banking services in rural areas were virtually non-existent.

Financial System for Rural Credit in India after Independence: The last four-decade period witnessed a rapid growth of commercial banking network in India under the guidance and initiative of the Reserve Bank of India (RBI). A vast co-operative branch banking network was developed in the fifties and sixties for purveying agricultural credit. The nationalization of the Imperial Bank of India in 1955, 14 major commercial banks in 1969 and another 6 commercial banks in 1980, the setting up of the Farmers Service Societies (FSS) in 1973, and Regional Rural Banks (RRBs) in 1975 enabled the creation of an extensive financial infrastructure for taking banking to the far- flung rural areas.

### *Nationalization of Banks*

Nationalization of Banks speeded up the pursuit of national objectives, namely rural development for stimulating growth by strengthening agriculture, small scale and rural industries, thereby leading to employment generation. This was considered important to achieve faster, balanced and integrated development. The banks were also being credited with designing and implementing a wide range of social banking policies and products that supported vital sectors of rural development. The banking resources were in turn directed in meeting the credit needs of rural masses. It is fair to say that banking industry is the mirror of any rural economy. The last fifteen years or so have perhaps been the most important phase in the annals of our country when a number of economic reforms were initiated that stimulated high trajectory growth that we are now witnessing. With the rural economy on turbo, the banking industry too witnessed rapid transformation through deregulation and various liberalization measures, many of which were recommended by the Narasimham Committee, resulting in greater flexibility and financial stability.

Since the second half of 1960s, banks/financial institutions have been playing an important role in the socio-economic transformation of rural economy. Besides actively implementing Government sponsored lending schemes, Banks have been providing direct and indirect finance to support economic activities. Mandatory lending to the priority sectors has been an important feature of Indian banking. Commercial Banks, Co-operatives and Regional Rural Banks are the three major segments of rural financial sector in India. Rural financial system, in future has a challenging task of facing the drastic changes taking place in the banking sector, especially in the wake of economic liberalization. There is an urgent need for rural financial system to enlarge their role functions and range of services offered so as to emerge as "one stop destination for all types of credit requirements of people in rural centres".

A giant stride in banking was the Nationalizations of 14 commercial banks on July 19, 1969 - marking a turning point in the history of the Banks in India. The main objectives were to reduce regional imbalances and to be responsive to the needs of national development and aspirations of the common man. It imparted new ethos to Indian Banking. This was also the early phase of the green revolution in India. During this period, nationalized banks attempted to mop up new rural liquidity. The declared objectives of the new policy, known as social and development banking, were the following: to provide banking services in previously unbanked or under-banked rural areas; to provide substantial credit to specific activities including agriculture and cottage industries; and to provide credit to certain disadvantaged groups such as, for example, Dalit households. The Government of India and the Reserve Bank of India (RBI) issued, from time to time, specific directives regarding social and development banking. These included setting targets for the expansion of rural branches, imposing ceilings on interest rates, and setting guidelines for the sectoral allocation of credit. Given the new farming practices associated with the green revolution, the first post-nationalization phase of expansion in rural banking saw growth in credit to agriculture. Specifically, a target of 40 per cent of advances for the priority sectors, namely agriculture and allied activities, and small-scale and cottage industries, was set for public sector banks. The period after nationalization was characterized by an expansion of bank credit to rural areas.

The impact of bank nationalization on the growth of banks in rural areas is clear: The number of bank branches increased from 8,262 in 1969 to 68,682 as on 31-03-2007, of which rural area branches are 30,572 constituting of 45 per cent of the branches. The share of rural bank offices in total bank offices jumped from 17 per cent in 1969 to 36 per cent in 1972 and present is 45 per cent. The proportion of credit disbursed to rural areas tripled in the 1970s, and continued until 1980s. After 1980, however, the share of total bank credit that went to rural areas declined, from 15 per cent in 1987 to 10 per cent by March 2000, and further declined to 8 per cent in 2007. This is due to overall increase of industrial credit in the country. Rural deposits also grew rapidly after nationalization; their share of aggregate deposits doubled in the 1970s, from 6 per cent in 1969 to 13 per cent by 1980, continued to grow, reached 16 per cent by 1990 and declined to 11 per cent in 2007. However, the credit-deposit ratio in rural areas which was only at 25 per cent in 1969 rose to 56 per cent by 2007.

## Multi-Agency Approach to Rural Credit

A multi agency approach has been adopted for rural credit delivery, involving commercial banks, RRBs and co-operatives. A vigorous rural branch expansion programme by commercial banks and RRBs was undertaken to increase the rural credit flow. The main emphasis is on the spread of banking network and introduction of new instruments, credit packages and programmes, and sectoral and institutional 'bench-marks' was to make financial system responsive to the needs of the weaker sections in the society comprising small and marginal farmers, rural artisans, landless agricultural non-agricultural labourers and other small borrowers falling below poverty line.

### *Priority Sector Lending: Focus on Poor*

Commercial banks are required, as per the directions of RBI, to provide loans to the priority sector comprising agriculture and allied activities, small, tiny, cottage and village industries, rural artisans, etc., to the extent of 40 per cent of their credit portfolio. This includes 18 per cent of lending exclusively to agriculture and allied activities. Further, 10 per cent of their loan portfolio is required to be provided to weaker section of the society covering scheduled castes, scheduled tribes, small and marginal farmers, agricultural labourers, rural artisans, etc.

One of the objectives of banking policy after nationalization was to expand the flow of credit to agriculture and small industries, or what were termed priority sectors. The share of these sectors in the total advances of banks rose from 14 per cent in 1969 to 21 per cent in 1972 then went up to 33 per cent in 1980 and as of March 2007 it is 42 per cent. The RBI set a target of 40 per cent for priority sector lending and by the mid-1980s this target was met. From 1985 to 1990, in fact, the target was over-achieved, that is, more than 40 per cent of total advances went to those sectors. As on March 2007, banks have disbursed Rs.4, 10,379 crores under priority sector achieving 40.3 per cent, however, agriculture constitutes only 15.2 per cent as against the target of 18 per cent.

It may be seen from the foregoing that for banking with the poor, micro-finance has been an essential aspect of the banking policy. Though in the present scenario banks are serving a variety of clients, they continue to play an important role in the area of micro finance. Therefore, it is apt to consider banks as one of the major micro finance service providing institutions, though not exclusive micro finance institutions.

## Micro-finance Structure in India

Micro-finance institutions (MFIs) are those which provide thrift, credit and other financial services and products of very small amounts, mainly to the poor in rural, semi-urban and urban areas for enabling them to raise their income levels and improve their living standards. Defined thus, MFls in India fall under two broad sectors formal and non-formal Commercial banks, Regional Rural Banks (RRBs) and co-operative banks constitute the formal sector. In non-formal sector, three major organizational forms are observed:

(a) Not-for profit MFIs (NGOs; trusts, and certain forms of companies);

(b) Mutual benefit MFls (state credit co-operatives, national credit co-operatives and mutually aided co-operatives);

(c) For profit MFls (non-banking financial companies). Of these, the first and last categories mutually aided co- operatives (MACs) may well be considered as innovative institutional arrangements in the arena of financial intermediation.

After Independence, the Government of India (GOI) appointed a number of committees like Rural Banking Enquiry Commission (1949), All-India Credit Survey Committee (1951), All-India Credit Review Committee (1966), Working Group on Rural Banks (1975), Committee to Review Arrangements for Institutional Credit for Agriculture and Rural Development (1979) and Agricultural Credit Review Committee (1986), to review the arrangements for institutional credit delivery. The main focus of these committees was sector-oriented rather than people-centered, possibly because of the then prevalent view that the development of agricultural and rural sectors was closely inter-linked with the goals of poverty eradication. The reduction in social economic inequalities was expected to take place as a result of the "trickle down" effect. The recommendations of these committees, therefore, dealt more with the need for streamlining the flow of credit to the rural sectors, mainly agriculture sector, through appropriate institutional arrangements than with providing access to institutional credit for the asset-less rural poor.

It is estimated that there are about 7000 micro-finance institutions around the developing world. There is no comprehensive number of MFIs in India and the extent of intermediation carried out by them. This could partly be due to the variety of institutional forms and the resultant difficulties in collating their financial statistics. Given the available data in India, the total number of MFIs in the non-formal sector by the end of 2007 could be put at around 1,600. This is an indicative number arrived at, by taking into account the approximate numbers of NGOs participating until then in the NGO-SHG-Bank linkage programme of the NABARD, partners of the Grameen Trust, MACs and NBFCs. It may be noted that current focus of micro-finance policy in India is on the non-formal sector. The Reserve Bank of India through a circular issued in February, 2000 tried to mainstream micro-credit as a priority sector lending. The emerging rural micro finance sector in India, despite initiatives to promote linkages between the formal and non-formal sectors, has a dualistic structure. The formal banking institutions form the legal and regulated component of the micro-finance sector and largely function as the providers of bulk credit and other services. The NGOs, SHGs and federations of groups, who serve as non-formal intermediaries, operate outside the legalized structure, largely surviving on the gaps and loopholes within the formal system. The most noteworthy point about this intermediary layer is that it has demonstrated considerable organizational flexibility and dynamism in responding to the demands at the grass-roots.

As for the flow of funds, the major institutional sources of bulk credit in India are NABARD and SIDBI. There is also government initiated NGO, the Rashtriya Mahila Kosh (RMK) under the Department of Women and Child Development - that extends credit support to NGOs and Women Economic Development Corporations. Thus, in the micro-finance sector in India the formal funds get into the non-formed channels before they reach the desired segment of the clientele. The entry of a new set of players in the financial system has definitely eased a lot of delivery obstacles, by externalizing a part of banks' responsibilities in the spheres of identification of clients, assessment of their risk profile, loan monitoring and recovery, which, in turn, may result in a reduction in transaction costs. According to the study conducted by NABARD, there has been a 40 per cent reduction in transaction costs due to SHG intermediation and the consequent reduction in time spent by the bank staff. Similarly, the borrower's transaction costs have been found to have declined by 85 per cent with the elimination of complex documentation and procedures, and reduction in time and cost incurred in repeated visits to banks.

### *Micro-finance by Banks*

Self-help Group Bank linkage is being adopted by all public sector banks and was successful in reaching the poor rural women and their empowerment. Micro-finance is usually associated with very small loans, no collateral, borrowers from among the rural and urban poor, loans for income-generation through market-based self-employment, the formation of borrower groups and privatization, generally through the mechanism of NGO control over disbursement and the determination of the terms and conditions attached to each loan. In India, as we have noted, micro-finance has been described as the way to go with respect to rural banking for the poor. Micro-finance is the favoured alternative to the present system because, it is assumed that the transaction costs of banks and other financial institutions can be lowered significantly if these costs are passed on to self-help groups. The characteristic features of micro credit operations are small loans to poor households in rural and urban areas for income generation through self-employment.

India is one of the largest potential markets for micro-finance in the world; still, 36 per cent of rural poor are not getting access to services through the financial system. There is wide gap between demand and supply. The micro-finance is popular in few states such as Andhra Pradesh, Gujarat,

Tamil Nadu and Rajasthan due to respective State Governments' encouragement. Among the different models of micro-finance, SHG-bank linkage programme has emerged as the major micro-finance programme in the country, which is being adopted by commercial banks, RRBs and cooperative banks.

**SHG Bank Linkages in India**

Micro-finance is the provision of a broad range of financial services such as deposits, loans, payment services, money transfers, and insurance to poor and low-income households and, their micro enterprises. The basic idea of micro-finance is that; if poor people are provided access to financial assistance, including credit, they may be able to start or expand a micro-enterprise that will allow them to break out of poverty. Despite vast expansion of the formal credit system encompassing spheres of social and mass banking, the dependence of the rural poor on moneylenders still continues in many areas, especially for meeting their emergent needs. Under the circumstances, a non-formal agency for credit supply to the poor, in the form of Self Help Groups, emerged as a promising partner to the formal credit system. SHGs are part of micro credit.

In India, a variety of micro-finance schemes and various approaches have been practiced by both Governmental and Non-governmental. Leading national financial institutions like, the National Bank for Agriculture and Rural Development (NABARD), the Small Industries Development Bank of India (SIDBI) and the Rashtriya Mahila Kosh (RMK) have played a significant role in making micro credit a real movement in India. Professional Assistance for Development Action (PRADAN), International Centre for Entrepreneurship and Career Development (ICECD), Mysore Resettlement and Development Agency (MYRADA), Self Employed Women's Association (SEWA); act as resource organizations

**Table 2.12**
**State-wise Growth trends in the SBLP for 2006-07 (Rs in millions)**

| *Region / State* | *Cumulative groups up to 31-03-06* | *Groups linked during 2006-07* | *Groups provided with repeat finance dur 2006-07* | *Cumulative no. of groups, with bank loanUp to 31-03-2007* | *Cum-ulative bank loan up to 31-03-2006* | *Bank loan during 2006-07* | *Of column 7 repeat bank loan* | *Cumulative bank loan up to 31-03-2007* |
|---|---|---|---|---|---|---|---|---|
| *1* | *2* | *3* | *4* | *5* | *6* | *7* | *8* | *9* |
| **Northern Region** | | | | | | | | |
| Himachal Pradesh | 22,920 | 4,879 | 2,282 | 27.199 | 863.98 | 388.27 | 153.60 | 1,252.25 |
| Rajasthan | 98,171 | 39,666 | 3,692 | 137,837 | 2,447.94 | 1,447.40 | 191.53 | , 3895.34 |
| Haryana | 4,867 | 1,966 | 1,821 | 6!833 I | 316.01 | 183.31 | 69.86 | 499.32 |
| Punjab- | 4,561 | 1,893 | 517 | 6.454 | 238.86 | 147.74 | 29.24 | 356.60 |
| Jammu and Kashmir | 2,354 | 405 | 199 | 2,759 | 100.48 | 44.25 | 15.83 | 144.73 |
| New Delhi | 224 | 112 | | 336 | 18.58 | 8.65 | | 27.23 |
| **TOT AL** | **133,097** | **48,921** | **8,511** | **182,018** | **3,985.85** | **2,189.62** | **460.05'** | **6,175.47** |

*(Contd...)*

| 1 | 2 | 3 | 4 | 5 | 6 | 7 | 8 | 9 |
|---|---|---|---|---|---|---|---|---|
| **North Eastern Region** | | | | | | | | |
| Assam | 56,449 | 25,005 | 160 | 81,454 | 1,423.98 | 194.40 | 2.91 | 2,218.38 |
| Meghalaya | 735 | 476 | 0 | 1,211 | 16.19 | 17.40 | 0.00 | 33.59 |
| Tripura | 1,996 | 910 | 57 | 2,906 | 31.12 | 18.40 | 1.48 | 49.52 |
| Sikkim | 127 | 33 | 0 | 160 | 1.86 | 1.12 | 0.00 | 2.98 |
| Manipur | 1,468 | 1,215 | 0 | 2,683 | 71.85 | 40.80 | 0.00 | 112.65 |
| Arunachal Pradesh | 346 | 101 | 0 | 447 | 13.49 | 5.72 | 0.00 | 19.21 |
| Nagaland | 422 | 576 | 10 | 998 | 34.38 | 33.50 | 2.97 | 67.88 |
| Mizoram | 974 | 921 | 0 | 1,895 | 64.14 | 70.56 | 0.00' | 134.70 |
| **TOT AL** | **62,517** | **29,237** | **227** | **91.754** | **1,657.01** | **981.89** | **7.36** | **2,638.90** |
| Eastern Region | | | | | | | | |
| Orissa | 180,896 | 53,555 | 28,806 | 234,451 | 4,754.65 | 3,274.27 | 1,409.33 | 8,028.92 |
| Bihar | 46,221 | 26,118 | 1,306 | 72}39 | 1,052.19 | 9t!°.28 | 211.15 | 2,012.47 |
| Jharkhand | 30,819 | 6;498 | 1,153 | 37,317 | 1,114.60 | 391.96 | 84.21 | 1,506.56 |
| West Bengal | 136,251 | 45,312 | 22,014 | 181,563 | 2,424.52 | 2,060.64 | 888.40 | 4,485.16 |
| **UT of A and N Islands** | **164** | **47** | **30** | **211** | **8.23** | **4.58** | **3.40** | **12.81** |
| **TOT AL** | **394,351** | **131,530** | **53,309** | **“525,881,** | **9,354.19** | **6,691.72** | **2.596.50** | **16,045.91** |

| | | | | | | | | |
|---|---|---|---|---|---|---|---|---|
| **Central Region** | | | | | | | | |
| Madhya Pradesli' | 57,125 | 13,787 | 1,726 | 70.912 | 1,666.86 | 499.23 | 65.12 | 2.166.09 |
| Chhatisgarh | 31,291 | 10,412 | 1,330 | 41,703 | 337.81 | 218.44 | 27.51 | 556.25 |
| Uttar Pradesh | 161,911 | 36,676 | 2,873 | 198,587 | 5,153.54 | 1,778.48 | 192.43 | 6,932.02 |
| Uttarakhand | 17,588 | 3969 | 1;288 | 21.527 | 891.86 | 382.69 | 225.64 | 1,274.55 . |
| **TOT AL** | **267.915** | **64.814** | **7,217** | **332,729** | **8050.07** | **2,878.84** | **510.69** | **10.928.91** |
| **Western Region** | | | | | | | | |
| Gujarat | 34,160 | 9,412 | 64 | 43,572 | 1,244.51 | 885.46 | 4.69 | 2,129.97 |
| Maharashtra | 131,470 | 94,386 | 19,382 | 225,856 | 3,951.67 | 2,983.86 | 841.01 | 6;935.53 |
| Goa | 624 | 395 | 142 | 1,019 | 55.21 | 28.28 | 9.03 | 83.49 |
| **TOT AL** | **166,254** | **104,193** | **19,588** | **270,447** | **5,251.39** | **3,897.60** | **854.72** | **9,148.99** |
| **Southern Region** | | | | | | | | |
| Andhra Pradesh | 587,238 | 96,381 | '262,895 | 683,619 | 43.455.18 | 27,154.55 | 23'.536.74 | 71,209.73 |
| Karnataka | 224.928 | 92,708 | 56,717. | 317,636 | 9.927.53 | 8,163.89 | 3,239.26 | 18,091.42 |
| Karla | 86,988 | 30,925 | 13,559 | 117,913 | 4,821.48 | 2,889.40 | 1,067.68 | 7.710.88 |
| Tamil Nadu | '312,778 | 87,699" | 35.387 | 400,417, | 27.121.87 . | 10,984.48 | 3,721.55 | 38.106.35 |
| UT of Pondicherry | 2,499 | | | 2.499 | 350.86 | | | 350.86 |
| **TOT AL** | **1,214,431** | **307 713.** | **368.558** | **1,522,144** | **85,676.92** | **49,792.32** | **31,565.24** | **135.469.241** |
| **GRAND TOTAL** | **2,238,565 .** | **686.408** | **457,410** | **2,94,9'13** | **113,975.43** | **66.431.99** | **35,994.56** | **180.407.42** |

## Table 2.13
## Progress of SHG-bank Linkage Programme in India: 1992-93 to 2006-07

| Year | SHGs Linked *1 | | Bank's Loans to SHGs *2 | | NABARD'S Refinance to Banks | |
|---|---|---|---|---|---|---|
| | Number | Cumulative Number | Amount (Rs. in crores) | Cumulative Amount (Rs. in crores) | Amount Rs. in crores) | Cumulative Amount (Rs. in crores) |
| 1 | 2 | 3 | 4 | 5 | 6 | 7 |
| 1992-93 | 225 (-) | 255 (-) | 0.29 (-) | 0.29 (-) | 0.27 (-) | 0.27 (-) |
| 1993-94 | 365 (43.14) | 620 (143.13) | 0.36 (24.91) | 0.65 024.90 | 0.19 (-128.73) | 0.46 (71.26) |
| 1994-95 | 1,502 (311.51) | 2,122 (242.26) | 1.79 (395.84) | 2.44 (275.38) | 1.84 (865.44) | 2.30 (401.74) |
| 1995-96 | 2,635 (75.43) | 4,757 (124.17) | 3.62 (102.12) | 6.06 (148.28) | 3.36 (82.10) | 5.66 (145.80) |
| 1996-97 | 3,841 (45.77) | 8,598 (80.74) | 5.78 (59.81) | 11.84 ( 95.44) | 4.99 (48.57) | 10.65 (88.12) |
| 1997-98 | 5,719 (48.89) | 14,317 (66.51) | 11.92 (106.15) | 23.76 (100.67) | 10.73 (115.07) | 21.38 (100.75) |
| 1998-99 | 18678 (226.59) | 32,995 (130.46) | 33.32 (179.44) | 57.07 (140.19) | 30.68 (65.02) | 52.06 (143.49) |
| 1999-00 | 81,780 (337.84) | 1,14,775 (247.85) | 135.80 (307.68) | 192.87 (237.95) | 98.07 (219.65) | 150.13 (188.38) |
| 2000-01 | 1,49,050 (82.26) | 2,63,825 (129.86) | 288.00 (112.08) | 480.87 (149.32) | 250.61 (155.54) | 400.74 (166.93) |
| 2001-02 | 1,97,653 (32.61) | 4,61,478 (74.92) | 545.47 (89.40) | 1 026.34 (113.43) | 395.73 (57.91) | 796.47 (98.75) |
| 2002-03 | 2,55,882 (29.46) | 7,17,360 (55.45) | 1,022.33 (87.42) | 2 048.67 (99.61) | 622.33 (57.26) | 1,418.80 (78.14) |

| | | | | | | | | | | | | |
|---|---|---|---|---|---|---|---|---|---|---|---|---|
| 2003-04 | 3,61,731 | (41.37) | 10,79,091 | (50.43) | 1,855.54 | (81.50) | 3904.21 | (90.57) | 705.90 | (13.43) | 2 124.70 | (49.75) |
| 2004-05 | 5,39,365 | (49.11) | 16,18,456 | (49.98) | 2,994.25 | (61.37) | 6,898.46 | (76.69) | 967.30 | (37.03) | 3,092.00 | (45.53) |
| 2005-06 | 6,20,069 | (14.96) | 22,38,525 | (38.31) | 4,498.94 | (50.25) | 11,397.40 | (65.22) | 1,064.56 | (10.05) | 4,156.56 | (34.43) |
| 2006-07 | 6,86,448 | (9.66) | 29,24,973 | (13.93) | 2922.00 | (41.26) | 14,319.40 | (25.63) | 1164.00 | (9.39) | 5320.56 | (28.00) |
| Mean | 159892.5 | | - | | 814.10 | | - | | 296.89 | | - | |
| S.D. | 21162.64 | | - | | 1381.63 | | - | | 387.36 | | - | |
| LGR | 28.13 | | - | | 0.0008 | | - | | 0.09 | | - | |
| t-value | 2.83** | | - | | 2.18* | | - | | 2.79* | | - | |

** Significant at 1%level * Significant at 5%level

*Notes:** 1 SHGs linked are new SHGs only, excluding existing SHGs *2 Bank loans to SHGs include loans to existing as well as new SHGs
3. Figures in the parenthess indicate percentage growth rates over the respective preceding year.

*Sources:* NABARD, Progress of SHG-bank Linkage in India; Its various yearly publications, Mumbai.

**Table 2.14**

**Regional Spread of SHG-bank Linkage: 1992-93 to 2006-07**

| Year | *N.R* | | *N.E.R* | | *E.R.* | | *C.R* | | *W.R* | | *S.R* | | *All* | |
|---|---|---|---|---|---|---|---|---|---|---|---|---|---|---|
| | *SHGs (Nos.)* | *Bank loan (Rs. in Crores)* | *SHGs (Nos.)* | *Loan (Rs.ln crores* | *SHGs (Nos.)* | *Loan (Rs.ln crores)* | *SHGs (Nos.)* | *Loan (Rs.ln Crores)* | *SHGs (Nos.)* | *Loan (Rs.in crores)* | *SHGs (Nos.)* | *Loan (Rs. in Crores)* | *SHGs (Nos.)* | *Loan (Rs. Crores)* |
| *1* | *2* | *3* | *4* | *5* | *6* | *7* | *8* | *9* | *10* | *11* | *12* | *13* | *14* | *15* |
| 1997-98 | 142 | 0.45 | 5 | 0.014 | 648 | 0.50 | 558 | 1.25 | 916 | 1.19 | 3,450 | 8.52 | 5,719 | 11.92 |
| | (2.48) | (3.77) | (0.09) | (0.12) | (11.33) | (4.18) | (9.76) | (10.48) | (16.01) | (9.98) | (60.33) | (71.47) | (100) | (100) |
| 1998-99 | 605 | 1.37 | 49 | 0.13 | 1,653 | 1.55 | 1,925 | 1.81 | 1,941 | 3.60 | 12,505 | 24.86 | 18,678 | 33.32 |
| | (3.24) | (4.11) | (0.26) | (0.39) | (8.85) | (4.65) | (10.31) | (5.43) | (10.39) | (10.81) | (66.95) | (74.61) | (100) | (100) |
| 1999-00 | 752 | 4.17 | 96 | 0.13 | 5,204 | 4.94 | 9,277 | 9.46 | 4,388 | 7.72 | 41,933 | 109.57 | 61,650 | 135.93 |
| | (1.22) | (3.07) | (0.15) | (0.10) | (8.44) | (3.63) | (15.05) | (6.96) | (7.12) | (5.68) | (68.02) | (80.56) | (100) | (100) |
| 2000-01 | 4,221 | 9.78 | 160 | 0.49 | 11,057 | 11.14 | 8,631 | 12.40 | 6,911 | 11.04 | 1,09,218 | 243.04 | 1,40,198 | 287.89 |
| | (3.01) | (3.40) | (0.11) | (0.17) | (7.89) | (3.87) | (6.16) | (4.31) | (4.93) | (3.83) | (77.90) | (84.42) | (100) | (100) |
| 2001-02 | 10,309 | 20.94 | 1,013 | 1.64 | 23,640 | 27.74 | 19,330 | 31.19 | 13,775 | 26.87 | 1,70,999 | 437.08 | 2,39,066 | 545.46 |
| | (4.31) | (3.83) | (0.42) | (0.30) | (9.89) | (5.09) | (8.09) | (5.72) | (5.76) | (4.93) | (71.53) | (80.13) | (100) | (100) |
| 2002-03 | 15,602 | 39.82 | 2,579 | 3.49 | 45,001 | 73.68 | 33,402 | 87.83 | 12,862 | 35.40 | 1,46,434 | 782.11 | 2,55,882 | 1,022.33 |
| | (6.10) | (3.90) | (1.01) | (0.34) | (17.59) | (7.21) | (13.05) | (8.59) | (5.02) | (3.46) | (57.23) | (76.50) | (100) | (100) |

| | | | | | | | | | | | | | | |
|---|---|---|---|---|---|---|---|---|---|---|---|---|---|---|
| 2003-04 | 17,473 | 55.23 | 8,209 | 14.18 | 67,344 | 140.07 | 45,426 | 131.58 | 12,635 | 53.97 | 2,10,644 | 1,460.50 | 3,61,731 | 1,855.53 |
| | (4.83) | (2.98) | (2.27) | (0.76) | (18.62) | (7.55) | (12.56) | (7.09) | (3.49) | (2.91) | (58.23) | (78.71) | (100) | (100) |
| 2004-05 | 33,622 | 107.16 | 21,960 | 81.75 | 1,07,391 | 257.80 | 70,356 | 225.13 | 41,451 | 154.19 | 2,64,585 | 2,168.22 | 5,39,365 | 2,994.25 |
| | (6.23) | (3.58) | (4.07) | (2.73) | (19.91) | (8.61) | (13.04) | (7.52) | (7.69) | (5.15) | (49.06) | (72.41) | (100) | (100) |
| 2005-06 | 47,039 | 158.92 | 28,279 | 63.74 | 1,28,723 | 417.12 | 70,550 | 303.55 | 69,988 | 230.06 | 2,75,490 | 3,325.55 | 6,20,069 | 4,498.94 |
| | (7.59) | (3.53) | (4.56) | (1.42) | (20.76) | (9.27) | (11.38) | (6.75) | (11.29) | (5.11) | (44.42) | (73.92) | (100) | (100) |
| 2006-07 | 48921 | 218.9 | 29237 | 98.10 | 131530 | 669.17 | 64814 | 287.88 | 104193 | 389.76 | 307713 | 4979.23 | 686408 | 6643.19 |
| | (7.12) | (3.29) | (4.25) | (1.47) | (19.16) | (10.17) | (19.44) | (4.33) | (15.18) | (5.86) | (44.82) | (74.95) | (100) | (100) |

*Notes:* 1. Figures in the parenthess are region wise percentages to row totals
2. Discrepancies in aggregate SHG figures for the years 99-00, 00-01and 01-02 in this table due to unrevised region wise breakups.

*Sources:* NABARD, Progress of SHG-bank Linkage in India; Its various yearly publications. Mumbai

and have been successful in replicating their experiences in other parts of the country without restricting to one area.

There are three models being followed in the area of Micro-finance in India. In model 1 banks they take up the work of forming and nurturing the self help groups, opening their accounts and providing them with bank loans. Up to March 2007, about 20 per cent of SHGs financed were from this category. In model 2, where SHGs are formed by formal agencies other than banks, NGOs and others, but directly financed by banks, have occupied the major share with 74 per cent of the total number of SHGs as on 31 March 2007. Model 3 consists of SHGs financed by banks using NGOs and other agencies as financial intermediaries. The share of cumulative number of SHGs linked to this model is relatively small i.e. six per cent.

### *Growth of SHGs Linked to Banks, Bank Loans and NABARD's Refinance*

Table 2.13 presents year-wise progress of SHG-bank linkage programme in India for 14-year period covering three dimensions namely annual and cumulative number of SHGs linked with banks, amount of bank loans and NABARD's refinance to banks. Annual growth rates of fresh and cumulative bank-linked SHGs are highest at 337.84 and 247.85 per cent respectively in the year 1999- 2000, and lowest at 9.66 and 13.93 per cent respectively for the year 2006-07. Annual fresh and renewal loans, and cumulative loans to bank- linked SHGs are highest at 307.68 and 237.95 per cent respectively in the year 1999-00 and lowest at 24.91 and 25.63 per cent in 1993-94 and 2006-07 respectively. Annual fresh and renewal, and cumulative NABARD's refinancing to banks linking SHGs, are highest at 219.65 and 188.38 per cent respectively in the year 1999-2000, lowest at 128.73 and 28.00 per cent in 1993-94 and 2006-07 respectively. From the preceding analysis it can be concluded with annual growth rates on all dimensions of SHG programme are impressive at national level.

**Table 2.15**
**ANOVA-test for Regional differences in SHG bank linkage**

| *Regions* | *Sum of squares* | *Df* | *Mean square* | *F* |
|---|---|---|---|---|
| Between Regions | 738737239060.635 | 6 | 73122873176.772 | 8.011** |
| Within Regions | 511134930399.111 | 56 | 9127409471.413 | |
| Total | 949872169459.746 | 62 | | |

** Significant at 1 per cent level

**Table 2.16**
**ANOVA-test for Regional differences in bank loans to SHGs**

| *Regions* | *Sum of squares* | *Df* | *Mean square* | *F* |
|---|---|---|---|---|
| Between Regions | 14533378.553 | 6 | 2422229.759 | 4.423** |
| Within Regions | 30668493.896 | 56 | 547651.677 | |
| Total | 45201872.448 | 62 | | |

** Significant at 1 per cent level

### *Regional Spread of SHG-Bank Linkage*

Regional spread of bank-linked SHGs and loans by SHG-linking banks are shown in the Table 2.14 in absolutes and per centage shares. The per centage shares of N.R., N.E.R., E.R., C.R., W.R, and S.R. in fresh SHGs in the initial year 1997-98 were 2.48, 0.07, 11.33, 9.76, 16.01 and 60.33 respectively, whereas in the terminal year 2006-07, the corresponding per centage shares were 7.12, 4.25, 19.16, 19.44, 15.18, and 44.82. Per centage shares of the regions in the fresh and renewal (or repeat) loans of the regions were

3.77, 0.12, 4.18, 10.48, 9.98, 71.47 respectively for the initial year 1997-98, whereas the corresponding per centage shares in the final year were 3.29, 1.47, 10.19, 4.33, 5.86 and 74.95. From the above analysis it can be concluded that all regions witnessed increase in these shares in fresh SHGs except S.R. with regard to per centage shares in fresh and renewal loans S.R., E.R. and N.E.R. experienced upward trend whereas N.R., CR. and W.R. downward trend.

## Financial Inclusion: A New Strategy

In spite of persisted efforts by Banks, Government of India, State Government Reserve Bank of India, NABARD, etc., the progress made under rural development was not substantial, so as to cover and include the entire rural population with banking services. In recent times, a multilateral approach was being adopted called financial inclusion for the underprivileged people in rural and urban areas, who were deprived of banking services. Financial inclusion is the delivery of banking services to the common man at an affordable cost to the vast sections of disadvantaged and low-income groups. Identifying the basic tenets of financial inclusion, the Financial Inclusion Task Force in the U.K. has cited three priority areas, viz., and access to banking, access to affordable credit and access to free face-to-face money advice.

Financial Inclusion is one of the anti-poverty strategies, which includes, Preventing individuals or families from falling into poverty, Provide routes out of poverty for individuals and families and Sustenance of individuals or families in a lifestyle free from poverty in rural areas. All public sector banks have started implementing the above strategy, i.e., opening of no frills accounts, issue of general credit cards, etc., which will have direct impact on the rural poverty. Government of India has constituted a Committee headed by Dr. Rangarajan and the Committee has submitted its Report during January 2008.

## Financial Inclusion for Inclusive Growth

The challenges of achieving more inclusive growth can be met by policies that encourage easier and affordable access to financial services. Both theoretical and empirical researches highlight the role of financial development in facilitating economic development at the cross-country level, evidence indicates that various measures of financial development are positively related to economic growth. Even the recent endogenous growth literature, building on 'learning by doing' processes, assigns a special role to finance.

From an annual average growth rate of 3.5 per cent during 1950 to 1980, the growth rate of the Indian economy accelerated to around 6.0 per cent in the 1980s and 1990s. In the last four years (2003-04 to 2006-07), the Indian economy grew by 8.8 per cent. In 2005-06 and 2006-07, the Indian economy grew at a higher rate of 9.4 and 9.6 per cent, respectively. Reflecting the high economic growth and a moderation in population growth rate, the per capita income of the country also increased substantially in the recent years. An important characteristic of the high growth phase in recent years is its resilience to shocks. The Indian economy, for instance, successfully avoided any adverse contagion impact of the East Asian crisis, sanctions like situation post-Pokhran nuclear test, and border conflict with a neighboring country during May-June 1999.

Despite the impressive numbers, growth has failed to be sufficiently inclusive, particularly after the mid-1990s. Agricultural sector which provides employment to around 60 per cent of the population lost its growth momentum from that point, though there has been a reversal of this trend since 2005-06. The per centage of India's population below the poverty line has declined from 36 per cent in 1993-94 to 26 per cent in 1999-2000. The approach paper to the Eleventh Plan indicated that the absolute number of poor is estimated to be approximately 300 million in 2004-05.

Concerns about financial exclusion, especially in rural areas have surfaced in India in recent years following the results of the NSSO's All-India Debt and Investment Survey (AIDIS), 2002. According to the Survey results, though the share of non-institutional sources of credit for the cultivator households had declined from 92.7 per cent in 1951 to 30.6 per cent in 1991, it had increased to 38.9 per cent in 2002 mainly due to increase in money lenders share. Simultaneously, the share of institutional sources such as commercial banks, co-operative societies, etc. increased from 7.3 per cent in 1951 to 66.3 per cent in 1991, before declining to 61.1 per cent in 2002. While data later than 2002 are not available in this regard, it is expected that the doubling of agriculture credit and other measures since 2004 would have led to some improvement in the share of institutional sources.

Over seventy per cent of people in India still live in villages. As per known macro economic facts, India has over 210 million households with more than 140+Mn households in the rural areas. These households and the people living in rural area remain excluded from the purview of the economic developments as they do not have easy access to the banking and financial transactions and related facilities, even after 60 years of Independence.

### *Finance Sector Policy and Regulatory Framework for Financial Inclusion*

The financial sector in India has been primarily dominated by the banking system. Scheduled commercial banks (SCBs) occupy a predominant position in the financial system, accounting for around three-fourths of the total assets. As at end-March 2007, the public sector banks (PSBs) accounted for 70 per cent of the total assets of SCBs. Foreign banks operating in India accounted for about 8 per cent of the assets of SCBs. The RRBs and the co-operative banks, with two broad segments of urban and rural co-operative banks also form an integral part of the Indian financial system.

Broadly speaking, one can observe two distinct phases in the developments relating to public policy objectives underlying banking policy. The first phase viz. the two decades since 1970 represented the period of State control over the banking system, pre-emption of the major part of bank resources by the public sector and directed lending with administered interest rates. During this period, the nationalization of major banks in 1969 saw banking policy giving a thrust to branch expansion in the rural and semi-urban areas and stepping up of lending to the so called priority sectors viz. agriculture, small scale industry, self-employed and small business sectors and weaker sections within these sectors.

As a result, the branches of scheduled commercial banks increased from 8,262 in June 1969 to 69,471 in March 2007. The average population per branch office decreased significantly from 64,000 to 16,000 during the above period, with the share of rural branches increasing from 22.2 per cent in June 1969 to a little over 51 per cent in March 1998. Lending to the priority sectors was increased to the mandated target of 40 per cent. Specialized Regional Rural Banks were set up in 1975, especially in backward and tribal districts to cater to the needs of the weaker sections amongst farmers and non-farm small businesses entrepreneurs. National Bank for Agriculture and Rural Development (NABARD) largely provided concesional refinance for lending done by the rural cooperative credit structure.

The second phase after the early 1990s, represents the period of financial sector reform, higher allocation of credit to the private sector, lower preemption by the government sector, moving away from administered interest rates to market determined rates even for government borrowing, introduction of international best practices and regulatory policies for strengthening the financial sector, increased competitiveness with entry of new private sector banks and more foreign banks, and allowing private shareholding in public sector banks. Listing of public sector banks on the stock exchanges made them consciously focus on bottom line, control NPAs, make investments in technology and skills and bring about other efficiencies. This period also saw consolidation of banking system in terms of branches. Although priority sector lending norms continued, the definitions became progressively wider with several sectors and activities getting included. In a sense, this period demonstrated the recognition that inclusive banking cannot be at the cost of weakening financial institutions and that policies for inclusive banking have to go hand in hand with encouraging strong and efficient financial institutions. The thrust of inclusive financing for the poor in this phase was mainly through government sponsored credit-cum-subsidy programmes. The recovery performance in these schemes was not encouraging and their success in achieving desired outcomes was also tepid.

A notable development in the second phase of inclusive banking was the launching of the SHG Bank Linkage programme by NABARD in 1992. The programme gained momentum when Reserve Bank allowed banks to open savings accounts for SHGs despite their not having any legal form. The group leaders operate the SHG accounts. SHGs facilitate collective decision - making and provide door step banking to the poor. The banks, as wholesalers of credit, provide the resources, while the NGOs are the agencies that organize the poor, build their capacities and facilitate the process of empowering them. Interest rates on loans granted by banks to SHGs are deregulated. Loans to SHGs of individual farmers are treated as direct agricultural finance, provided the details of such loans are maintained by the bank/SHG. As at March 31, 2007, over 2.9 million SHGs have been linked to banks

## Recent Strategies for Financial Inclusion

As the economy began to grow at higher rates, the regional and societal disparities called for new strategies to ensure that the banking system met the requirements of inclusive growth. Such strategies needed to be fashioned in a manner that they did not undermine the stability and efficiency of the financial system. Accordingly, over the last four years or so, several measures have been taken by the Reserve Bank and Government of India to ensure better banking penetration and outreach, particularly that the credit needs of agriculture and small enterprises are met while allowing sufficient flexibility to each bank to evolve its own policies and strategies for the purpose. We shall now discuss some of these initiatives.

Specific focus on financial inclusion commenced in November 2005, when Reserve Bank of India advised banks to make available a basic banking no-frills account with low or nil minimum balance as well as charges, with a view to expanding the outreach of such accounts. In such accounts, banks are required to make available all printed material used by retail customers in the regional language concerned. In order to ensure that persons belonging to low income groups, both in the urban and rural areas do not encounter difficulties in opening bank accounts, the know your customer (KYC) procedure for opening accounts has been simplified. Besides the Kisan Credit Cards (KCCs), banks have been asked to consider introduction of a General Purpose Credit Card (GCC) facility up to Rs.25000 at their rural and semi urban braches. This facility is in the nature of revolving credit, which entitles the holder to withdraw up to the limit sanctioned. Based on assessment of household cash flows, limits are sanctioned without insistence on security or purpose. Interest rate on the facility is completely deregulated.

In January 2006, the Reserve Bank permitted banks to utilize the services of non-governmental organizations

(NGOs/SHGs), micro-finance institutions and other civil society organizations as intermediaries in providing financial and banking services through the use of business facilitator (BF) and business correspondent (BC) models. The BC model allows banks to do cash in-cash out transactions at a location much closer to the rural population, thus addressing the last mile problem. Banks are also entering into agreements with Indian Postal Authorities for using the enormous network of post offices as business correspondents for increasing their outreach and leveraging the postman intimate knowledge of the local population and trust reposed in him.

The Reserve Bank of India has been encouraging the use of Information Communication Technology (ICT) solutions by banks for enhancing their outreach with the help of their Business Correspondents. The BCs carry hand held devices, which are essentially smart card readers. The information captured is transmitted to a central server where the accounts are maintained. These devices are used for making payments to rural customers and receiving cash from them at their doorsteps. Mobile phones have also been developed to serve as card readers. Account holders are issued smart cards, which have their photographs and finger impressions. Pilot studies have clearly shown that the technology is practical and robust, besides being affordable. Scaling up is, at present, the challenge, and some States like Andhra Pradesh are keen that all Government payments should be routed through these accounts to ensure transparency and efficiency in such payments, apart from providing a huge opportunity for ensuring financial inclusion.

In the Union Budget 2007-08, the Government announced the creation of two funds - Financial Inclusion Fund and Financial Inclusion Technology Development Fund - for meeting the costs of development, and promotional and technology interventions as recommended by the Rangarajan Committee.

Recognizing that lack of awareness is a major factor for financial exclusion, the Reserve Bank of India is taking a number of measures for increasing financial literacy and credit counseling. A multilingual website in 13 Indian languages on all matters concerning banking and the common person has been launched by the Reserve Bank of India on June 18, 2007. Financial literacy programmes are being launched in each State with the active involvement of the State government and the SLBC. Andhra bank has opened the center at Srikakulam. Credit counseling services in addition to financial literacy and financial education are being perceived as important tools to enable people to overcome the problem of indebtedness and seek re-access to banking system. Each SLBC convener has been asked to set up a financial literacy-cum-credit counseling centre in one district as a pilot, and extend it to all other districts in due course.

In the context of the finding that the share of moneylenders in total dues of rural households had increased, the Reserve Bank constituted, in 2006, a Technical Group consisting of senior Reserve Bank Officers and Secretaries from select State Governments to review the efficacy of the existing legislative framework which governs money-lending, as also the enforcement machinery in different States. A model draft of legislation on money lending has been prepared by the Group for consideration and adoption by the State Governments for improving the legal and enforcement framework for protecting the interest of rural households. The model legislation provides for a hassle free procedure for compulsory registration with State Governments. The Group has also proposed establishing a link between the formal and informal credit providers, to be called 'Accredited Loan Providers' for use as an additional credit delivery channel. The report has been sent to the State governments for their consideration.

## Measures for Sustainability of Micro-finance Programmes

Financially self-sufficient and sustainable systems and institutions only can serve the poor effectively. There is a growing realization that large scale lending of small amounts to the poor cannot be accomplished through subsidies and grants. The successful examples of micro-finance programmes which have been able to reach large number of poor are those where no lending operations or little subsidy. It is clear that almost no donor or Government has the resources to subsidize lending to vast majority of the poor who suffer presently for lack of access. Self-sufficiency has also emerged from wide spread change in attitude arising from the debilitating effects of subsidized lending on both the lender as well poor alike.

Institutional sustainability in micro-finance programme primarily depends upon the convenient and low-cost operations with involvement of beneficiaries and the communities, increasing the scale of operations and reducing dependence on external subsidies and resources in the long-run. Important measures for achieving self-sufficiency and sustainability of micro-credit institutions are summarized below:

(1) To make the micro-finance system low-cost and effective, involve local communities and the beneficiaries in as many tasks as possible.

(2) To encourage local NGOs, Animators, Trainers, etc. as far as possible for economy as well as effectiveness.

(3) To make the procedures relating to savings, credit recovery, accounting etc. convenient, simple and manageable by the people themselves.

(4) To involve community and SHG members in appraisal, supervision and recovery of loan, this reduces the high transaction costs if the same is done through NGOs /MFls.

(5) To attain convenience and low transaction cost to the beneficiaries while borrowing and repaying in a prompt manner, which leads to greater demand and increased operations helping in sustainability.

(6) To limit doncrs / Government subsidy / grant, which should be used primarily towards technical assistance like motivation and organization of groups, capacity building of NGOs / SHGs, training, etc., over a period of time when the operations increase the cost per unit on this component will increase substantially and can be shared by the MFIs groups and beneficiaries.

**Micro-finance Policy and Strategy in India**

The past two decades have witnessed several interesting innovations in micro-finance First, a large number of NGOs, primarily engaged in bringing out social and economic upliftment of their clientele, have recognized the importance of micro-finance in this task, are actively engaged in promoting, SHGs, and many of them are also involved in linking the SHGs with banks linked with micro-finance, the SHG movement has now been accepted as an effective intervention strategy for poverty alleviation. Self-help group linked micro-finance includes such credits provided to rural poor on easy terms and conditions for several new income generation activities. Considering this the future strategy of rural credit institutions would have to include strengthening the credit delivery system for increasing employment opportunities in rural non-farm sector.

According to the plans of various apex-level financial institutions like NABARD, SIDBI, and RMK, some NGOs, NGO MFls and NGO-networks, over one-third of the entire rural poor population will be covered by micro-finance through the SHG strategy and other delivery mechanisms in about next ten years.

**Issues of Micro-Finance in India**

A lot of issues, funds and personnel are at stake in these initiatives. There is a strong case for a formal recognition of micro-finance, just like institutional credit, as a strategic tool for poverty alleviation and rural development, both at the policy and implementation level. The task force, therefore, recommends that Government of India (GoI) may consider making a suitable policy statement recognizing the role of micro-finance as a strategy for 'poverty alleviation on a sustainable and long-term basis'.

The task force considers that a good beginning has already been made in this direction by the GoI through the announcements made in the budget speeches of 1998-99 and 1999-2000 regarding SHG-bank Linkage programme. This endeavor may have to be carried further by recognizing the other initiatives of the voluntary sector in providing micro-finance services to the poor.

The acceptance and recognition of micro-finance as an essential tool for poverty alleviation envisages adoption of a national policy on micro-finance.

The major components of the national policy include:

(1) Encouraging initiatives and participation of different type's institutions in micro-finance;

(2) Bringing the micro-finance activities, irrespective of the type of institutions, with in the regulation and supervision by competent authorities;

(3) Creating policy environment for closer linkages of micro-finance sector with the formal banking channels; and

(4) Making available equity, start-up capital and capacity building funds for the existing and prospective institutions engaged in micro-finance including banks

and various micro-finance structures from institutional sources in the country.

## NABARD's Vision of Micro-finance

The approach and strategy for implementation of national policy on micro-finance may have to recognize and appreciate the need for:

(1) Encouraging innovations in delivery mechanisms, instead of adopting stereotypes, and participating agencies to innovate as per local requirements and develop their own programmes;

(2) Ensuring functional autonomy of MFls, giving freedom to NGOs and other agencies to decide the approach to be adopted in implementing porgrammes;

(3) Obtaining consensus in client selection among different ministries and departments of GoI need to have consensus and that the SHGs and other micro-finance delivery initiatives include that a major part of the social engineering processes are time-consuming and are not likely to respond well to any target approach.

## NABARD's Micro-finance Strategy

Its strategic elements include the following:

(1) Forming and nurturing small, homogeneous and participating self-help groups (SHGs) of the poor. Today, it has emerged as a potent tool for human development. This process enables the poor, especially the women from the poor households, to collectively identify and analyze the problems they face in the perspective of their social and economic environment. It helps them to pool their meager resources, human, financial, and prioritize their use for solving their own problems.

(2) Emphasis on regular thrift collection and its use to solve immediate problems of consumption and production.

It helps to meet their most urgent needs, but also trains them to handle larger financial resources more skilfully, prudently and with a more lasting impact.

(3) Encouraging SHGs to become a forum for many social sector interventions.

(4) Facilitating SHGs to access credit from formal banking channels. SHG - bank Linkage programme has proved to be the major supplementary credit delivery system with wide acceptance by banks, NGOs and various government departments.

(5) NABARD intensified efforts for roping in new partners. It is for promotion and linkage of groups in regions where the growth of groups has not been commensurate with potential.

(6) Assigning priority to awareness building and for identification of NGO and other partners in 13 priority states, which account for 70 per cent of rural poor in the country.

(7) Provision of training inputs on SHG financing to training establishments of participating banks, to help them to internalize the training requirements at their level.

(8) Support help to banking institutions, especially RRBs and co-operative banks, to take on the role of self-help promoting (SHPs) institutions.

(9) Technical support to banks to evolve suitable intermediate structures like farmer's clubs to increase the outreach of their branches in promotion and linking SHGs.

(10) Provision of necessary assistance to the governments for dovetailing micro-finance practices with the poverty alleviation programmes.

(11) Co-ordination of the micro-finance activities in India at international/national / state / district level by organizing international/national workshops, seminars, etc., for experience sharing, organizing National and State level meets of bankers and NGOs, etc.

## Micro-finance Bill

The Finance Minister, Mr P. Chidambaram, tabled the Micro-financial Sector (Development and Regulation) Bill 2007, in the Lok Sabha on Tuesday. The Bill makes the National Bank for Agriculture and Rural Development (NABARD) the regulator for the micro-financial sector.

On its enactment, the Bill makes registration of micro-finance organizations with NABARD mandatory and no institution (including existing) can carry out business of offering thrift services without obtaining certificate of registration. For seeking registration, the organization should have minimum net owned funds of Rs five lakh.

The Bill qualifies any amount not exceeding Rs 50,000 as a micro-finance service, with this limit set at Rs 1.50 lakh for housing purposes. For safeguarding interests of the people depositing their money, the Bill proposes constitution of a reserve fund, where minimum 15 per cent of the net profit or surplus realized out of thrift services will be parked.

The Bill also empowers NABARD to frame a scheme for the appointment of one or more Micro-finance Ombudsmen for settlement of disputes between clients and micro-finance institutions. NABARD is working on micro-finance bill.

Micro-finance in India is at a take off stage now. The prosperity generated by software and service sector boom need be supplemented by rural development. A boom in rural areas especially through micro-finance would lead to sustained growth in the long run leading to the Age of High Mass Consumption. Thus growth in micro-finance is essential to ensure inclusive and sustained economic growth.

**Some Programmes/Models in India**

Thorough discussion of international scenario as well as the micro-financing operation as well as activities is giving a sense to understand the multifarious micro financing models operating in a diversified country like India. The following section is discussing some of the important models of micro-finance adopted by leading micro-financing institutions in India.

**AKRSP's Micro-finance Programme**

Aga Khan Rural Support Programme's (AKRSP) savings and credit programme started off by conserving "programme savings". The initial groups formed were for a given village and had a membership of around a 100 people. The formation of the groups were more on the basis of the other work undertaken by the beneficiaries, rather than on an explicit need of having to save and rotate money amongst themselves. AKRSP has been working on watershed management, natural resource management and management of waste-lands and forest resources in its area. Several of these activities require the involvement of the stakeholders. The involvement includes labour contribution. One common method followed by AKRSP, is to get the communities involved in soil and water conservation by constructing check dams and undertaking contour bunding. If AKRSP is undertaking the activity of watershed management with the involvement of the communities, it is expected that the community contributes part of the labour free and a part of the labour is paid for. AKRSP might also bear some other out-of-pocket costs. Whenever there was work undertaken on a common property a component is paid to the community as wages.

In order to encourage the habit of thrift, AKRSP had initiated the practice of dividing up the wages into three components. For every payment of Rs.50 to be made Rs.35 was paid out to the workers in cash while Rs.10 was put into a common fund to take up activities benefited to the village at large and Rs.5 was retained in the name of members as voluntary savings. All these savings – though termed "voluntary" are as a result of check-offs from wages. Since these were check offs from payments related to programme implementation, these were called as programme savings. The above fund till recently was managed with the village as a unit. These groups undertook lending among themselves. Here, the micro-finance programme (having both the savings and credit component) was an integral part of the other programmes carried out by AKRSP.

## SEWA Bank Model

The SEWA Bank is, termed as one of the oldest micro-finance institutions in India. It had developmental roots, but was set up in the commercial arena as a co-operative, rather than a NGO. The second levels of NGOs help the poor by taking up sectoral economic activities. They satisfy the conditions laid out earlier purpose is developmental, focus is poor and working in the alternative sector.

## Experience of SIFFS

SIFFS was established in 1983. It is a society and an apex body of a three-tier structure for artisan fishermen. At village level there are more than a hundred fishermen's societies in six districts of Kerala, Tamil Nadu and Pondicherry. SIFFS works with a membership base of 6,000 who are directly members of the village societies and also around 14,000 crewmembers that work as a part of the team.

The objectives of SIFFS are to work with poor fishermen and provide marketing and technological support to them. Initially, SIFFS was mainly involved only in technology development for the artisan sector. Now, SIFFS continues to be active in technology development and dissemination. The activities of SIFFS can be categorized as commercial and non-commercial. The commercial aspect of the programme includes a network of 12 boat building centers and the micro-finance programme for fishermen.

The credit activities were started by the individual fishermen's societies even before the federation came into being, as early as the 1970s. The first stage was resorting to savings check-offs. This was done on payments due for fish at the end of the day. It was dovetailed into the economic activity. When the Federation was established, the activity reached the second stage, where it actively worked with the local banks in providing linkages with the societies and then with the fishermen. The third stage (late 80s) was when SIFFS turned out to be the guarantor for the loans given by the bank. This was the stage when SIFFS realized that the amount of loan forthcoming from the banks were insufficient and several times inefficient. The fourth stage was establishing revolving funds at the district level. In the fifth and the final stage SIFFS directly entered the arena by providing bulk loans. This is a clear indication of the increasing importance of micro-finance in this sector and how a "promoter" organization eventually turned out to be a "provider." SIFFS is one of the few institutions in India that undertakes micro-finance activities predominantly with men. Most of the other programmes are targeted at women.

# 3

# Micro-finance: An Experience of Andra Pradesh

## Background

A little over a third of the geographical area is tilled under agriculture and 22 per cent of the area is under forest cover. Forests occupy 63,814 sq. km with rich flora and fauna. The State has a coastline of 974 kilometres. The Krishna and Godavari rivers account for 84 per cent of the total riparian water resources of the State. Major and medium irrigation schemes utilize 55 per cent of the total state irrigation potential. Andhra Pradesh boasts of some of the best sun touched beaches in the country. Quite similar to some other beaches of the country, the beaches of Andhra Pradesh truly have golden sands against a backdrop of bright blue waters of the Bay of Bengal.

Although the interior is mountainous, Andhra Pradesh is largely on a coastal plain drained by the Penner, Krishna, and Godavari rivers. Andhra Pradesh can be broadly divided into three regions, namely Coastal Andhra, Telangana and Rayalaseema. *Coastal* Andhra occupies the coastal plain between Eastern Ghats ranges. *Telangana* lies west of the Eastern Ghats on the Deccan plateau. The Godavari and

Krishna rivers rise in the Western Ghats of Karnataka and Maharashtra and flow east across Telangana to empty into the Bay of Bengal in a combined river delta. *Rayalaseema* lies in the southeast of the State on the Deccan plateau, in the basin of the Penner River. It is separated from Telangana by the low Erramala hills and from Coastal Andhra by the Eastern Ghats.

Nearly three quarters of this population live in rural areas. The Krishna and Godavari rivers together irrigate thousands of square kilometres of land, and create the largest perennial cultivable area in the country. Andhra Pradesh leads in the production of rice (paddy) and is called India's Rice Bowl.

The important crops of the state are rice, sugarcane, peanuts, and cotton. The main ores available in the region are coal, chrome, and manganese. The State has a major port of international dimensions, facilities and standards at Visakhapatnam and a satellite launch center is on Sriharikota Island. Gas striking in the Krishna-Godavari basin has opened up unimaginable possibilities for the rapid development of Andhra Pradesh.

Andhra Pradesh falls under the semi-arid region of peninsular India and has a typical tropical climate of hot summers but relatively pleasant winters, especially in the plains of the interior. South-west and north-east Monsoons are the two important periodic winds which are the important sources of rain. The south-west monsoon is spread over the period commencing from June and ending with September and north-east monsoon from October to December.

## Micro-finance System in Andhra Pradesh

Most micro-finance programmes implemented by voluntary sector in India adopt group approach for lending. Several promotional agencies in the government sector have promoted and inspired formation of diverse kinds of thrift and credit groups to channelise the various State sponsored poverty alleviation and social development programmes. These groups vary widely in terms of their membership, size, decision making processes, methods of group action, etc. The salient features of these groupings and their relevance in the state of Andhra Pradesh are briefly given here as under:

### *Self-managed Thrift and Credit Groups:*

*Self-help Groups*

SHGs are small, economically homogenous and affinity groups of rural poor voluntarily formed to save and mutually agree to contribute to a common fund to be lent to its members as per group decision. These groups are usually formed by Governmental or Non-Governmental organizations with emphasis on both thrift and credit activities. All financial decisions are taken by the groups through a consensual approach.

*DWCRA Groups*

Groups with maximum membership of 15 women were formed by the Department of Rural Development under the erstwhile "Development of Women and Children in Rural Areas" (DWCRA) Programme of IRDP. Thrift was used as an entry point to weave women groups. Government through District Rural Development Agencies release maximum Revolving Fund Assistance (RFA) / matching grant of Rs. 15,000 per group to enable DWCRA groups to take up income generating activities. Even though IRDP and DWCRA have since been subsumed under SGSY since 1999, the SHGs formed by DRDAs in the state continue to be stated as DWCRA groups. At present, DWCRA groups and SHGs are synonymous in the state. Under the programme, banks also extend credit facilities to such groups for meeting their fund requirements.

*Podupulakshmi Groups*

Podupulakshmi Groups are DWCRA groups functioning on the lines of SHGs. Thrift is an entry point activity for these groups which is put to rotation among the group members as micro loans based on the priorities decided by the group members. DRDAs have been extending matching grant assistance to such groups based on their thrift, credit and repayment records. The matching grant received from the Government is completely funded with the groups' corpus. Banks have also been extending loans to the groups, enhancing overall fund base to enable internal lending of higher order for meeting both consumption and production credit requirements of the members.

*Avval Committees*

Avval Committees are women thrift and credit groups formed in tribal areas of Adilabad District under the aegis of Integrated tribal Development Agency. These groups have rudimentary elements of SHGs. Sri Saraswati Grameena Bank took the initiative of restructuring and strengthening these groups on the lines of SHGs by extending need based financial assistance to the groups while introducing the self management concepts in the field of thrift and credit activities.

### *Self Managed Networks*

*Mutually Aided Cooperatives Societies (MACS)*

Government of Andhra Pradesh has, in 1995 enacted the Andhra Pradesh Mutually Aided Cooperative Societies Act. The Act provided for voluntary formation of cooperatives as accountable, competitive, self-reliant business enterprises based on thrift, self-help and mutual aid. They are owned, managed and controlled by members for their economic and social betterment. Several coalitions and networks of women SHGs have institutionalized themselves under the new enactment. Under these MACS, the members continue to be with the groups they belong to, to ensure collective responsibility, endorsing loan transactions, providing moral security for repayment of loans and participation of all members in every activity of the society. At time groups are federated at village level in the form of Mahila Mandals/ Village Organizations which act as intermediaries between Mandal Level MACS and members, by collecting/ recommending loan applications from individual members to MACS, monitoring loans and facilitating default management. However, in some places village organizations are also registered as MACS, providing financial services to the members through SHGs.

*Groups of Working Women's Forum*

Women groups of membership not exceeding ten members have been formed by the Chennai-based voluntary agency in a few parts of Andhra Pradesh. These groups are given intensive training to advocate and manage social, political and economic issues pertaining to rural women. The women members are extended small loans for taking up house hold industrial activities backed by personal surety of the leader concerned, while the leader's loan itself is guaranteed by the forum's organizer sponsoring the group. Under the system, the leader based on her organizing potential can graduate to the organizer level for promoting several such groups. The groups formed by the Working Women's Forum are federated as India Cooperative Network of Women, which is a cooperative owned and managed by member women.

***Externally Managed Thrift and Credit Groups***

*Grameen Groups*

These groups are formed by Grameen Bank model (Bangladesh) replicating agencies. Under this system, five persons are formed into a group with thrift as entry point. The groups are given intensive training in credit management and group management. They are put through a Group Recognition Test before they become eligible to access credit for income generating activities. The credit terms like quantum of loan, interest rate, repayment period etc. are determined by the credit agencies. The loaning to members is done on staggered basis 2-2-1 with the leader of the groups getting the loan last. Each loan is secured by personal surety of two other members of the group. However, the group is empowered to prioritize the persons to be covered in the initial loaning.

*Rashtriya Mahila Kosh (RMK) Groups*

Though there is no such nomenclature as RMK groups, they are essentially those groups promoted by NGOs which have accessed assistance from Rashtriya Mahila Kosh, an organization set up by Government of India for assisting women in taking up income generating activities. The RMK has formulated a set of schemes for NGOs for on-lending to SHGs. The schemes delineate the type of activities eligible for finance, quantum of finance, interest rates and repayment terms. In practice, credit is directly extended to individual women in group mode on the recommendation of group leaders.

### *Activity Management Groups*

*Anganwadi Groups*

Anganwadi groups are women groups formed by Department of Women and child Welfare at habitation level for implementing their health, nutrition and literacy programmes for rural women. These women are encouraged to take up income generating activities for which loans are extended for setting up individual or group enterprises.

*Joint Forest Management (JFM) Groups*

The communities in notified forest areas are formed into Vana Samarakshana Samithis (VSS) or Joint Forest Management Groups to protect and conserve forest wealth.

Group action being core to the concept in Joint Forest Management, Government of Andhra Pradesh has chosen SHG route for social mobilization under the programme. Inculcation of thrift and credit habit in such groups will go a long way in sustaining their income levels.

*Watershed groups*

The farmers in micro watershed area are formed into groups for implementing technology package for watershed development with intervention of facilitating agency, normally an NGO. While on-farm development activities are funded through grant support, these groups have also been availing loans from formal credit agencies under the various Government sponsored programmes for raising crops, animal husbandry, non-farm activities etc. Some of such groups have also been formed with thrift as entry point activity.

*CJFS Groups*

There are more than 2400 Cooperative Joint Farming Societies (CJFSs) in the state. A cooperative farming society is deemed as a voluntary organization based on the principle and ideals of self-help and mutual help in the agricultural community. The members pool their agricultural land (allotted to them by the government), resources and their manual labor to cultivate jointly to facilitate a more rational use of the land to increase agricultural production and income. With a view to reviving these cooperatives, the state government has taken initiative to form SHGs from among the members of these societies, by inculcating the virtues of savings and internal lending among them and finally facilitating their linkage with banks for access to institutional credit. So far, a few hundred SHGs have been formed under these societies.

## *Evolution of SHGs in Andhra Pradesh*

*Development of Women and Children in Rural Areas*

The evolution of group concept goes back to 1982-83 with the implementation of the "Development of Women and

Children in Rural Areas (DWCRA) as a sub component of the Integrated Rural Development Programme (IRDP) by Government of India with the support of the State Governments and UNICEF. The objective of DWCRA programme was 'to empower the rural women living below the poverty line by way of organizing them into groups to create sustainable income generating activities through self employment. Women living in neighbourhoods with similar socio economic background were formed into groups of 25 members each to take up an economic activity suited to their skills and resources. In Andhra Pradesh, the programme was initially implemented in Adilabad, Kadapa and Srikakulam Districts and thereafter was extended in a phased manner to other districts. By 1994-95, all the districts were covered under the programme. Government of Andhra Pradesh took up re-modeling of DWCRA groups in the State into SHG with the help of NABARD in November 1996.

*Women's Groups under the Total Literacy Campaign*

In early 1990s, women were organized into Mahila Mandalis as part of Total Literacy Campaign. These women groups spearheaded the anti-liquor movement in Nellore District. The savings movement of 'Save a Rupee a Day' started thereafter by these Mahila Mandals which later led to *'Podupu Lakshmi'* (Podupu means savings and Lakshmi is the goddess of wealth) movement. Women came together and formed themselves groups of 10 to 30 with regular meeting and a common agenda. The District Administration provided the *'Podupu Laxmi'* movement with the initial support and acted as facilitators. Volunteers, animators, trainers and instructors in the Total Literacy Campaign acted as Podupulaxmi organizers. Several districts followed suit and" promoted thrift groups with different names such as Anantalakshmi (Anantpur district), Gramalakshmi (Chittoor), Maalakshmi (Mahabubnagar), Mahila Shakti (East

Godavari), Podupujyothi (Rangareddy), Swayam Shakti Sangaham (Srikakulam) etc. These groups after reaching the maturity were converted into DWCRA groups.

*South Asia Poverty Alleviation Programme*

The South Asia Poverty Alleviation Programme (SAPAP) was implemented during 1995-2000 by the UNDP in 20 mandals of three drought prone districts, viz, Kuroool, Mahbubnagar and Ananthpur of the state of Andhra Pradesh. The objective of the programme was to combat rural poverty through social mobilization and active participation of beneficiaries in grass roots. It relied on a three-pronged strategy, i.e., social mobilization of the poor, skill development and capital formation. The poor were organized at three levels: hamlet/sub-hamlet level through small homogenous SHGs, village level through village level organizations and the Mandal level through the Mahila Mandal Samakhyas. Development programmes like literacy, preventive health care, girl child education, elimination of child labour etc. were dovetailed to the SHG concept under the programme.

*Indira Kranti Patham Project (IKP)*

The SHG movement took a firm root in the state with the implementation of World Bank assisted poverty reduction project, Indira Kranti Patham (IKP), a scaled up versions of the SAPAP model with more focus on livelihood component. The project aims to build strong institutions of the rural poor and enhance their livelihood opportunities so that the vulnerability of poor is reduced. IKP consists of two projects, viz, Andhra Pradesh District Poverty Initiatives Project (APDPIP) and Andhra Pradesh Rural Poverty Reduction Project (APRPRP) and is implemented in 864 Mandals out of a total 1127 Mandals in the State. The project has a total outlay of Rs.21, 400 million with 56 per cent of the project outlay meant to support the sub projects of the poor through Community Investment Fund (CIF). Government of Andhra

Pradesh has decided to cover the entire state under the IKP Programme from the financial year 2006-07 by dovetailing the funds from State Government and Government of India. Society for Elimination of Rural Poverty (SERP), an autonomous body registered under the Societies Registration (Telangana) Act, has been established for management of IKP, which is implemented by SERP through DRDAs at the district level. The project is being managed with a large complement of staff consisting of Community Coordinators, Assistant Project Managers, and District Project Managers.

**Micro-finance Institutions in A.P.**

Andhra Pradesh has occupied an important place in the map of Indian Microfinance Institutions and Hyderabad has become popular as 'Macca of Microfinance'. More than 3/4$^{th}$ of Microfinance Institutions in India are located in Andhra Pradesh. Many MFI have extending credit facility to more than 1 lakh members through promotion of Joint Liability Groups (JLGs) and Individual lending. As the sector growing, many issues are emerging on MFI operations from Government and other stake-holders because of non-observance of prescribed norms in reaching their goals.

There are around 16 micro-finance institutions in the state of Andhra Pradesh registered under section 4 of Trust Act section 9 of Cooperative Societies Act, Section 2 of NBFC, Section 1 of Local Area Bank. Some of the established MFIs in the field are BASIX Group of Institutions, Share Micro-finance, Spandana Group of Institutions, etc. The MFIs have adopted various lending approaches such as lending to individual, SHGs, Joint Liability Group, Grameena Bank mode, etc. At the end of March, 2007, it is reported that MFIs in the State have mobilized savings aggregating to Rs.32.55 crores with cumulative borrowings aggregated to Rs. 458.89 crores. MFIs in the state are supporting nearly 5.50 lakh clients.

Micro-finance Institutions like SPANDANA, SHARE MOOLA, SUSMITHA etc in West Godavari, Krishna, Guntur, Prakasam and in some other districts in Andhra Pradesh are extending micro-finance to the poor and Self Help Groups, who were already financed by commercial banks. Private sector Banks like ICICI, HDFC, IDBI etc have since designed innovative products and lending to these MFIs, keeping in view this sector a good business proposition. The interest rate charged by MFIs is exorbitant, and it is reported that the interest rate charges varying between 40-50 per cent including group insurance premium, processing/appraising charges etc., thereby many poor people are unable to repay the loan and some of them are committing suicides. The District Collector, Krishna, has closed down a number of branches of MFIs, such as SPANDANA, SHARE operating in the district and proceeded legally against the alleged MFIs, who are not following RBI guidelines in extending finance.

MFI model is comparatively costlier in terms of financial services. It has been observed that the interest rates charged by the MFIs are very high. For poor, the rates of interest may not be an immediate concern as long as they get quick access to smaller but adequate and short duration loans. Yet cost of credit becomes an important issue, once their credit needs graduate to a higher level for undertaking investment activities.

### MFI lending in Andhra Pradesh *vis-à-vis* Banks

| *Details* | *MFIs* | *Banks* |
|---|---|---|
| **Group formation** | Don't do formation of groups | By NGOs, banks, Govt. |
| **No. of groups** | Do not bother about no. of members in the group. | Finance to groups members ranging 10-15 only |

(Contd...)

| *Details* | *MFIs* | *Banks* |
|---|---|---|
| **Savings** | Forcible | Voluntary |
| **Period of saving** | Not required | After 6 months only lending will start |
| **Focus on type of people** | Lend to men and women | Lend to women only (95 per cent) |
| **Lending to** | Individuals and groups | Mainly focus on groups |
| **Interference** | Too much interference | Less interference |
| **Type of lending** | Lend to mainly consumption (specific purpose) | Lend to all purpose |
| **Amount of lending** | Finance how much members wants | Basing on savings i.e. 1:4 on first dose, 1:10 on second dose etc.. |
| **Insurance products** | Forcibly cover | Optional to the members |
| **Insurance in the name of** | Member on Ac of MFI | In personal name of members |
| **Risk coverage** | Only on life | On life and health also |
| **Profitability** | Profit motive | Non profit motive |
| **Interest rates** | High | Low |
| **Type of recovery** | Forcible | Voluntary |
| **Defaults** | **More.** Lending is more than the requirement (Excess lending) | **Less.** Recovery per cent is high |
| **Recovery duration** | weekly | Monthly |
| **Control** | High control | Moderate control |
| **Rating of groups** | No rating | Critical rating index by NABARD |
| **End use of funds** | Not obtained | Banks see end use of funds |
| **Interference** | More | Less |

## Institutional Support to MFI

NABARD has initiated various steps for linking MFIs through rating with a view to promoting flow of commercial loans from banks to MFIs. A scheme was launched by NABARD during 2005-06 to provide financial support to banks through rating of MFIs by CRISIL. This scheme has since been revised to be operational up to 31 March 2008 and banks can now avail the services of other credit rating agencies viz., M-CRIL, ICRA, CARE and Planet Finance including CRISIL. Further the quantum of assistance has been increased to 80 per cent of the cost up to a maximum of Rs.80,000. This scheme would help MFIs in accessing commercial loans from banks.

## Capital/Equity Support to MFIs

In view of the announcements made by the Hon'ble Finance Minister in his Union Budget 2005-06, a scheme called "Capital / Equity Support to MFIs from MFDEF" has been announced under which Capital/ equity support to various types of MFIs would be provided by NABARD to enable them to leverage capital / equity for accessing commercial and other funds from banks. This would help MFIs in providing financial services at an affordable cost to the poor

## Self-help Promoting Institutions in Government Sector

Several promotional agencies in the government sector have promoted and inspired formation of diverse kinds of thrift and credit groups to chanelize the various state sponsored poverty alleviation and social development programs. These groups vary widely in terms of their membership, size, decision-making processes, methods of groups' action, etc. The phrase "savings and credit group" (SCGs) is used to include all variations, including the groups formed under the programme for Development of Women and Children in Rural Areas (DWCRA), as well as self-help groups (SHGs) formed by NGOs and linked with banks.

**Micro-finance Delivery Models in A.P.**

During the last few years several innovations were made by participating banks for financing SHGs in Andhra Pradesh. Interestingly, it is the only State where a number of models of delivering credit to rural poor through SHG system have been evolved and tested successfully for replication. Several models of credit delivery through SHG system practiced in Andhra Pradesh are as follows:

i. Financing SHGs directly by banks without any intervention/facilitation of any SHPI.

ii. Financing SHGs directly by banks with intervention/ facilitation of non governmental organizations.

iii. Financing SHGs directly by banks with intervention/ facilitation of governmental agencies.

iv. Financing SHGs with financial intermediation of non-governmental agencies.

v. Financing SHGs with financial intermediation of NGOs/ SHG cluster associations/ mutually aided cooperative societies.

**SHG-bank Linkage Programme**

Over the years the linkage programme grew in leaps and bounds. As on 30th September, 2007, cumulative amount of Rs.4, 682 crores has been disbursed by 24 commercial banks, 16 RRBs and 14 DCCBs to nearly 11.93 lakh SHGs in partnership with 22 DRDAs and 91 NGOs in Andhra Pradesh. The success of SHGs-bank linkage programme in A.P. is attributed to the existence of strong institutions involved in social intermediation, which help in the formation of SHGs. The East Godavari district continued to be the number one district in SHG financing in the state in the year with credit linkage of Rs.16, 453.69 lakhs in respect of 26,099 SHGs followed by West Godavari and Chittoor. It is estimated that around 60 per cent of SHGs may be utilizing the loans for productive purposes. Based on the potential assessed by NABARD in the district - wise potential linked plans (PLPs) for the year 2007-08, it is estimated that the projected ground level credit disbursement under SHG-bank linkage programme will be Rs. 7,000 crore including fresh and renewal loans.

## SHGs and Bank Linkage (2001 to 2008)

Andhra Pradesh is the front-runner state in SHG promotion and bank-linkage programme in South India and India as a whole. The status of self-help group and bank linkage is visibly depicted in Table 3.1.

## Regional Spread of SHGs and Access to Credit

Integrated SHG-BL across the districts and regions of the state is giving a very glossy picture of the MFI programme in the state. The current section is attempting to gives regional information on the SHGs as well as the credit leveraged. Spread of SHG-bank linkage programme region-wise in A.P. is shown in the Table 3.2 both in absolutes and relative terms.

## Methods of Bank Lending to SHGs

A banker is expected to provide credit in bulk directly to the group, which may be formal or informal (i.e. registered) one. The group in turn would undertake on - lending to the members. It would be necessary that the group prepares a simple credit plan for its members and an aggregate of that is submitted to the bank. The bank is expected to under take critical appraisal of self-help group and take appropriate credit decision. A few banks have developed rating norms for assessing the performance of the groups. However, a simple rating index has been designed in the state with participation

## Table 3.1
## Year-wise SHG Bank linkage Progress from 2001- 2002 to 2007-08 in Andhra Pradesh
### (Rs. In. Lakhs)

| Sl. No. | District | 2001-2002 | | 2002-2003 | | 2003-04 | | 2004-05 | | 2005-06 | | 2006-07 | | 2007-08 | | Total No of SHGs inthe State |
|---|---|---|---|---|---|---|---|---|---|---|---|---|---|---|---|---|
| | | *Groups covered* | *Credit Acc-essed by the groups* | *Groups covered* | *Credit Acc-essed by the groups* | *Groups covered* | *Credit Acc-essed by the groups* | *Groups covered* | *Credit Acc-essed by the groups* | *Groups covered* | *Credit Acc-essed by the groups* | *Groups covered* | *Credit Acc-essed by the groups* | *Groups covered* | *Credit Acc-essed by the groups* | |
| | 1 | 2 | 3 | 4 | 5 | 6 | 7 | 8 | 9 | 10 | 11 | 12 | 13 | 14 | 15 | 16 |
| 1 | Adilabad | 4504 | 1005 | 5388 | 1421 | 7611 | 2352 | 8024 | 2777 | 6742 | 4305 | 9632 | 7591 | 11443 | 13038 | 22460 |
| 2 | Anantapur | 4476 | 999 | 4168 | 1049 | 6862 | 2124 | 10105 | 3546 | 12308 | 6036 | 14019 | 9769 | 20038 | 32847 | 38543 |
| 3 | Chittoor | 5132 | 1146 | 7709 | 2664 | 14986 | 5635 | 12416 | 6067 | 15444 | 11139 | 20067 | 19604 | 20353 | 35453 | 39197 |
| 4 | East Godavari | 12766 | 2850 | 22194 | 6544 | 28119 | 10629 | 32139 | 12925 | 25517 | 17500 | 28991 | 26442 | 36170 | 50711 | 59117 |
| 5 | Guntur | 5072 | 1132 | 6286 | 2325 | 9463 | 4264 | 14242 | 8360 | 13852 | 9738 | 22240 | 13261 | 25226 | 28664 | 38578 |
| 6 | Kadapa | 1689 | 377 | 4329 | 1544 | 5870 | 2910 | 5553 | 3083 | 8467 | 10000 | 12605 | 10078 | 17345 | 19977 | 27693 |
| 7 | Karimnagar | 4260 | 951 | 9302 | 1829 | 9037 | 2135 | 15024 | 4544 | 15085 | 7543 | 17660 | 12571 | 17317 | 20629 | 33058 |
| 8 | Khammam | 6442 | 1438 | 8484 | 1851 | 17436 | 3342 | 17035 | 4182 | 15300 | 6217 | 21296 | 12763 | 21435 | 25182 | 31412 |
| 9 | Krishna | 6540 | 1460 | 5197 | 1607 | 11565 | 3814 | 14149 | 5106 | 15861 | 9000 | 23857 | 16920 | 29407 | 37048 | 35148 |
| 10 | Kurnool | 3494 | 780 | 8846 | 2632 | 16692 | 5215 | 14303 | 5952 | 12103 | 9706 | 15176 | 12086 | 17177 | 26975 | 26061 |
| 11 | Mahabub-nagar | 5380 | 1201 | 6940 | 2241 | 10613 | 4010 | 10794 | 6202 | 13386 | 12200 | 13314 | 8694 | 15871 | 14527 | 30789 |
| 12 | Medak | 4001 | 893 | 3328 | 1651 | 8429 | 3105 | 10962 | 4343 | 10940 | 6900 | 13805 | 9653 | 17339 | 24100 | 29925 |

| | | | | | | | | | | | | | | | | |
|---|---|---|---|---|---|---|---|---|---|---|---|---|---|---|---|---|
| 13 | Nalgonda | 4704 | 1050 | 4727 | 1550 | 9992 | 3618 | 19165 | 8901 | 17529 | 10025 | 14464 | 7709 | 21397 | 23489 | 33669 |
| 14 | Nellore | 2661 | 594 | 2650 | 1545 | 4816 | 2464 | 4192 | 2043 | 9242 | 6500 | 15718 | 17130 | 15735 | 25370 | 22505 |
| 15 | Nizamabad | 5015 | 1119 | 6358 | 1883 | 7322 | 3161 | 8211 | 3074 | 9065 | 4918 | 14472 | 14012 | 20058 | 28338 | 26269 |
| 16 | Prakasam | 4299 | 960 | 5293 | 1965 | 9936 | 4147 | 12989 | 6399 | 11630 | 8563 | 13885 | 12240 | 20281 | 27996 | 30127 |
| 17 | Ranga Reddy | 2928 | 654 | 4459 | 1499 | 5775 | 3631 | 5367 | 2844 | 7794 | 7285 | 8475 | 11290 | 9461 | 17883 | 19407 |
| 18 | Srikakulam | 11178 | 2495 | 14303 | 3226 | 15974 | 6115 | 14149 | 6538 | 13610 | 10600 | 14221 | 15079 | 17235 | 24162 | 27288 |
| 19 | Visakhapatnam | 6400 | 1429 | 7756 | 1889 | 8689 | 3356 | 11842 | 6568 | 11987 | 12284 | 13399 | 16760 | 18984 | 25837 | 35332 |
| 20 | Vizianagaram | 2639 | 589 | 6147 | 1501 | 8963 | 2713 | 10291 | 5568 | 10801 | 8555 | 13831 | 19441 | 12797 | 25537 | 21694 |
| 21 | Warangal | 10012 | 2235 | 11178 | 2870 | 12100 | 5266 | 13773 | 4681 | 12211 | 5928 | 19187 | 12502 | 18175 | 19665 | 33960 |
| 22 | West Godavari | 3760 | 839 | 10051 | 2390 | 18118 | 5816 | 24513 | 10138 | 19837 | 15200 | 26175 | 20792 | 28271 | 40851 | 48083 |
| | Total | 117352 | 26195 | 165093 | 47676 | 2E+05 | 89822 | 289238 | 123842 | 288711 | 200142 | 366489 | 306387 | 431515 | 588278 | 710315 |

*Source:* SERP, GOAP

**Table 3.2**
**Region-wise SHG Bank linkage Status (2001-02 to 2007-08 in Andhra Pradesh**
**(Rs. In. Lakhs)**

| Sl. No. District | 2001-2002 | | 2002-2003 | | 2003-04 | | 2004-05 | | 2005-06 | | 2006-07 | | 2007-08 | |
|---|---|---|---|---|---|---|---|---|---|---|---|---|---|---|
| | Groups covered | Credit Accessed by the groups | Groups covered | Credit Accessed by the groups | Groups covered | Credit Accessed by the groups | Groups covered | Credit Accessed by the groups | Groups covered | Credit Accessed by the groups | Groups covered | Credit Accessed by the groups | Groups covered | Credit Accessed by the groups |
| 1 | 2 | 3 | 4 | 5 | 6 | 7 | 8 | 9 | 10 | 11 | 12 | 13 | 14 | 1 |
| **Coastal** | | | | | | | | | | | | | | |
| Srikakulam | 11178 | 2495 | 14303 | 3226 | 15974 | 6115 | 14149 | 6538 | 13610 | 10600 | 14221 | 15079 | 17235 | 24162 |
| Visakhapatnam | 6400 | 1429 | 7756 | 1889 | 8689 | 3356 | 11842 | 6568 | 11987 | 12284 | 13399 | 16760 | 18984 | 25837 |
| Vizianagaram | 2639 | 589 | 6147 | 1501 | 8963 | 2713 | 10291 | 5568 | 10801 | 8555 | 13831 | 19441 | 12797 | 25537 |
| East Godavari | 12766 | 2850 | 22194 | 6544 | 28119 | 10629 | 32139 | 12925 | 25517 | 17500 | 28991 | 26442 | 36170 | 50711 |
| Guntur | 5072 | 1132 | 6286 | 2325 | 9463 | 4264 | 14242 | 8360 | 13852 | 9738 | 22240 | 13261 | 25226 | 28664 |
| Krishna | 6540 | 1460 | 5197 | 1607 | 11565 | 3814 | 14149 | 5106 | 15861 | 9000 | 23857 | 16920 | 29407 | 37048 |
| Prakasam | 4299 | 960 | 5293 | 1965 | 9936 | 4147 | 12989 | 6399 | 11630 | 8563 | 13885 | 12240 | 20281 | 27996 |
| Nellore | 2661 | 594 | 2650 | 1545 | 4816 | 2464 | 4192 | 2043 | 9242 | 6500 | 15718 | 17130 | 15735 | 25370 |
| West Godavari | 3760 | 839 | 10051 | 2390 | 18118 | 5816 | 24513 | 10138 | 19837 | 15200 | 26175 | 20792 | 28271 | 40851 |
| **Total** | 55315 | 12348 | 79877 | 22992 | 115643 | 43318 | 138506 | 63645 | 132337 | 97940 | 172317 | 158065 | 204106 | 286176 |
| **Rayalseema** | | | | | | | | | | | | | | |
| Anantapur | 4476 | 999 | 4168 | 1049 | 6862 | 2124 | 10105 | 3546 | 12308 | 6036 | 14019 | 9769 | 20038 | 32847 |
| Chittoor | 5132 | 1146 | 7709 | 2664 | 14986 | 5635 | 12416 | 6067 | 15444 | 11139 | 20067 | 19604 | 20353 | 35453 |

| | | | | | | | | | | | | | | |
|---|---|---|---|---|---|---|---|---|---|---|---|---|---|---|
| Kadapa | 1689 | 377 | 4329 | 1544 | 5870 | 2910 | 5553 | 3083 | 8467 | 10000 | 12605 | 10078 | 17345 | 19977 |
| Kurnool | 3494 | 780 | 8846 | 2632 | 16692 | 5215 | 14303 | 5952 | 12103 | 9706 | 15176 | 12086 | 17177 | 26975 |
| **Total** | 14791 | 3302 | 25052 | 7889 | 44410 | 15884 | 42377 | 18648 | 48322 | 36881 | 61867 | 51537 | 74913 | 115252 |
| **Telangana** | | | | | | | | | | | | | | |
| Karimnagar | 4260 | 951 | 9302 | 1829 | 9037 | 2135 | 15024 | 4544 | 15085 | 7543 | 17660 | 12571 | 17317 | 20629 |
| Khammam | 6442 | 1438 | 8484 | 1851 | 17436 | 3342 | 17035 | 4182 | 15300 | 6217 | 21296 | 12763 | 21435 | 25182 |
| Mahabubnagar | 5380 | 1201 | 6940 | 2241 | 10613 | 4010 | 10794 | 6202 | 13386 | 12200 | 13314 | 8694 | 15871 | 14527 |
| Medak | 4001 | 893 | 3328 | 1651 | 8429 | 3105 | 10962 | 4343 | 10940 | 6900 | 13805 | 9653 | 17339 | 24100 |
| Nalgonda | 4704 | 1050 | 4727 | 1550 | 9992 | 3618 | 19165 | 8901 | 17529 | 10025 | 14464 | 7709 | 21397 | 23489 |
| Nizamabad | 5015 | 1119 | 6358 | 1883 | 7322 | 3161 | 8211 | 3074 | 9065 | 4918 | 14472 | 14012 | 20058 | 28338 |
| Ranga Reddy | 2928 | 654 | 4459 | 1499 | 5775 | 3631 | 5367 | 2844 | 7794 | 7285 | 8475 | 11290 | 9461 | 17883 |
| Warangal | 10012 | 2235 | 11178 | 2870 | 12100 | 5266 | 13773 | 4681 | 12211 | 5928 | 19187 | 12502 | 18175 | 19665 |
| Adilabad | 4504 | 1005 | 5388 | 1421 | 7611 | 2352 | 8024 | 2777 | 6742 | 4305 | 9632 | 7591 | 11443 | 13038 |
| **Total** | 47246 | 10546 | 60164 | 16795 | 88315 | 30620 | 108355 | 41548 | 108052 | 65321 | 132305 | 96785 | 152497 | 186850 |
| **Grand total** | **117352** | **26195** | **165093** | **47676** | **248368** | **89822** | **289238** | **123842** | **288711** | **200142** | **366489** | **306387** | **431515** | **588278** |

***Source:*** SERP, Govt. of AP

of all practitioners to capture both the structural and functional aspects of self-help groups. The state government has since issued a government order making it virtually mandatory for all SHPIs to follow the rating norm as specified.

In the case of SHGs where the local bank branch does not have adequate confidence in lending to them, or in cases where SHGs for various reasons are not willing to be linked directly with the bank, the bank may finance such SHGs through the Voluntary Agency (VA) or the self-help promoting institution (SHPI) that has promoted the self-help Groups. Further if some members of SHGs require large loans than that could be covered under the savings-related loaning, the SHG could appraise the requirement and recommend the proposal to the bank for directly lending to the members concerned. In such cases, the SHG should be willing to accept the responsibility for proper credit utilization and repayment by the members and for monitoring the same. It may be observed from the above discussion that there are essentially two methods for lending to SHGs-direct and indirect methods.

***Direct Method of Lending***

Under direct method, SHGs have direct access to loans from financing banks based on their independent credit standing, and savings/ loan accounts of the groups are maintained and operated at the financing branch. As a corollary, credit decisions of the banks are made based on the appraisal of individual SHGs. The credit risk under this method is borne by the financing bank. There are very few SHGs which have autonomous origin. Generally, there is a definite support mechanism from SHPI to facilitate interaction between financing bank and the groups.

***Indirect Method of Lending***

In the absence of necessary confidence for lending directly to SHGs, indirect methods are adopted to route finances through intermediation of non- governmental organizations/ SHPIs. As indicated earlier, RBI/NABARD have also recognized indirect financing of SHGs as an important method for reaching the rural poor under SHG-Bank linkage programme. Under this method savings accounts are maintained and operated by SHGs at the financing branch, whereas the loans are extended to SHPI acting as financial intermediary on behalf of SHGs. While primary credit risk is that of intermediary (usually an NGO), the banks will bear only a secondary risk. Since the banks will be extending loans to an intermediary agency, it will have to primarily appraise the credit standing of that agency. However, the quantum of credit will be based upon the strengths and weaknesses of borrowing SHGs, the resources mobilized and rotated by them. Their credit requirements, systems and procedures adopted by them for managing savings and loan portfolios, etc.

## Synergy through SHGs Network

With the proliferation of large number of thrift and credit groups, new coalitions and network are fast emerging in the SHG scene of Andhra Pradesh. As a result mature SHGs are getting networked to obtain synergies through sharing of information, resources and wisdom. The organization resulting from such networking effort will either have unitary or federal character depending upon the nature of group interests, its social composition, methods of operations and systems and procedures adopted in each formation. While doing so, it is to be ensured that power relationships and resources do not gravitate to a few individuals or groups. The corporate status to such structures is provided by the appropriate enactment under which they are registered. The financing banks may have to, therefore, keep in view these evolutionary trends in SHGs and adopt appropriate financial instruments to reach the rural poor.

In the initial stages, SHGs are brought on a common platform like village, cluster or Mandal level conventions to facilitate cross-selling of experiences and ideas among them. These conventions gradually got formalized in the form of appropriate associations where the groups win evolve methods for sharing community and group resources. While SHGs operate independent of other groups and maintain their respective group savings account at the local bank branch, they also contribute a part of their resources to the village, cluster level organization to access various financial and non -financial services available for the members. This transfer mechanism helps the groups to moderate the surpluses or deficits at the group level. Here again, the banks have an option to finance either the groups directly or choose village, cluster level organization as an intermediary. A few banks have opted for the latter route to obtain advantages of twin peer pressure from both - within and across the groups. Wherever such financing was attempted, the banks have to ensure that the village, cluster level organization enforces uniformity in methods of operation at each of the groups belonging to it, develop suitable accounting systems and appropriate vigilance mechanism.

A few cluster-level organizations have enlarged, aligned, consolidated or amalgamated their operations with other counterparts in nearby areas and formed mutually aided cooperative societies (MACS). Government of Andhra Pradesh has enacted Andhra Pradesh Mutually Aided Cooperative Societies Act, 1995 which provides corporate status to these organizations. Unlike informal SHGs, the structure and functions, roles and relationships and rights and obligations of members in MACS are clearly predefined which may add to the confidence of funding agencies. Under this system SHGs may not have any relationship with local banks and their savings may be pooled with MACS and loaning decisions are taken at group/MACS level depending upon the nature and size of credit. However, responsibility of loan assessment, monitoring and supervision is cast upon the respective groups. The extent and nature of financial assistance from banks to MACS is generally determined based on its cash flows; lending programme and resource gap. Non-governmental organization/professional and development agencies have been actively associating with formation, nurturing and management of these societies. At the same time, many MACS, especially those promoted by DRDAs, are facing financial crunch and are waiting for bank finance.

## Financing Self-help Groups

Despite vast expansion of the formal credit system encompassing spheres of social and mass banking, the dependence of the rural poor on money lenders still continues in many areas, especially for meeting their emergent needs. Under the circumstances, a non-formal agency for credit supply to the poor, in the form of Self-help Groups, emerged as a promising partner to the formal credit system. The objectives of Self-help Groups are to:

- Inculcate saving and banking habits among the poor;
- Secure them with financial, technical and moral strengths;
- Enable availing of loan for productive purposes and repaying the same over a period of time, and in the process
- Gain economic prosperity;
- Gain from collective wisdom in the financial matters in organizing and managing their own finance and distributing the benefits among themselves.

The Self-help Groups consist of the members who are poor, having low savings capacity and who depend on money lenders or private sources for meeting their consumption needs and other pressing obligations. In other words, a typical Self-help Group would comprise like minded individuals who regularly save small amounts of money. To facilitate group processes and ensure transparency of operations, group meetings are regularly convened at a pre-determined place, date and time. The thrift amounts are pooled during group meetings and given out as loans to members for consumption, production or investment purposes based on the priorities decided by the group. The loans are need based and provided in time. The group members take collective decision on all matters keeping in view the welfare and prosperity of the members. More often, lending decisions like purpose, size, interest rate and repayment period for loans are decided case by case, paramount consideration being given to needs and aspirations of individual borrowing members. Therefore, these groups play a role more than that of a middle man or money lender. The procedures for sanction of loan adopted by the groups are very simple and the loans are provided on the basis of mutual trust among the members.

Since it is members' thrift that is given out as loans to some members at each meeting depending upon the priorities set by the group, members exercise close supervision on utilization of loans. Similarly, peer or moral pressure is exerted on members to continue savings to provide every member an opportunity to avail loans. Likewise, prompt on-time repayments of loans are also insisted upon by remaining members in their anxiety to avail loans of higher order. As a result, at any given point of time all members in Self-help Group may not be borrowers, even if all of them are borrowers, their loans out standings would not be equal. Several interesting features have been observed in the financial dynamics of group where there is evidence in qualitative shift in loans portfolio in favour of productive purposes as against consumption loans availed earlier. So is the case with the size of the loan.

SHG formation necessitates an all encompassing environment for conscious leadership development, decentralized decision making, transparency in transactions, peer pressure for sustainable group action and enterprise development among rural poor. The fungibility of credit and savings cycles in SHGs consolidates group behavior while enhancing the capacity of individual members to manage scarce financial resources. Though equitable distribution of pecuniary benefits to the members of SHGs are ensured, such benefits are not based on any entitlement mechanism but are determined by the absorption capacity and managerial ability as perceived by the group. As a corollary, all policy decisions related to fund mobilization and management are with SHGs, unlike in other formations where the lending decisions and credit entitlements are pre-decided by promotional agencies.

Nevertheless, it must be understood that the concept of self help and mutual help is not alien to other formations but that it has only been relegated to the background. There is a definite scope to synthesize group based thrift and credit programmes with the SHG concept. To achieve this, special efforts are required to harmonize the group dynamics by providing homogeneity in the membership, rotation of leadership, transparency in decision making and fungibility of savings and credit cycles in the said groups. Here it must be emphasized that such groups should be given complete autonomy with regard to fund management, credit discipline, prioritization and allocation of resources, etc. Any external assistance to these groups must be accessed by a group of individuals and not individuals - in - group mode. As a prelude to synthesizing efforts, there is a need to prepare the groups to handle managerial responsibilities besides sensitizing all functionaries concerned on concepts of SHGs. In essence, strength of SHG concept lies in its democratic character, decentralized decision making, and financial discipline coupled with sound systems and procedures, lending transparency to all its transactions.

## SHG-Bank Linkage Programme - NABARD Guidelines

NABARD introduced in 1992, a "Pilot Project for Linking SHGs with Banks" to encourage thrift and savings amongst the rural poor and to supplement their funds to meet credit needs through the banking system. With a view to studying the functioning of SHGs and NGOs and for expanding their activities and deepening their role in rural sector, RBI constituted a Working Group in November 1994, comprising eminent NGO functionaries, academicians, consultants and bankers under the Chairmanship of Shri S.K. Kalia, the then Managing Director, NABARD. The Working Group submitted its report, recommending for treating the linkage programme as a business opportunity for reaching rural poor. Based on the recommendations of the Working Group, the RBI, in 1996, decided to extend SHG linkage programme beyond the pilot phase and advised the banks to make it a part of their mainstream lending operations. Some of the salient features of SHG-Bank Linkage Programme are:

*Criteria for Selecting SHGs*

The group should have been in active existence for at least a period of six months. The group should have successfully undertaken savings and credit operations from its own resources. Democratic working of the group wherein all members feel that 'they have a say' should be evident. The group is maintaining proper accounts/records. The banker should be convinced that the group has come into existence realizing the genuine need to help each other and work together with participation of all its members. The SHG members should preferably have homogeneous background and interest. The interest of the NGO or the Self-help Promoting Institutions (SHPI) concerned/in the group is evident and the agency is helping the SHG by way of training and other supports for skill up gradation and proper functioning.

*Estimation of credit requirements*

The quantum of credit is determined in multiples of the savings pooled by the group and the proportion of savings to credit could vary from 1:1 to 1:10 depending on the assessment of the SHG by the bank. Greater the degree of confidence of bank on the SHG, greater could be the proportion of loan. The activities or purposes and size of loans, which the group proposes to lend, should be left to the common wisdom of the group.

*Extent of refinance*

NABARD provides 100 per cent refinance to all banks for the loans disbursed to SHGs

*Repayment Period*

The repayment period for the loans extended by SHG to its members will be determined by the group. However, the banks could give a longer repayment period for the loans extended by them to SHGs, for allowing rolling over of funds by the groups leading to greater internal capitalization of their fund base. In other words, the SHGs should be able to service their debt without having any depletion of its resources built up with own funds. As regards repayment of refinance by the banks to NABARD, it is generally repayable over a period of 2 to 5 years depending upon the requirements of each case.

*Interest Rates*

The present interest rate structure stipulated by NABARD/RBI at different levels under the SHG-Bank Linkage Programme is as under:

| | | |
|---|---|---|
| NABARD to Banks | - | 9 per cent |
| Banks to SHG | - | To be decided by bank within the scope of RBI directives |

| | | |
|---|---|---|
| Banks to NGO/MCO* | - | Bank free to decide |
| NGO/MCO* to SHG | - | NGO/MCO free to decide |

* NGO - Non governmental Organization and MCO-Micro Credit Organization

- A SHG is free to determine the rate of interest of the loans granted by it to its members.

*Security*

SHGs might not be in a position to offer any collateral security other than the savings under rotation within the group. Peer pressure among members is the alternative for the collaterals. RBI has therefore relaxed the security norms and classified loans under the programme as "Advances to Weaker Sections".

*Eligible Agencies*

Commercial banks, Regional Rural Banks, Cooperative Banks and Primary Agricultural Credit Societies.

### Promoting Self-help Groups and Inculcating Best Practices

It has been observed that group approach is a cost-effective, equitable and sustainable way to channelising developmental efforts. But the rural poor may not be able to form groups by themselves and would require the services of developmental agencies for support. There is, thus, a need for promotional agencies which can function as catalysts and facilitators to act as intermediate link, between the poor and the formal credit agencies. Voluntary agencies can help the poor organize themselves into groups, assist in their organizational, managerial and financial matters, upgrade their skills and wherever necessary, counter the pressures from the vested interests. Realizing the potential of the SHGs in implementing community development programmes, state government and several development organizations have also started promoting SHGs. Also, RRBs and DCCBs in different parts of the country, are attempting formation of groups on their own to increase their business and clientele. Thus both governmental and non-governmental sectors have been instrumental in promotion and nurturing of SHGs. The institutions promoting such groups are called Self-Help Promoting Institutions (SHPI).

SHPIs play a vital role in mobilizing the poor in groups, nurturing them and building their capabilities in group processes, functional areas of management, skill development, technology up gradation, market support, etc. The groups are also guided in improving their standard of living by dovetailing literacy, health and nutrition, housing and sanitation ecological conservation and restoration programmes.

## Disturbing Trends in SHGs in A.P.

### *Dormancy in SHGs*

It was found that the groups linked earlier have also gone dormant, while some of them make regular repayment of bank loans (post. linkage inertia). Perhaps, this will deal a fatal blow to the credit linkage programme. The initiatives for revival of dormant groups could include group counselling by DRDA staff, sharing of experiences by active groups, village- level interface meets involving DRDA, banks, SHGs, etc, loan disbursement function at the village/habitation level, joint monitoring along with the SHPI, etc., DRDA and local banks can emphasize on benefits of SHG-bank linkage programme and benefits of adopting best practices. Banks may prepare a list of inoperative savings bank accounts of SHGs and forwards the same to DRDA-Velugu for necessary action.

### *NPAs in SHGs*

A high recovery rate of SHG loans has been the hallmark of the credit linkage programme in A.P. It should be the constant endeavor of everyone to keep the recovery rate at

97+ per cent under this programme at all costs. In many branches, as the portfolio is not sizeable as compared to other business, visit to groups is not being done even in case of defaults. Of late, there is an increase in level of NPAs in SHG portfolio of some banks, though the same are still insignificant. The banks may institute a mechanism to collect details of such defaults from branches on a regular basis and initiate follow-up action for recovery of dues. The banks may also forward the same to SHPIs i.e. PD, DRDA-Velugu and NGOs for necessary action. The issue needs to be discussed regularly in JMLB/SC/DCC meetings.

***Over-dues in SHGs***

In some cases over dues are being identified and the reasons for over-dues are:

i. Misappropriation of SHG Credit/funds

ii. Migration of Members of the SHG Group to other villages and towns

iii. Group defunct

iv. Wilful defaulters

v. Misappropriation of funds by Group Leaders

vi. Involvement of men / outsiders in the affairs of the group

vii. Death of members

viii. Officials of DRDA are not supporting / involving in recovery of loans

ix. All Government Programmes are routing through SHGs irrespective of their managerial abilities like Indiramma And Pasukranthi padhakam

x. Political interference

xi. Misunderstanding among the members in repayment of interest of SHG loans and differences in internal lending

xii. Non-recovery of internal lending amount to the outsiders i.e., farmers

**Measures for Accelerating SHG-Bank Linkage Programme in Andhra Pradesh**

Some of the measures contemplated for consolidating Self-help Group Movement in the state are as follows:

i. Consolidating the SHG movement with focused efforts on capacity building of SHG especially in the areas of self management, leadership development, financial management, etc.

ii. Building up capacities of NGOs and GOs for forming, managing and developing SHGs in sustainable manner.

iii. Dovetailing groups formed under Indira Mahila Yojana, Joint Forest Management and Watershed Programmes to Self-help Group concept.

iv. Fostering fresh group mobilization efforts for stretching out to un-reached particularly tribal and deprived segments of rural societies through Andhra Pradesh District Poverty Initiatives Project (APDPIP), Joint Forest Management, and Integrated Tribal Development Agencies.

v. Aiding the efforts of NGOs in strengthening of DWACRA groups on lines of SHG concept.

vi. Supporting SHG networking initiatives in NGO and government organisation sectors for salubrious growth of micro-finance movement in the state through member based institutional development and encourages self review against consensual performance benchmarks.

vii. Collaborating with agencies like National Institute of Small Industry Extension and Training (NISIET), Andhra Pradesh Industrial Technical Consultancy Organization (APITCO), etc, for designing an innovative and fully participatory modules for micro-Entrepreneurship Management, Skill Up gradation Programmes and Project Opportunity Guidance.

viii. Assisting NGO and other resource institutions for taking up programmes for Self Help Groups on business skill promotion, MEDPs, Skill up gradation skills, etc.

ix. Promote training research on ongoing basis for training needs assessment, designing of training modules and development of training aids. These efforts can converge with internalization of finding of studies conducted by NABARD for drawing district specific strategies for improving quality of SHGs and linkage practices.

x. Initiating policy research in areas relating to management of micro-finance programmes, measures for promoting their economic and financial efficiencies, new product development, etc.

xi. Strengthening the data base on various mF programmes in the state to document best practices to vogue.

xii. Selectively support institutional structures for capacity building and monitoring of SHG.

# 4

# SHG Financing: Role of Andhra Bank

## PROFILE AND PERFORMANCE OF ANDHRA BANK

### Evolution of Banking

Banking in its crude form is an age-old phenomenon. Prof. Marshall in his book *Money, Credit and Commerce* (1923) write about the activities of money-changers in the temples of Olympia and other sacred places in Greece, around 2000 B.C. To quote:

> " Private money changers began with the task of reducing many metallic currencies, more or less exactly, to a common unit of value, and even to accept money on deposit at interest, and to lend it out at higher interest, permitting mean while drafts to be drawn on them".

As a matter of fact, the origin of banking lies in the business of money changing in ancient days. Another fact that supported the emergence of banks in the early period was the need for borrowing by the monarchical governments from the finance companies. In the middle ages, in Italy, the first bank called the "Bank of Venice" was established in 1157 on this ground, particularly, when the authorities of the state of Venice were in finance trouble due to war. In England, however, the bankers of Lombardy had taken the initiative to start modern banking along with their trading activities in London. But, commercial banking began there only after 1640, when goldsmiths started receiving deposits from the public for safe custody and issued receipt for acknowledgement, which were being used as bearer demand notes later on.

In India, however, modern banking started when the English agency houses in Calcutta and Bombay began to serve as bankers to the East India Company and the Hindustan Bank was the first banking institution of its kind to be established in 1779.

## Historical Background

The Andhra Bank Limited, an offshoot of National Movement was established by Dr.Bhogaraju Pattabhi Sitaramayya, an ardent Freedom Fighter, a great Intellectual and a multifaceted Genius. The Andhra Bank Ltd. was registered on November 20, 1923 and commenced business on 28th November, 1923, at Machilipatnam - a Port Town in Coastal Andhra. By setting apart 50 per cent of its advances for the farmer, the trader, the artisan and the craftsman in rural areas at the time of inception, the Bank proved its commitment for the development of the less privileged sections of the Society. Some of the landmarks in the history of the Bank are listed hereunder.

i) The Bank attained the status of Scheduled Bank in the year 1943.

ii) The Bank opened first branch (outside Andhra Pradesh) in Madras in the year 1945 and in Berhampur in 1946.

iii) The Bank attained the status of *A Class Bank* in 1964.

iv) The Bank absorbed Bharata Lakshmi Bank, another offspring of National Movement, in 1964 to consolidate its position further in Coastal Andhra Pradesh.

v) The Bank opened its first of all Women Branch in Hyderabad in 1964.

vi) The Bank opened its 100th Branch at Calcutta in 1964.

vii) The Bank opened its first Branch in the Nation's Capital - 'Delhi', in 1966.

viii) After the Nationalization of 14 major banks in the country in 1969, the bank remained as largest private sector bank in the country and retained the same position till its nationalization in 1980.

ix) Even as a private sector bank, the bank assumed Lead Bank responsibilities in 5 districts - four in Andhra Pradesh (Guntur, West Godavari, East Godavari) and one in Orissa (Ganjam).

x) The bank surpassed Rs. 100 crore deposits mark in 1972.

xi) The bank was nationalized in the year 1980. The Andhra Bank Ltd., thus has become Andhra Bank, wholly owned by the Government of India.

xii) The Bank celebrated its Silver Jubilee in 1948, Golden Jubilee in 1973, Diamond Jubilee in 1983 and Platinum Jubilee in 1998, continuing its march ahead to carve a niche for itself in the New Millennium and racing towards Centenary.

xiii) The Bank attained "Autonomy" in the year 1998 by fulfilling the eligibility criteria laid down by Government of India and since then continued to enjoy autonomy.

**Overall Performance of Andhra Bank between 1969 and 2008.**

***Capital, Reserves and Surplus***

Capital, reserve and surpluses are the important parameters of performance measurement of any financial institutions. Andhra Bank during the reporting period has shown phenomenal growth in all parameters. The net worth of the Bank increased from Rs. 2,894 crore to Rs.3,156 crore during 2006-07. There is an improvement of Rs.262 crore over previous year, with a growth of 9.05 per cent. The reserves and surplus position increased from Rs.2, 409 crore as on 31.03.2006 to Rs.2, 671 crore, registering an increase of 10.88 per cent.

***Capital to Risk Assets Ratio (CRAR)***

Andhra Bank has retained the CRAR norm of Reserve Bank of India to withstand to all kinds of unforeseen risks and certainties. The CRAR of the Bank is 11.33 per cent as on 2007 as against the prescribed RBI norm of 9 per cent. The CRAR was at 14 per cent in 2006, which is a very positive sign of the institution to absorb the market as well as natural risks.

***Total Business***

The total volume of business recorded by the Bank during the financial year 2006-07 was Rupees 69,687 crores, is far better a business recorded upon the last years.

***Resource Management***

The total Assets / Liabilities of the Bank increased to Rs.47, 541.00 crore as on 31.03.2007. Bank's Loan Portfolio increased by 25.57 per cent to reach Rs.28, 233 crore as on 31.03.2007, as compared to Rs.22, 484 crore as on 31.03.2006, with an incremental growth of Rs.5, 749 crore. The focus during the year was on qualitative and balanced Credit growth. The Credit Portfolio was managed in such a way that a major portion of incremental Credit flow is diverted to Productive Sectors, viz., Agriculture, Industry and Service Sectors. As on 31st March 2007, the Total Investments (Net of Depreciation) of the Bank stood at Rs.14, 300.72 crore as against Rs.11, 444.15 crore as on March 31, 2006.

Total Deposits of the Bank stood at Rs.41, 454 crore as on 31st March 2007 from a level of Rs.33, 922 crore as on 31st March 2006, with an incremental accretion of Rs.7, 532 crore and a growth of 22.20 per cent. The Low Cost Deposits Portfolio at Rs.14, 314 crore increased by 16.21 per cent over March 2006 level of Rs.12, 317 crore and accounted for 34.53 per cent of the Total Deposits.

### *Advances to Priority Sectors*

Lending to Priority Sectors is one of the thrust areas for the Bank during the year. Priority Sector Advances stood at Rs.11, 427 crore as on 30.03.2007 (Last Reporting Friday of March 2007) achieving 41.14 per cent of the adjusted Net Bank Credit, thereby surpassing the stipulated norm of 40 per cent.

### *Agriculture*

The Annual Policy Statement of the Reserve Bank of India in May 2004 and Hon'ble Finance Minister's announcement in June, 2004 have emphasized the need to improve the flow of credit to agricultural sector and to double agricultural credit in three years by achieving 30 per cent compounded growth every year. Bank has implemented these directives proactively. The total agricultural advances increased from Rs.4, 064 crore as on March 2006 to Rs.5, 150 crore as on March 2007 recording a growth of Rs.1, 086 crore in absolute terms and 26.72 per cent in percentage terms. The share of agricultural advances to adjusted net bank credit was 18.54 per cent as on last reporting Friday of March 2007.

There are one lakh and Twenty-one thousand new farmers were financed as against the targeted level of 73,400 farmers during 2006-07. In 2006-07, the Bank has disbursed more than 5.25 lakh Pattabhi Agri Cards against the target of 5 lakh. The client base under Agricultural Sector surpassed one million mark. Bank entered MoU with tractor manufacturing companies for sourcing of proposals through their respective dealers' network. During the year, financial assistance was extended for 1532 tractors amounting to Rs.45.96 crore.

Rates of interest, Margin and Collateral security norms were rationalized / liberalized for many Agricultural Credit Products. Through Kisan Vikas Card Scheme of the Bank, the Agricultural Credit Cards issued by the Bank are made ATM compatible. Under *Rythu Mitra* more than 3,045 groups were financed to an extent of Rs.45.32 crore. To take the technology to the door steps of the farmers, several farmer meets were conducted with the help of Research Institutions, Krishi Vignan Kendras and Farmer Training Centers.

During the year, the Bank has also assisted 58,701 farmers in distress. It has provided interest relief to distressed farmers to the tune of Rs.97.52 crore in 31 districts, viz., 16 districts in A.P., 6 districts in Karnataka, 3 districts in Kerala and six districts in Maharashtra States. Further, the Bank has rescheduled Loans to an extent of Rs.135.70 crore.

***Other Priority Sectors***

The Other Priority Sector (OPS) Advances during the Financial Year 2006-07 registered an increase of Rs.1,091 crore going up from Rs.3,643 crore to Rs.4,734 crore, registering a growth of 29.95 per cent. Housing loans (direct) increased from Rs.1,572 crore as on 31$^{st}$ March 2006 to Rs.1,774 crore as on 31st March 2007, registering a growth of 12.85 per cent. Educational loans increased from Rs.677 crore to Rs.905 crore, registering a growth of 33.68 per cent.

### *Lending to Women*

With a view to encourage women entrepreneurs to become self-supportive, Bank has improved the flow of credit to women beneficiaries from Rs.1,427 crore (31.3.2006) to Rs.1,586 crore (31.3.2007).

### *Advances to Weaker Sections and Minority Community*

Going by the mandate to help assist the weaker sections of the society to come out of poverty through fruitful and gainful employment opportunities, the bank has given priority lending facility to the section. As a result, the assistance to Weaker Sections as on 31-03-2007 stood at Rs.2,649 crore. Advances to SC/ST Beneficiaries as on 31-03-2007 stood at Rs.452 crore and the recovery portion is 34 per cent to demand. Similarly the financial assistance given to the minority communities stood at Rs.211 crore as at the end of March 2007.

### *Self-help Groups (SHGs)*

Self-help Group formation and linkage has acquired a significant status in Bank's endeavor to uplift the weaker sections of the society. Linkage of SHGs has been seen as an important activity for the economic development of rural areas and for reaching the rural poor. During the year 2006-07, 57,168 SHG groups have been financed and 1, 12,926 groups outstanding have been linked with financial assistance to the extent of Rs.521 crore. All the SHGs financed were Women Self Help Groups. Bank also took lead in extending SHG Concept to Urban Areas and assisted formation of 10479 women SHGs in Urban Areas. The concept of SHG Credit Card was popularized. As announced in the Budget by Hon'ble Union Finance Minister, Bank introduced comprehensive health insurance scheme for all credit linked groups under "Swasthya Bima Yojana".

### *Government of India Sponsored Schemes and Lead Bank Schemes*

Besides Central Sponsored Schemes like Prime Minister Rozgar Yojana (PMRY), Swarna Jayanthi Gram Swarozgar Yojana (SGSY), Swarna Jayanthi Shahari Rozgar Yojana (SJSRY), etc., many State Specific Schemes are being implemented. The Bank is having Lead Bank responsibilities in six districts in the country, viz., Guntur, West Godavari, East Godavari and Srikakulam Districts in the State of Andhra Pradesh and Ganjam and Gajapathi districts in the State of Orissa. In all the six districts, District Credit Plans for the year 2007-08, were launched well before 31st March, 2007. In all the 23 districts of Andhra Pradesh, District Credit Plans for the year 2007-08 were launched before 31st March, 2007.

### *State Level Bankers' Committee*

The Bank took over the Convenorship of State Level Bankers' Committee (SLBC) from State Bank of India in 1984 and since then 159 SLBC meetings were organized by the Bank in the State besides several meetings of the Standing/ Steering Committee. In the Financial Year 2006-07, a total of 32 Meetings were convened (as against the prescribed level of 12 meetings in a year) including Two State Level Bankers' Committee Meetings. There is continuous, regular and timely follow-up and review of Progress in implementation of Government Sponsored Schemes.

### *Rural Development Institutes*

With the objective of providing training to youth in rural and semi-urban areas to take up self employment ventures, Bank is conducting various vocational and human resource development training programmes and also providing consultancy services, through its nine Rural Development and Self-Employment Training Institutes. So far, 58,555

Participants have been trained in Self-Employment Ventures and capacity building and are gainfully engaged through some Income Generation Activities.

### *Regional Rural Banks (RRBs)*

The Bank has two RRBs, viz., Chaitanya Godavari Grameena Bank located in Guntur covering Guntur and Godavari Districts of Andhra Pradesh and Rishikulya Gramya Bank in Ganjam District of Orissa State. The combined business of the two RRBs stood at Rs.1, 438.74 crore with a total branch network of 164. Both the RRBs are making profit with an aggregate net profit of Rs.5.45 crore as on March 2007.

### *Industry*

India is fast emerging as an industrial hub. In a scenario where manufacturing industry is occupying increasing importance, the credit deployed to this sector is to be increased proportionately. Andhra Banks' credit to industry sector has registered a growth of 38.83 per cent, with an absolute growth of Rs.2, 962 crore. The industry-wise exposure of credit above Rs.100 crore as on March 2007 is depicted in Table 4.1.

### *Small and Medium Enterprises*

Keeping in view the important role of Small and Medium Enterprise (SME) in the growth of the economy, Government of India announced a "Policy Package for stepping up credit to Small and Medium Enterprises" in the year 2005. Government of India also advised Public Sector Banks to fix their own targets for funding SMEs, in order to achieve a minimum of 20 per cent year-on-year growth in Credit to SMEs, so as to double the exposure within a period of 5 years. As per the said Guidelines of Government of India, Bank's Exposure to SMEs should increase from Rs.1,915 crore (31.3.2005) to Rs.3, 830 crore by the year 2009-10.

**Table 4.1**
**Industry-wise credit exposure of Andhra Bank**
**(Rs. in Crore)**

| *Industry / Sector* | *Fund Based Exposure Exposure* | *per cent to to GBC* |
|---|---|---|
| Power | 2040.46 | 7.22 |
| Textiles | 1663.70 | 5.89 |
| Iron and Steel | 1240.11 | 4.39 |
| Construction and Contractors | 809.74 | 2.87 |
| Rice Mills | 863.40 | 3.06 |
| Real Estate and Hotels | 617.98 | 2.42 |
| Petroleum Products | 703.13 | 2.49 |
| Engineering (Heavy and Light) | 647.61 | 2.29 |
| Diamonds, Gems and Jewellery | 553.07 | 1.96 |
| Drugs and Pharmaceuticals | 533.35 | 1.89 |
| Sugar | 387.23 | 1.37 |
| Educational Institutions | 281.67 | 1.00 |
| Cement and Cement Products | 122.56 | 0.43 |
| Tobacco | 169.68 | 0.60 |
| Hire Purchase and Leasing | 142.81 | 0.51 |
| Hospitals | 119.11 | 0.42 |
| **Total** | **10895.61** | **38.59** |

*Source:* Compiled from various annual repots of Andhra Bank.

In tune with the Government policy, Andhra Bank has initiated several measures to augment credit flow to SME Sector. Consequently, the outstanding credit to the sector increased from Rs.1,915 crore (31.3.2005) to Rs.3,250 crore as at the end of March 2007, with a growth rate of 58.92 per cent within a period of two years, as against the prescribed growth of 40 per cent. Andhra Bank has surpassed credit targets both under Small Scale Industries and Medium Enterprise Sectors for the year 2006-07.

As on 31st March 2007 advances to SSI Sector stood at Rs.1,581 crore as against the target of Rs.1,509 crore, resulting a growth of 29.91 per cent over March, 2006. Similarly, advances to medium enterprise stood at Rs.1,669 crore, as against the target of Rs.1,612 crore, with a growth of 36.54 per cent over March, 2006. In all, outstanding credit to SME Sector has increased by Rs.811 crore during the year 2006-07 registering a growth rate of 33.25 per cent over the year 2006.

In tune with the guidelines of Government of India, pricing of credit to SME is being done through a transparent Credit Rating System. Borrowers are also encouraged to get themselves rated by SME Rating Agency of India Ltd. (SMERA) and 50 per cent of the rating fee (Maximum Rs.5,000) is being reimbursed. Further, to encourage Women Entrepreneurs, a concession of 0.50 per cent in the rate of interest is also being given.

### *Corporate Banking*

The Bank has two Specialized Corporate Finance Branches, which are catering exclusively to the needs of Corporate Clientele. The Bank has provided Corporate Terminals to high value Corporate Customers.

### *Retail Banking*

Credit under Retail Banking has increased to Rs.6, 623 crore as on March 2007 from Rs.5, 050 crore as on March 2006.

### *Asset Quality Management*

Measures such as due diligence in selection of borrowers, adherence to systems and procedures, enhanced prudence in asset monitoring and administration and unrelenting focus on recovery of NPAs helped the Bank to contain NPA below the level of last year. Bank is benefited immensely from the policy environment and utilized legal means such as Lok Adalats and SARFAESI Act extensively to its best advantage.

The Gross NPAs of the Bank registered a decline from Rs.436.91 crore in 2006 to Rs.397.01 crore in 2007. Gross NPAs as a percentage to Gross Advances came down from 1.94 per cent in 2006 to 1.41 per cent as on March 2007 and Net NPAs as a percentage to net advances stood at 0.17 per cent for the year ended March, 2007, as against 0.24 per cent in the year 2006. The percentage of standard assets to total assets registered improvement from 98.06 as on March 2006 to 98.59 as on March 2007. The provision coverage ratio stood at 86.52 per cent as at the end of March, 2007.

***Provisions and Contingencies***

Andhra Bank has made the following major provisions as on 31st March 2007:

- Rs.61.62 crore as Depreciation on Investments.
- Rs.97.49 crore towards Non-Performing Assets (NPAs).
- Rs.238.91 crore towards Income Tax.
- Rs.46.00 crore towards Standard Assets.
- Rs.8.09 crore towards Deferred Tax Asset / Liability.

***Treasury***

Bank's Treasury, while integrating the management of domestic and foreign exchange funds and investment operations centrally, focuses on profit maximization, through diligent control of liquidity and proper compliance with regulatory requirements.

As on 31st March 2007, the Total Investments (Net of Depreciation) of the Bank stood at Rs.14, 300.72 crore as against Rs.11,444.15 crore as on March 31,2006. The Investments comprised Government Securities (79.42%), Other Approved Securities (1,04%), Shares (1.51%), Debentures and Bonds (6.62%) and others (Subsidiaries and/ or Joint Ventures, IDBI Deposits, Indira Vikas Patras, Units of UTI and MFs and RIDF) 11.41 per cent. While the SLR Securities constituted 78.54 per cent of the Total Investments, Non-SLR and Recapitalization Bonds were to the tune of 21.46 per cent. The average yield on investment was 7.34 per cent during 2006-07 in comparison to 7.29 per cent during 2005-06.

Prudential norms prescribed by RBI were strictly adhered to by the Bank. Statutory prescriptions relating to CRR and SLR are also maintained. Risk Management in Treasury Operations has been strengthened further by undertaking the stress testing and back testing of the Investment Portfolio at quarterly intervals besides daily monitoring of Duration and Value at Risk (VaR). External Rating Migration of the Bonds and Debentures Portfolio is also being monitored on quarterly basis. The Capital charge has been computed for market risk for Investment Portfolio under AFS and HFT (including the derivatives transactions for trading purposes and the hedging positions whose underlying are in AFS) for the year ended March 31, 2007, as per RBI Guidelines. Bank has already integrated the Domestic and Forex Operations of Treasury.

***Forex Business***

Systems have been put in place for management of Country Risk, Exchange Risk and other Forex Risks. The Country Risk Exposures for Single Country Risk Limit and Aggregate Risk Limits for the Group of Countries under each Risk Category are fixed and are being monitored on daily basis.

The Merchant Turnover was Rs.20,858 crore during 2006-07 as against Rs.14,705 crore in the previous year. Inter-Bank Turnover was Rs.1, 25,306 crore during 2006-07 compared to Rs.87,528 crore in the previous year. The Profit on Exchange Operations achieved improvement of Rs.38.05 crore as on March 31, 2007 when compared to Rs.27.71 crore in the previous year.

Bank has 47 Authorized Dealer Branches to conduct Foreign Exchange Business and has rupee drawing arrangements with 5 Exchange Houses. Bank introduced Speed Remittance Facility under Tie-up with one of the Exchange Houses.

***Cross-Selling and Utility Payments Business***

Keeping in view the increasing strain on margins, Bank has been focusing on augmenting Non-Interest Income through diversification of Income streams by taking up marketing of Life and Non-Life Insurance Products, Mutual Fund Products, collection of - telephone bills, Direct Taxes, Municipal Taxes, utility payments and arrangement with Western Union Money Transfer, payment of remittances, Sale of Government of India Bonds, Demat Accounts, etc.

Bank is selling insurance policies through a 'Corporate Agency' arrangement with LIC for life cover and with United India Insurance Company Ltd. for sale of non-life insurance products. Bank is also selling Mutual Funds Products of PNB Principal Mutual Fund, SBI Mutual Fund, UTI Mutual Fund, Tata Mutual Fund and Sundaram Mutual Fund. Credit Card Facility is provided through tie-up arrangements with HPCL and ICFAI.

Bank is offering Depository Services to the Public by acting as Depository Participant (DP) with Central Depository Services (India) Limited (CDSL) with the brand name "AB Demat". Bank has also commenced Depository Services as a DP with National Securities Depository Limited (NSDL). Bank has designated 20 Branches as Back Office Branches for offering Depository Services.

***Cash Management System***

Andhra Bank Cash Track is the premier Cash Management System, being extended to various Corporate Clients all over India for collection of their receivables. The Bank had 113 clients as on 31st March 2007, who have availed the facility. During the year 2006-07, the business turnover under this head is Rs.1,523 crore. Number of Branches covered under CMS Facility across the country stood at 128.

### *Financial Inclusion*

As a part of Financial Inclusion, Bank adopted two Districts, i.e., Srikakulam in Andhra Pradesh and Ganjam in Orissa State and achieved 100 per cent coverage in Srikakulam District and 95 per cent in Ganjam District so far. The Bank has opened around 1,19,000 Accounts by the end of March 2007.

### *Financial Service Centres*

The Bank has 16 Financial Service Centers across the country, which is providing varied financial products and services under one roof. These FSCs help in increasing the Clientele base for the Bank and maximizing Customer Satisfaction. These FSCs also enable the Bank to earn Fee Based Income.

### *Credit Card Business*

Andhra Bank has achieved a Credit Card Business Turnover of Rs.1,184 crore for the period ended 31.03.2007 as against the previous year's business of Rs.995 crore, registering a growth of 418.99 per cent.

### *ATM and Debit Cards*

Number of ATM / Debit Cards stood at 2.34 million as on 31.03.2007. The Bank has its own ATMs numbering 505 with sharing arrangements with SBI, HDFC Bank, IDBI Bank, Indian Bank, UTI Bank, etc., offering more than 17000 ATMs available for use by Customers.

### *Innovations*

In order to suit the varying needs of customers and to achieve the customer delight, the Andhra Bank has been marketing many innovative products and services from time to time. A few of the innovations of the Bank are as below:

1. To inculcate savings habit among 'Future Citizens' of the country, the Bank launched an exclusive Savings Scheme for Children under the title "Kiddy Bank" in the year 1970. The cute Kiddy Bank doll designed by the Bank invoked enthusiastic response and the scheme remained as a household name.

2. The bank pioneered the concept 'Bank on Wheels (Cluster Banking)' to take banking to the door-steps of people in interior villages.

3. Even before the Housing Loans Activity (HLA) was taken up by the public sector banks under the present-day Retail Lending (RL), Andhra Bank had long way back designed, formulated and implemented the Novel "Gruhakalpa Loan-Linked Deposit Scheme" for disbursement of housing loans in the country.

4. Andhra Bank was the first to launch credit card Scheme in the Indian Banking Sector in 1981. The Bank had tie-up with 2 International giants in credit card business, viz., VISA International and Master Card.

5. The Bank was the first Bank to market Insurance Linked Savings Products in the Country on a large scale.

6. The Bank was the first Bank in the Country to launch an innovative and farmer friendly Credit Card Scheme under the title 'Andhra Bank Pattabhi Agri-Card'.

7. Andhra Bank always played a proactive role in Poverty Alleviation. The Bank retained its No.1 Position in SHG-Bank Linkage Programme in the State of Andhra Pradesh and was conferred the Best

Performance Award by NABARD continuously for the last four years in the State of AP for financing maximum number of SHGs.

8. The Bank launched various Schemes for financing Agriculture such as Rural Godowns, Agri-Clinics and Agro-Services Centres, Agricultural Produce Loans, etc. Andhra Bank stood first in financing Rural Godowns in AP State.

9. The Bank introduced various Products in response to changing needs. The ATM/Debit Card Initiatives, Cash Management Services, Jeevan Abhaya, Arogyadaan, Jeevan Prakash, Jeevan Prakash Plus, Kisan Green Card, Student Care, Flexi-Deposit - Current and Savings Bank Account, Freedom Schemes, etc. Further, Andhra Bank Multicity Cheque Book and Corporate Salary Account Schemes are on the anvil.

10. Andhra Bank is the first Public Sector Bank to go in for Securitization of Housing Loan Portfolio. A Memorandum of Agreement between Andhra Bank and National Housing Bank was signed on 13th March 2004. Andhra Bank has identified Housing Finance as a Thrust Area and Securitization of Home Loan Portfolio as a strategic move to improve spread management, enhance competitive abilities in the Area of Housing Finance besides upgrading the quality of Balance Sheet Management.

In order to diversify the Income Streams leading to increase in Non-Interest Income and thereby Profitability, the Bank has affected changes in its activities and introduced by designing and marketing several customer friendly and innovative Products and Services to boost its Fee-Based Income over a period of time, some of which are :-

1. The Bank has obtained Corporate Agency from United India Insurance Company to sell their Non-Life Insurance Products.
2. The Bank has also tied up with Principal PNB Mutual Fund, UTI Mutual Fund, TATA Mutual Fund, SBI Mutual Fund and Sundaram Mutual Fund to market their Products.
3. The Bank has also tied up with Life Insurance Corporation of India to market the LIC Policies.

### *Customer Service*

Bank is committed to create a customer centric organization with a deep sense of social responsibility and to continuously leverage technology to World class standards of performance. Bank is the coordinating Bank for the 'Customer Service Centre' for all the Branches of Public Sector Banks and Jammu and Kashmir Bank Limited in Andhra Pradesh.

Bank became a member in the Banking Codes and Standards Board of India (BCSBI). 'Code of Commitment to Customers' of BCSBI has been printed in Hindi, Telugu and English and circulated. The position of 'Customer Complaints' and 'Awards passed by the Banking Ombudsman' is as under:

### *KYC and AML Standards*

In terms of RBI directives, Bank's Policy on 'Know Your Customer (KYC)' is revised as 'Know Your Customer (KYC)' Guidelines – Anti-Money Laundering (AML) Standards. All Branches and Offices of the Bank were strictly advised to adhere to KYC and AML Guidelines without any deviation, before accepting the prospective Customers into the Bank's fold.

### *Risk Management*

The Bank has a well defined and Board approved Policy on Integrated Risk Management covering Credit Risk, Market

Risk and Operational Risk. Broad guidelines are put in place for managing various risks through appropriate risk-return trade-off which helps in maximizing the Shareholders' value.

*Credit Risk*

Bank has a well defined Loan Policy duly approved by the Board. To guard against credit concentration and to have a well-diversified credit portfolio, the bank has prescribed industry-wise and constitution-wise exposure limits. Credit Committees have been set up at Head Office Level and Zonal Office level. Such Committees analyze and ensure the quality of Credit proposals and assist Board / Executives in taking prudent credit decisions. Bank has in place comprehensive risk rating system for various levels of exposures which are rated under the CRAS model developed in-house. Bank utilizes Industry reports from CRISIL and the Industry Risk Scores services from CRISINFAC for updating the knowledge of Officers/Executives at all levels. These are made available through the Bank's Intranet Portal.

*Market Risk*

A high level Executive Committee oversees the Asset Liability Management in the Bank and deliberates liquidity and interest rate scenario in the market. The Liquidity Risk is measured and managed through Gap Analysis for maturity mismatches based on residual maturity. For assets and liabilities, which are of non-maturity nature, Bank is conducting behavioral studies and factoring the observations in the Gap Analysis. The behavioural study findings are back tested and validated regularly. Prudential limits are fixed for net gaps and also for cumulative gap up to one year and these limits are measured and monitored regularly. Liquidity profile of the Bank is also measured regularly through various liquidity ratios and monitoring of the same is done with the help of prudential limits fixed thereon.

The Interest Rate Risk is managed through Gap Analysis and Duration Gap Analysis. Tolerance limits have been fixed for impact on Net Interest Income (NII) due to adverse changes in interest rates. To measure the impact of interest rate changes on Equity, Duration Gap Analysis is done and prudential limit is fixed for Modified Duration cf Equity, which has been well within the prudential limit fixed.

*Operational Risk*

Operational Risk Management Committee (ORMC) is reviewing, monitoring and managing the Operational Risk and issuing necessary directions from time-to-time. Operational Risks in the areas of Credit Management, Internal Control, HRD and Technology are reviewed monthly by obtaining MIS from all the 16 Zonal Offices of the Bank.

The Bank has developed a robust system of collecting data on Operational Losses from the Zones and Head Office departments by stipulating an elaborate list of Operational Loss events. The data so collected is analyzed and preventive measures are suggested to avoid recurrence of the loss events to the maximum extent possible. With the data base of over three years, the Bank is confident of moving over to the Advanced Measurement Approach. The Bank is in a position to provide Capital for Operational Risk under the Basic Indicator Approach and is in the process of moving towards Advanced Approaches as per the guidelines of Reserve Bank of India.

**Basel-II Preparedness**

As per the New Capital Adequacy Framework guidelines, Bank has been implementing the capital charge guidelines for HFT, Open positions in Gold and Foreign Exchange, trading positions in derivatives and derivatives entered into for hedging trading book exposures since 2006. For implementing Standardized Approach for credit risk, the

Bank has modified the branch level accounting software for capturing the exposures into various categories as suggested in the approach. While implementing the parallel run of the New Capital Adequacy Framework from 2006, capital charge for operational risk is also provided as per the Basic Indicator Approach. The Bank is in a position to implement the New Capital Adequacy Framework on the appointed date.

Capital Adequacy Assessment Process (CAAP) is established for assessing in an on-going manner, the additional capital requirements for meeting the increased business. The deliberations of the officer level committee are reviewed by the General Managers' Committee and the necessary actions are taken well in advance with the approval of board. The assessment is reviewed at quarterly intervals based on the actual business levels. Market discipline is being ensured by disclosure of key information on capital risk exposures, risk assessment processes, capital adequacy etc., as per the Disclosure Policy approved by the Board.

For moving to advanced approaches for Credit Risk, Andhra Bank has developed a robust BASEL-II compliant credit risk rating model with the consultancy assistance of NIBM and is developing a Loss Given Default (LGD) Model. Bank is in the process of segregating the gross income into 8 business lines for capital charge for operational risk.

**Information Technology Management**

Bank has been leveraging technological advantage for maximizing customer satisfaction, higher productivity and minimizing operational costs. All the 1289 Branches, 99 Extension Counters, 15 Service Centers, and 27 currency Chests are fully computerized and all the technology enabled services are offered to the Customers at these Units. Out of these Units, 1023 Branches, 90 Extension Counters, all the Service Centers and Currency Chests are connected over Wide Area Network. Bank has adopted a unique model of Cluster-based Core-Banking. As on date, 79 per cent of Bank's Units and 93 per cent of Bank's Business is under Cluster Based Core Banking Solution.

All the Customers of the Bank at Cluster-connected Branches are offered a large array of technology-driven products and a wide choice of channels like ATMs and internet channel. Any Branch Banking services are offered to Customers enhancing the status of the Customer from being a "Customer of a Branch" to "Customer of the Bank". The Customer can draw cash, effect funds transfer and query balances from any of the Cluster Connected Branches. Multi-city-cheque option is given to desired Customers.

Inter-branch remittances are rendered easier and faster with Instant Funds Transfer (IFT) Product, a facility that is available at all Cluster Connected Branches. Inter-Branch advices are sent on-line which enables speedier credits to Customers.

ATM delivery channel emerged as a popular channel in the Bank. The number of ATMs has increased to 505. Around 17000 ATMs of various Banks accept Bank's ATM, Debit and Credit Cards on shared payment network. Bank has bilateral arrangements with Banks like State Bank of India, HDFC, UTI, Indian Bank, etc.

Apart from the existing services like cash withdrawal, funds transfer, Donations to TTD, Shirdi Sai Trust, payment of prepaid mobile cards, etc. Now, Cardholders can also use Bank's debit cards for booking railway tickets through IRCTC website and make payments for King Fisher Airline tickets through Bank's ATMs. The Bank is also a Pioneer in introducing Biometric ATM which caters to rural and illiterate customers through voice enabled services.

Reserve Bank of India's initiatives with respect to payment solutions like RTGS and NEFT are implemented at all the eligible branches. Customers across the Bank are using these products. Bank has also taken a decision for migrating to Core Banking with Centralized Database and the process of identification of system Integrator is in progress.

In the context of fast developing technology, Information Security assumed greater importance. The aspect of security is being given due weightage while designing, implementing and operating various information technology solutions. Interests of the Customers and the organization are duly protected while meeting regulatory and legal requirements.

**Vigilance**

Bank recognizes Vigilance as an integral management function. Bank oversees three primary aspects of Vigilance, viz., Preventive, Detective and Punitive. Greater emphasis is being laid for implementation of Preventive Vigilance measures at all levels.

Bank is monitoring the implementation of the Ghosh Committee Recommendations. The Bank has prepared Best Practices Code for Customer related transactions as per the recommendations of 'The Mitra Committee on Legal Aspects of Bank Frauds' and the 'High Level CVC Group'.

In tune with CVC guidelines, a three member Committee of General Managers has been constituted to scrutinize and determine existence of vigilance angle in various cases / complaints. All cases of frauds involving Rs.One lakh and above are being individually reviewed by the Audit Committee of the Board. Bank has constituted a Board Level Special Committee to review large value frauds involving Rs.100 lakhs and above.

**Inspection and Audit**

Bank is evolving and monitoring various inspections and audits of the Branches, Departments, Zonal Offices, sponsored

RRBs and Farmers Service Coop. Societies, etc. Bank is focusing on the statutory, regulatory and internal compliances, to assess the level and direction of various risks involved in banking business.

Besides regular inspection of Branches including Computer Audit, Off-Site Surveillance and On-Site IS Audit of select Branches by Internal IS Audit Team and by qualified Audit Firms were conducted.

**Reconciliation**

In terms of RBI Guidelines, Scheduled Commercial Banks are required to reconcile the inter-branch entries within a period of six months. Bank was able to strictly adhere to the above time frame and is able to reconcile the items accordingly without any deviation.

**Business Strategy and Marketing Strategies**

The Bank's strategy to diversify into streams of related and specialized domains has brought immense success and made the bank pioneer of many innovative Products and decisions in the Banking Industry. The Business strategy is compatible with the changing times and the focus was laid on clientele expansion, product diversification, and value addition to shareholders, best practices and augmentation of business. In tune with the business strategy, the Bank designed various innovative products tailored to meet varied Customer needs from time to time due thrust is given to the various initiatives through Financial Service Centres and Marketing Officers to boost the Bank's core banking business and non-interest income.

Low Cost Deposits growth remains the Key Area along with Non-Interest Income, which is derived mainly through Commission and Exchange and other Fee-Based Income. Low Cost Deposits increased by Rs.1392 crore, registering 16.25 per cent and constituting 36.15 per cent of the Total Deposits.

Low Cost Deposits is considered as a Potential Area, as the Bank has shown appreciable performance in growth of Low Cost Deposits among all Public Sector Banks over the years.

## Performance Trend of Andhra Bank

### *Branch Expansion*

Andhra Bank has started in 1923 in a small town called Machilipatnam in Andhra Pradesh. The performance of Andhra Bank since inception till 2008 has been thoroughly analyzed following different parameters in the following sections and sub-sections.

**Table 4.2**
**Andhra Bank Performance Analysis Since Inception Till 2008**

| *Year* | *No. of branches* | *Growth % over previous 10 years* | *Deposits* | *Growth % over previous 10 years* | *Advances* | *Growth % over previous 10 years* |
|---|---|---|---|---|---|---|
| Prior to 1963 | 162 | — | 27 | — | 16 | — |
| 1973 | 307 | 32.57 | 114 | 22.22 | 82 | 412.5 |
| 1983 | 852 | 177.52 | 1090 | 56.14 | 669 | 715.85 |
| 1993 | 1040 | 22.06 | 4189 | 84.31 | 1908 | 185.20 |
| 2003 | 1100 | 5.76 | 21062 | 402.79 | 11513 | 503.40 |
| 2008 | 1366 | 24.18 | 49437 | 134.72 | 34238 | 197.38 |

*Source:* Compiled from Various Annual Reports of Andhra Bank.

Table 4.2 shows that Andhra Bank Performance since inception till the year 2008 with intervals of 10 years was good and follows an almost upward increasing trend. The data compiled to Number of branches, deposits and Advances. The percentage of growth during 1983 is more in number of branches with 177.52 percent, deposits with 56.14 percent and advances 715.85 percent. During 2003 period the number of branches is with 5.76 per cent, deposits with 402.79 percent and advances with 503.40 percent.

Figure 4.1 shows that the number of branches has increased from 162 to 1366 till 2008. The decade 1973 to 1983 has witnessed a massive many fold scale up of branch network, which ranges from 307 in 1973 to 852 in 1983. Branch expansions in rest of the decades are more or less at the same pace and spirit.

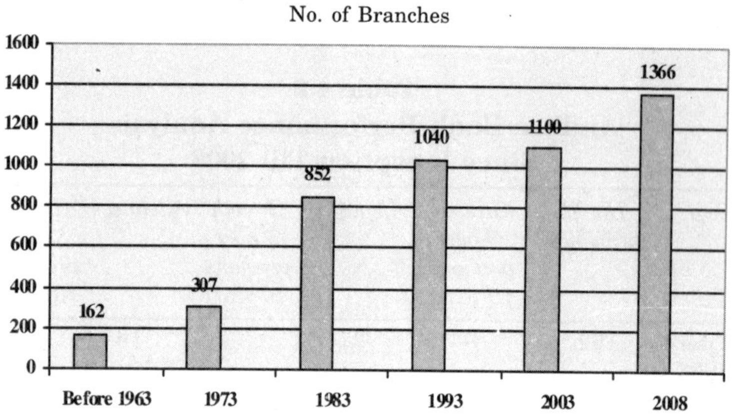


**Fig. 4.1: Year-wise status of Branch Expansion of Andhra Bank**

## Bank Deposit

Deposit with the bank is one of the important parameter of functionality of the bank. With the expansion of branch network, the savings mobilization also grown in the similar way.

Figure 4.2 shows that the Total Deposits have increased from Rs. 26.77 crores in 1963 to the tune of Rs.49, 437 crores by 2008. There is an increase of total deposits during the ten year period of 1993 to 2003 i.e. from Rs.4189 crores to Rs.21062 crores. This is primarily due to the vast expansion of bank branches to all over the country.

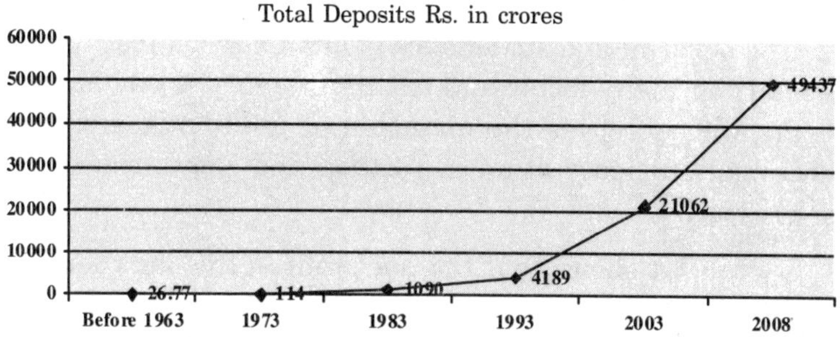


**Fig.4.2: Total Deposits of Andhra Bank since beginning till 2008**

## Total Advances

Mobilization of deposit is one aspect of the whole functional gamut of any financial institutions so also it matter for Andhra Bank too. Advances of credit do form the other pillar of bank functionality and the more the liquidation the more is the efficiency of institutional performance. The performance of the bank is thoroughly analyzed on the efficiency of the bank to advance credit to multi-farious needs of the people.

Figure 4.3 shows that the total advances since inception till 2008 March have increased from Rs. 16 crores to Rs.34238 crores till 2008. There is an increase of Advances during the ten year period of 1993 to 2003 i.e. from Rs.1908 crores to Rs.11513 crores. This is due to vast expansion of the branches all over the country. More growth in the country towards agriculture industry etc. has made the loans to grow up.

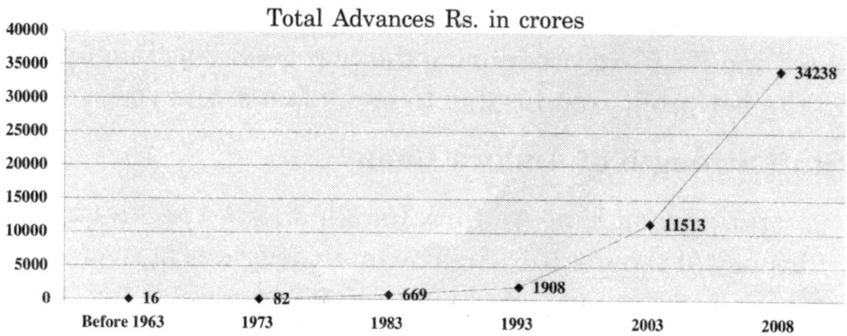


**Fig. 4.3: Total Advances of Andhra Bank since beginning till 2008**

## Analysis of Net Profit

The survival and sustenance of any financial institution depends on many factor and net profitability is one among them. And moreover the quantum of profit indicates the functional efficiency of an institution and shows the seeds for prosperity.

Figure 4.4 shows that the net profit of the bank for the past seven years has increased from Rs. 121 crores to Rs. 520 crores in 2005 and was decreased to Rs. 486 crores during the year 2006 and increased to Rs. 576 crores during the year 2008.

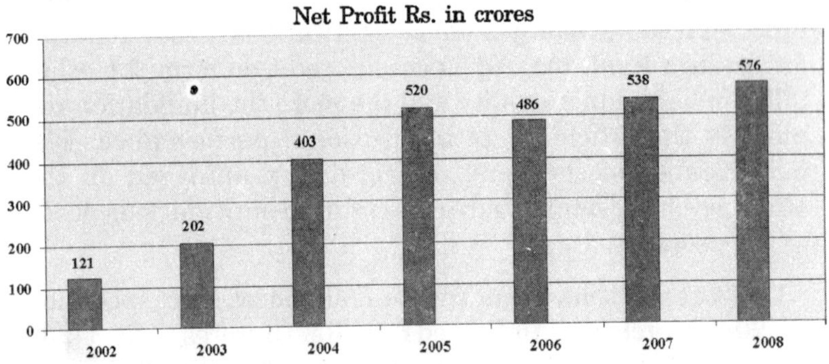


**Fig. 4.4: Andhra Bank Net Profit from 2002 to 2008**

The Net profit is Rs. 121 crores during the year 2002, Rs. 202 crores during the year 2003, Rs. 403 crores during the year 2004, Rs. 520 crores during the year 2005, Rs. 486 crores during the year 2006, Rs. 538 crores during the year 2007 and Rs. 576 crores during the year 2008. The fluctuation in the net profit trend is due to many factor and risks.

## Staff Strength of Andhra Bank

Staff strength of Andhra Banks shows the functional efficiency of the institution. The manpower strength started with a good strength of close to 13,000 and that has been maintained persistently.

Figure 4.5 shows that the staff strength of the bank for the past seven years. The staff is increased from 12798 employees in the year 2002 and increased to 13,387 in 2008. The staff strength is decreasing due to Voluntary retirement Scheme in the bank. The staff indices as given in the figure above more or less confirms to the fact that Andhra Bank was able to retain a good number of manpower to offer best of the service to the people on a persistent and time bound manner.

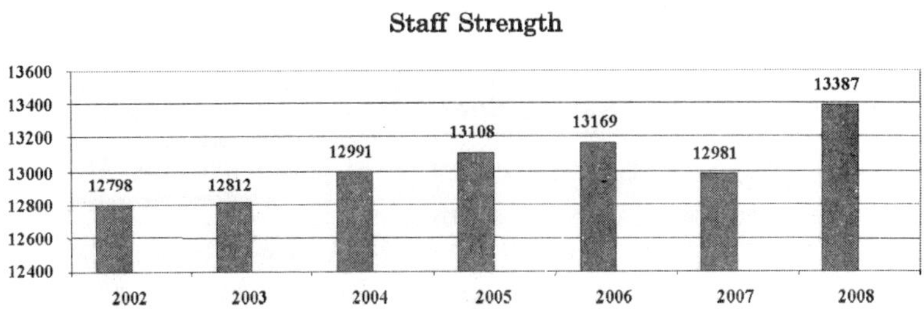


**Fig 4.5: Andhra Bank Staff Strength from 2002 to 2008**

## Innovative Schemes Developed by Andhra Bank

### *SHG Credit Cards*

Andhra Bank is the first bank in the country to introduce the credit card facility with many user friendly features for SHGs. SHGs who have availed finance from the bank and have repaid the same within stipulated time, and SHGs who qualify under category 'A' (70-100 marks) and 'B 'category (50-70 marks) as per critical rating index norms are eligible for accessing the credit card service. The Card will be issued to those groups which have reached to third/fourth level of finance with a limit of Rs.3.00lacs with validity of three years. The facility is in the form of cash credit. During this period, the SHG can utilize / draw the limit and credit the surplus as per the SHGs convenience. The bank does not take any security up to Rs.5 lacs. The additional benefit due to these cards is that all the members of SHG will get an additional benefit of coverage of Life insurance. The bank finances to

SHGs for the purpose to supplement the corpus of the SHG for their internal lending purposes and to take up micro enterprises / economic activities by the SHG or its members.

The advantages to SHGs includes that the card will be useful for immediate identification at counter of the branch, as it contains Loan No., S.B A/c No., and names of all SHG members. The card will serve as identification of SHG, to all concerned Govt. departments and in the public functions. The bank has issued 4238 cards with an amount of Rs. 92.14 crores so far.

***Janashree Bima Yojana Scheme***

The scheme is tied up with LIC of India. Andhra Bank would like to cover all SHG members who are aged between 18 to 59 years. The member of the Self Help Group (SHG) has to submit a data cum application to the SHG and SHG will submit the information to the bank. The annual premium payable is Rs.100 per each member. An equal amount of premium Rs.100 will be adjusted from the Social Security Fund set up by the Corporation making the total premium Rs. 200. Risk will be covered on the life of member from the date of collection of premium from the SHG. The claims will be settled on receipt of the information of death or accident of the SHG members with LIC. The members will get a death benefit of Rs. 20,000 upon premature natural death. The bank has financed around 15,210 policies to SHG members.

***Swasthya Bima Policy***

The scheme will be operated jointly with M/s United India Insurance Company Ltd. The policy cover is available for Members of SHG and other credit linked groups who are below poverty line and availed credit from Andhra Bank with the age group of 15 - 65 years. The annual premium payable per member is Rs.140. The benefits to SHG members includes meeting hospitalization expenses up to an amount of

Rs.10,000. The claim is settled after the receipt of the intimation from the SHGs.

***Solar Cookers for SHGs***

This is a scheme of Ministry of Non-conventional Energy Sources (MNES) Government of India, New Delhi for promoting use of solar water heating systems and Solar Cookers in the Country. This scheme is being implemented as Soft Loan scheme for Solar Cookers (SC) under the Interest Subsidy. Under the scheme of MNES, soft loans are provided by Andhra Bank for installation of/purchase of Solar Cookers. This is a solar device, which cooks food with the solar energy. The loan amount includes maximum of Rs.1,500 for Solar Cooker with electrical back up with three years repayment.

***Financing to Village Organizations /Federations***

Village Organizations /Federations are SHGs federated at village level. On an average there are 10-15 SHGs operating in a contiguous area are federated in to institution to get advantage of representation of many to get financial assistance from any formal and semi-formal institutions. The group of village organizations in Mandal level are federated and commonly known as Mandal Samakhya and also called as Mutually Aided co-operative societies (MACS) in Andhra Pradesh.

The bank sanctions Village Organizations (VO) one or two credit limits i.e. for trading activity and also for onward lending to SHGs as per the proposal submitted by the VO/ Federation. The VOs who are having bank account for the period of 6 months are eligible for the finance. The federation should have mobilized the share capital (thrift) in full from member SHGs and there should be no arrears in its collection. The quantum of finance will be 10 times of the net worth of the V.O (or) 80% of estimated/projected micro credit plan, whichever is less. The loan is given with 20% margin. The corpus and the book debts available with the federations will be both primary and collateral security for the limit to be financed by the bank as the federations will not have any fixed assets.

### *Scheme for Financing Matured SHGs for Farm Production and Investment Activities*

The scheme is formulated with an objective of the scheme to facilitate the members of matured SHGs to meet their credit requirement for farm production and investment activities and to enable them to diversify their income generating activities. Bank extends finance to target group of all matured SHGs, which are three years old or have availed a minimum of two cycles of bank loan and repaid successfully are eligible. The scheme includes the insurance coverage of Individual Self Help Group members with Janashree Bima Policies, which covers their life and also with Swasthya Bima Policies which covers their health.

### *Andhra Bank Mahila Soubhagya - Debt Swapping to Rural and Urban SHGs*

In order to provide institutional credit to SHGs to repay loans of their members taken from non-institutional lenders (private money lenders), Andhra Bank has devised the scheme to give financial leverage to all SHG closely working with the bank. The scheme is launched with an objective to facilitate the members of SHGs to meet their debts (from non institutional lenders) through bank linkage. Advantages of the scheme includes to make the SHG members to come out of the clutches of money lenders and replacement of high cost loans with bank finance.

The eligibility of the loan is as per the corpus and (or) Micro Credit Plan (Note: Micro Credit Plan includes the components like Investment credit needs for economic activities and Social needs like Health, Education, marriage, house, house repair etc., which is subject to maximum of 10% of investment credit needs as calculated above). Fifty per cent of the eligible loan amount as calculated above, (or) to the extent of debt which ever is lower, as additional term loan. New SHGs completing six months of their existence with regular savings and internal lending are eligible for the service. The eligibility of loan is four times of savings/corpus (or) Rs: 50,000/- which ever is higher. Fifty per cent of the eligible loan amount as calculated above (or) to the extent of debt which ever is lower, as additional term loan. The loan is repayable in three to five years in monthly installments with gestation period of six months. The bank does not take collateral security up to Rs.5 lakhs per group. Individual Self Help Group members are covered with Janashree Bima Policies, which covers their life and are also covered with Swasthya Bima Policies with their health. Andhra Bank has financed to the tune of Rs.105 crores under debt swapping.

***Rythu Mithra Groups***

Andhra bank has adopted RMGs with group guarantee under the guidance of AP Government and established linkage with these groups through extending financial support. The scheme is launched with an objective to serve as a conduit for technology transfer, facilitate common access to market information and market.

RMGs function like SHGs where all marginal, small and tenant farmers including women farmers in a village are eligible to become members of RMGs. The Optimum number of members in each group should not exceed 15. The convener and the co-convener co-opted by the members will operate the Bank account and facilitate thrift and credit activities. RMG will mobilize a minimum monthly thrift of about Rs.50 per member. The State Government will be giving initial grant assistance of Rs.2,500 on formation of RMG for capacity building, exposure visits, purchase of records etc and formation expenses. After reviewing the performance of the

RMG over 6-9 months period and depending on their savings, matching grants of Rs.15000 will be provided. Group dynamics on the lines of SHGs and active existence for at least six months, may not be insisted upon for the present as RMGs are in process of evolving. However, once credit linked, the RMGs must follow banks' guidelines as made applicable to SHGs including record keeping. Therefore for the present they are to be treated more like informal groups and RMG members will be accessing credit by virtue of being farmers collectively. RMGs will prepare a micro credit plan and submit the same along with loan application.

The groups formed generally include SF/MF/Women/ Tenant farmers/Share croppers/Oral Lessees that are fairly homogenous in nature with focus on uncovered borrowers. RMGs will certify proof of lease of members. A letter of self-declaration has to be obtained from each tenant farmer (member) to this effect. For the purpose of financing, the land cultivated by tenants should be restricted to the norms applicable for Small and Marginal farmers viz., 5.00 acres of dry land and 2.50 acres of wet land, inclusive of own land of the tenant. The group will decide on the quantum of loan to be given individual members out of the limits sanctioned by the Bank to RMG. There is no collateral security required up to Rs. 5.00 lakhs per group. RMGs will be covered under Bank's ICD scheme of insurance cover. Andhra Bank has so far bank financed to 5475 RMGs with an amount of Rs.90.95 crores.

### *Recovery in Written off Accounts through SHGs*

The scheme is applicable to advances made by Rural and Semi-urban branches and which were written off up to Rs. 1.00 lakh. Self Help Groups, whose dealings have been satisfactory, can be used under this scheme. The amount of commission will be paid @ 10% on the amount recovered to SHGs.

## Information Technology Enabled Schemes/ Programmes

### *Rural Connectivity*

Several projects are now attempting to provide information and services to rural citizen-consumers via human-mediated intranet systems. These include the Village Knowledge Centres Project in Pondicherry, the Warana Wired Village Project in and around Warana, and the Gyandoot Project in Dhar. Important lessons learnt from each of these initiatives, concerning, for example: the appropriate role of NGOs, the private sector and the State, the financial and entrepreneurial models which can make such infrastructure development feasible, and the socio-economic impact of such projects upon the village communities in which they are located.

The Sustainable Access in Rural India Project in Madurai is a newer, more ambitious project in the planning stages. It seeks to wire up all 1000 villages in the district using WLL technology developed out of IIT-Chennai. Tarahaat.com is a new company seeking to build branded computer kiosks in relatively prosperous rural areas. The NIIT 'Hole-in-the-wall' and Kiosks Project consists of unattended point-and-click devices in urban slums.

### *E-Governance*

Some of the rural ICT projects mentioned above offer limited e-governance functions or services. With the exception of the Gyandoot project in Dhar, however, these remain very rudimentary, and may be restricted to printing out standard government forms. Several State governments have announced high-profile projects to put their land records online, including Karnataka (Bhoomi; revdept.kar.nic.in) and Andhra Pradesh (CARD; The computerization of land records is an extremely labour - and time-intensive process, the rewards of which are very long in the coming.

Computerized land records are available on an experimental basis for a number of districts in these two States.

***Wired Micro-credit/Micro-finance/Micro-ecommerce***

There is no doubt that the computerization of micro-finance and micro-credit records could result in savings of time and effort, and generally facilitate the maintenance of these accounts. However, the real transformative effect of this technology will be seen only once micro-credit accounts come to be used for online or distance transactions amongst or within village communities at the grassroots. This will allow rural entrepreneurs and crafts persons the same savings of time, travel and effort that the internet has afforded individuals and institutions in the industrialized world. These possibilities have not yet been charted in any rural ICT project.

The Swayam Krishi Sangam (SKS) project is recording transactional information on optical ID cards for micro-finance, as well as for education and healthcare. Dr Mohammed Yunus, founder of the Grameen Bank of Bangladesh, has notably called for the establishment of an 'International Centre for Information Technology for the Elimination of Global Poverty'. A related agency, Grameen Telecom has attempted to provide mobile telephones to rural consumers through existing MFI/MCI networks.

***Technology Application Models in Andhra Bank***

The technology application model is premised on providing financial services in the rural areas through the BC Model using low cost and simple IT-based solutions. There has to be a central system which could be a shared infrastructure providing for economies of scale and conseq-uential cost benefits, and a field system which enables access to the central computer by the business correspondents. The account holders have a Multi-application Smart Card that leverages technology and takes mainstream banking and financial services along with other non-financial services having a social impact, to the customer last mile in a cost effective manner. Biometric-enabled smartcards will be enabled for various financial and non-financial transactions in the field through multiple handheld devices that will be carried by the agent. The backend transaction processing system will cater to the processing and settlement of the transactions captured on the field. While the models which are prevalent in the market today allow a shared infra-structure, they differ widely in the field systems which enable access through simputers, and other hand held devices including mobile phones accessing the central system through fixed lines or mobile technology.

*Various models have the following essential components:*

1. A customer with a Multi-application Smart Card which can be a contact card or a contact-less card,
2. BC with a simputer / hand held terminal / mobile phone enabling banking services,
3. Merchant establishments as points of sale with a terminal,
4. A CPU,
5. The bank,
6. A centralized card management for each of the above systems.

### *Initiatives by Andhra Bank through the Use of Smart Card Facility*

#### *Andhra Bank Smart Card*

The bank has launched a pilot project in April 2007 to include the excluded sections of population of Geesukonda Mandal of Warangal in Andhra Pradesh. Bank has appointed a NGO named Zero Mass as its business correspondent (BC).

Zero Mass initially started with coverage of 27 villages. Each village is served through a CSP (Customer Service Point), who is a BC. The CSP is the face of BC in the village, a banking outpost delivering banking services to the customers.

*The process of enrolment of beneficiaries for issue of smart cards is as under:*

1. Andhra Bank smart card enrolment forms are distributed by the CSPs,
2. Prospective customers come to the CSP with filled forms,
3. CSP collects the forms, enters the data in a personal computer, captures one photo and two fingerprints of each customer,
4. Enrolment data are sent to card production centre,
5. Printed cards are dispatched to the CSP, and
6. CSP hands over card to the customer after verifying the fingerprint and photo.

The registered customers are issued a card with 10 years validity. The cards are built on new generation NFC mobile phone technology and store extensive identity profile including bio-metric finger print data, multiple accounts, last known balance and history of recent transactions. The BC carries portable equipment - NFC mobile, fingerprint unit and transactions printer - which operate on portable battery with a stand-by time of up to 10 days.

Customer identification takes place by matching of photo and fingerprint. The finger print unit matches the fingerprint on the card with client fingerprint. Once authenticated, the chip embedded in the card gets charged. When the card with charged chip is brought close to the mobile phone, message templates for deposit, withdrawal and balance enquiry are generated in the mobile. The BC needs to select the relevant option and feed the amount of transaction through the mobile keypads and send the message to the backend server. The server authenticates the message, processes the transaction and sends an update back to the mobile, which in turn writes back to the card. When the card is brought close to the printer, a transaction report is printed in triplicate. The available services include savings product micro credit, micro-insurance, cash withdrawal and can be used for routing Government payments.

*Payments of Social Security Payments of GoAP through Smart Cards*

The GoAP has successfully launched a pilot project on routing social security Payments to widows, handicapped, old and eligible weavers through the use of smart cards and BCs. The pilot involves six banks - SBI, Union Bank of India, UTI Bank, State Bank of Hyderabad, Andhra Bank and Andhra Pradesh Grameen Vikas Bank. The first phase of the pilot was successfully launched on April 30, 2007, wherein three banks - SBI, Union Bank of India and UTI Bank disbursed social security payments to 127 beneficiaries in 3 villages through intermediaries. Payments were made to more than 2000 beneficiaries of these villages in this stage during the first week of May 2007. Andhra Bank has launched the pilot project on 1st June 2007. With the inclusion of Andhra Pradesh Rural Employment Guarantee Scheme, the fully scaled up project is expected to cover 5 million beneficiaries. Discussions with GoAP revealed that all the Government payments would be routed through this mechanism. The CSPs have been selected from the existing VOs.

The project is the first experiment in routing Government payments through use of intermediaries and smart card technology. Its successful launch reflects the potential of the model in routing other Government payments through the use of such technology. The decision of the Andhra Pradesh

Government to meet a substantial portion of the card and device cost has helped to nurture the pilot project.

*Rural Kiosks*

AP Government has launched Rajiv (Rajiv Internet Village programme) financing to kiosks is an innovative and revolutionary project with components, which includes electronic delivery of Services through 6000 Rural kiosks, set up through SHG by December 2004 under the aegis of Rural Development department. The aim of the scheme is to improve the quality of life of rural people by providing them with IT-enabled education, health care, and better governance. The technology will be useful for rural citizens in increasing their agricultural yields, enhancing their income levels, and to lead a comfortable and decent life. Rural Kiosks under this scheme, deliver a host of services related Agriculture, Health, Education, Gram Panchayat, Rural development and welfare schemes and collection of power bills, taxes etc., The wide usage of Telugu in Information Technology will be promoted. The bank is providing computers to SHGs. Kovvali village, the centre stage of the new IT programme of Andhra bank. SHG women of Velugu would own and operate rural kiosks in villages. Thus it is a means of livelihood as well a channel for delivery of Government services and information. These kiosks render immense benefit to rural citizens like:

a. Easy access to information on agriculture, education, health etc.,

b. Market prices, cropping pattern, weather forecast, agriculture extension through Kisan and AP Online.

c. *Agricultural marketing:* getting better prices for produce

d. Examination results, computer-assisted learning through azim Premji Foundation,

e. Health Extension and Immunization through UNICEF, Telemedicine with the help of CDR Hospitals etc.,

f. Access to all Forms, copies of land records, applications, certificates etc., through AP Online

g. *Collection of bills:* electricity, telephone etc., through AP Online

h. *Private Services:* Insurance of ICICI and Birla Sun life, e-commerce, Western Union Money Transfer, Bharat Matrimony etc.,

Following the success of e-Seva centres in the urban and semi-urban areas of the State, the Andhra Pradesh Government has planned to set up around 6,000 rural e-Seva centres in the form of touch-screen kiosks such that the SHG members will get benefit.

**Mobile ATM: An ATM plus Marketing Point**

Andhra Bank the pioneer in several banking services and products, also brings banking services to the doorsteps of customers. Mobile ATMs, apart from expanding the reach of the bank, will also effectively function as a market point offering multiple services even in remote areas. The facility will provide multiple benefits such as: (i) balance enquiry, (ii) cash withdrawals, (iii) mini Statement, (iv) funds Transfer, (v) cash against Credit Cards, (vi) mobile recharge, (vii) ATM Cards of SBI, Indian Bank, UTI, IDBI, HDFC Banks and (viii) utility payments.

***Advanced Technology - To Meet Customer Needs***

ATM Mobile works on advanced CDMA technology, and is designed with inbuilt security features. Computers and wireless connectivity ensures that records were also updated immediately at these mobile locations. The front portion of the custom built vehicle will have an ATM, while the rear portion will be used for customer service, by the bank staff. ATM Mobile will reach out to the rural areas, giving the farmers and people from the rural sectors, an opportunity to access the most modern banking services, virtually at their doorsteps.

The ATM Mobile will also be used as a product information delivery system and as a drop box for collection of cheques, providing multiple services even in the remote areas. The flexibility to serve the customers at temporary venues like events, concerts or games will also be available. ATM mobile will also serve as moving hoardings, creating great awareness in the general public of the bank's products

### Mobile Biometric ATMs

Andhra Bank is the first bank in the country to launch mobile biometric ATMs. Sri K Rosaiah, Hon'ble Minister for Finance, Andhra Pradesh flagged off Andhra Bank's "Mobile Biometric ATMs" in Hyderabad on 21-05-2007. The Bank has rolled out two mobile biometric ATMs here, one each for Hyderabad and Secunderabad, which would stop at locations scheduled by the RBI. For biometric access, customers have to register their finger prints with the branch in which they maintain their accounts. The mobile ATMs would identify the customer based on his/her finger print. However, personal identification number (PIN) facility would also be available. The customer would also be guided by voice in local languages on how to use the ATM. "Besides, many educated customers prefer biometric ATMs as it adds to the safety and security of their money. The mobile biometric ATMs would go a long way in achieving the financial inclusion.

## SELF-HELP GROUP FINANCING OF ANDHRA BANK

### Introduction

Andhra Bank is one of the nationalized banks, actively participating in the development of economy. Through implementation of various Government sponsored programmes, the bank is achieving social obligations. From 1993 the bank is actively participating in SHG bank linkage. Bank's Delivery Channels are spread over 22 States and 2 Union Territories. The Business Delivery Channels comprise 1366 Branches, 68 Extension Counters, 38 Satellite Offices and 656 ATMs. Bank has specialized outlets like SME Branches, Personal Banking Centers, Financial Service Centers, Agricultural Finance Branches, Micro-finance Desks to cater to the specific banking needs of various Clientele.

***Micro-finance by Banks in India and by Andhra Bank***

For the purpose of providing Micro-finance, not only the SHGs were linked to Banks, but also they link to Regional Rural Banks and Cooperative Banks. Up to the year 2006-07, nearly 44362 branches of 547 banks have participated in the SHG-Bank Linkage programme. All the 27 public sector banks and 20 private sector banks and the cooperative banks had participated in this linkage programme. State Bank of India credit linked the highest number of SHGs followed by the Indian Bank and Canara Bank. During that year, Indian Overseas Bank, Punjab National Bank, Andhra Bank, Bank of India, Bank of Baroda registered impressive growth in SHG-Bank Linkage.

Rural indebtedness is one of the main reasons for backwardness of the rural sector in the underdeveloped countries. It has remained as the most persistent constraint for the development of rural economy in India. Andhra Bank is one of the strong sources of financial support to rural women. Bank is operating through 388 rural branches and 337 semi urban branches in SHG bank linkage.

Andhra bank since 1998 has been actively participating in SHG-Bank Linkage Programme. Bank received the Best Performance award from NABARD consecutively for the years 2000-2001, 2001-2002, and 2003-04.

### *Multiple Agencies Dealing with SHGs*

*Commercial Banks*

The SHG-Bank Linkage became a part of business for all the 27 public sector banks and 20 private sector banks. SBI credit-linked the highest number of SHGs (142,034) during 2005-06, followed by Indian Bank (30,632) and Canara Bank (18,445). During the years many banks registered impressive growth in SHG-Bank Linkage. These were Indian Overseas Bank, Punjab National Bank, Andhra Bank, Bank of India, Bank of Baroda. The private sector banks which significantly supported SHG financing were ICICI Bank Ltd (6746), Dhanalaxmi Bank (1201) followed by the Lord Krishna Bank (1181).

*Regional Rural Banks*

The Regional Rural Banks (RRBs) financed SHGs in a very significant way during 2006-07. All the 96 RRBs in the country participated in the SHG-Bank Linkage programme. During the year 2006-07, maximum number of SHGs have been linked by Pragjyotish Goanlia Bank in Assam (9190 SHGs) followed by Bolangir Anchlik Gramya Bank (7278 SHGs) in Orissa and Karnataka Vikas Gramin Bank (5819 SHGs) in Karnataka. The other RRBs showing significant achievement were Pandian Gramin Bank in Tamil Nadu, Nagarjun Gramin Bank, Sri Rayalseema Gramin Bank and Shri Vishakha Gramin Bank in Andhra Pradesh, Kalahandi Anchalik Gramya Bank in Orissa and Pragati Gramin Bank in Karnataka.

*Cooperative Banks*

Cooperative Banks, though comparatively late starters, have begun making forays into the micro-finance sector on a large scale. The amendments made by many of the States in their respective Co-operative Societies Acts enabled Co-operative banks to take up the activity of promotion and nurturing of SHGs. Influenced by the pioneering performance of District Central Cooperative Banks (DCCBs) like Hoogly (West Bengal), Chandrapur (Maharashtra) and South Canara (Karnataka) in the SHG-Bank Linkage programme, many other DCCBs also evidenced keen interest in SHG – Bank Linkage Programme. The number of partners for the SHG-Bank Linkage in the cooperative banking sector increased to 340 up to March 2006. During the year, maximum number of SHGs have been linked by Kolhapur (4229) in Maharashtra followed by Hooghly DCCB (4115 SHGs) in West Bengal, Chandrapur DCCB (4027 SHGs) in Maharashtra and Mursheedabad DCCB (3944 SHGs) in West Bengal. The other DCCBs showing significant achievement cumulatively were Hassan DCCB and South Canara DCCB in Karnataka, Thiruchirapalli DCCB in Tamil Nadu, Thrissur DCCB in Kerala, and Sangli DCCB in Maharashtra.

## Self-help Group – The Concept and Instrument for BL by Andhra Bank

### *Rooting Micro-finance – Experience of Andhra Bank*

The State of Andhra Pradesh takes the pride for successful implementation of micro-finance programme to alleviate poverty as well as empower poor women to lead a life with dignity and self-esteem and Andhra Bank plays a significant role. Andhra Bank has 1289 branches spread all over the country and there are 918 branches exclusively functioning in Andhra Pradesh. The rural and semi-urban branches constitute 59.89 per cent of the total branches giving an ample scope to be a forerunner in helping the poor and play a pivotal role in the mission of financial inclusion. The huge network of branches in rural/semi-urban areas provides a natural edge for the Bank besides its robust financials and dedication and committed workforce.

A SHG has an average size of about 15 people from a homogeneous class. They come together for addressing their common problems. They are encouraged to make voluntary thrift on a regular basis. They use this pooled resource to make small interest bearing loans to their members. The process helps them imbibe the essentials of financial intermediation including prioritization of needs, setting terms and conditions, and accounts keeping. This gradually builds financial discipline in all of them. They also learn to handle resources of a size that is much beyond individual capacities of any of them. The SHG members begin to appreciate the fact that resources are limited and have a cost. Once the groups show this mature financial behavior, banks are encouraged to make loans to the SHG in certain multiples of the accumulated savings of the SHG. The bank loans are given against group dynamics without any collateral security and at market interest rates. The groups continue to decide the terms of loans to their own members. Since the groups' own accumulated savings are part and parcel of the aggregate loans made by the groups to their members, peer pressure ensures timely repayments. Apart from financial help at the time of need, the group provides social security to its members.

### *Operational Design of SBLP of Andhra*

Unlike other financial institutions engaged in advancing financial support to self-help groups following the functionality norms of the institutions, the Andhra Bank has stipulated certain paraphernalia's and procedures for liquidating cash with the self-help groups. The operational design and norms followed by Andhra Bank contains the following features:

#### *Small and Fixed Savings at Frequent Intervals*

Small and fixed savings made at regular intervals coupled with conditions like compulsory attendance, penal provisions to ensure timely attendance, saving, repayment etc.

*Self-selection*

The members select their own members to form groups. The members residing in the same neighborhood ensure better character screening and tend to exclude deviant behaved ones.

*Focus on Women*

Regular meetings and savings are compulsory ingredients in the design and functioning of self-help groups. It is also envisaged that all women members are participating in the self-help group and it is purely a SHG of women. Andhra Bank believes that women are committed and adoptive of the changes and hence, they would be instrumental in effective use of fund for productive uses and timely repayment.

*Savings First and Credit Later*

The saving first concept enables the poor to gradually understand the importance of saving, appreciate the nuances of credit concept using their own money before seeking external support (credit) for fulfilling future needs. The poor tend to understand and respect the terms of credit better.

*Intra Group Appraisal Systems and Prioritization*

Essentials of good credit management like (peer) appraisal for credit needs (checking the antecedents and needs before sanction), (peer) monitoring- end use of credit; (peer sympathy) re-schedulement in case of crisis and (peer pressure) collateral in case of willful non-payment etc all seems to coexist in the system – making its one of the best approaches for providing financial services to the poor.

*Credit Rationing*

The approach of prioritization i.e. meeting critical needs first, serves as a useful tool for intra-group lending. This ensures the potential credit takers/users to meticulously follow up credit already dispensed, as future credit disbursals rely on repayments by the existing credit users.

*Shorter Repayment Terms*

Smaller and shorter repayment schedule ensures faster recycling of funds, greater fiscal prudence in the poor and drives away the slackness and complacency that tends to set-in, in long duration credit cycles

*Market Rates of Interest*

Self-determined interest rates are normally market related. Sub-market interest rates could spell doom; distort the use and direction of credit.

*Progressive Lending*

The practice of repeat loans and often-higher doses - is followed by SHGs in their intra-group loaning, thereby enticing prompt repayments.

*Multiple-eyed Operation*

The operations of the SHG are transacted in group meetings thus enabling high trust levels and openness in the SHG system. SHG members facilitating openness and freedom from unfair practices also generally conduct the banking transactions.

## Guidelines for SHG Bank Linkage

*Objectives of Linkage*

The scheme is evolved with objectives like evolving supplementary credit strategy for reaching rural poor, building mutual trust and confidence between banks and the rural poor and encouraging banking activities both thrift as well as credit.

*Advantages to the Bank*

The advantages to the bank include externalization of some of their credit activities viz., assessment of credit needs, appraisal, disbursal, supervision and repayment, reduction in the formal paper work leading to reduction in transaction cost and larger mobilization of small savings. Loans to SHGs can be categorized as "Weaker section finance under Priority Sector".

*Characteristics of SHG*

The SHG possess membership up to 20 and may be registered or unregistered. The group should devise a code of conduct to bind themselves and internal savings mobilized by its members is the core of SHG. The group has to decide the amount to be saved, its periodicity and the purposes for which loan can be given to members. The Group has to decide the rate of interest to be paid and/or charged on savings/ credit to members and should function in a democratic way allowing free exchange of views and participation by members. The group has also to maintain simple basic records such as Minute Book, Membership Register, Saving and Credit Registers and has to open a Savings Bank Account with the Bank.

*Records / Books of Account to be maintained by SHGs*

The records are to be maintained by SHGs includes: Attendance Register, Membership Register, Proceedings Book, Savings Register, Bank Borrowing/Deposit Register and Credit Register

*Selection Criteria for Linkage*

The broad criteria for linking self-help groups with Bank includes that the group size should be of 5-20 members. The members of group should have homogenous back ground, generally be in active existence for a period of at least for six months and should have successfully undertaken savings and credit operations from its own resources. The group should conduct periodical meetings, maintain proper accounts/records and the group can be guided by NGOs/Voluntary Agencies

(VAs) with the interest of NGO/VAs in the group be evident. The group formation should reflect genuine need to help each other and work together and the banker should be convinced about the genuineness of the group formation and its objectives.

*Assessing a Self-help Group*

The appraisal of self-help group is very important for ensuring the utility of the loan and repayment of the loan. Andhra Bank generally appraises the project and the borrower. In case of SHG financing, most of the project appraisal norms like assessing the cost benefit and profits will not be workable due to the peculiarities of SHG financing. SHG's being customers have to be appraised before extending credit facilities. The assessment of creditworthiness of a SHG is very different from that of an individual. SHGs are not to be assessed in terms of their ability to provide collateral or guarantees of net worth. Therefore SHGs are assessed in terms of group dynamics like cohesion, vibrancy, and goal-oriented action, participation of members, democratic decision and collective leadership. The appraiser has to see whether the group is functioning as a group and it is sustainable.

The basic principles on which the SHGs function are that the members of the group should be residents of the same area and must have an affinity. Homogeneity of relationship could be in terms of caste/occupation/gender or economic status. Savings first, credit thereafter is another important principle. SHGs should hold regular meetings and should maintain record of financial and other transactions. They should have norms regarding membership; meetings etc and group leaders should be elected by members and rotated periodically. Transparency in operations of the group and participatory decision making is also an important basic principle of SHGs. Rates of interest on loans should be decided by the group while group liability and peer pressure to act as substitutes for traditional collateral. Andhra Bank follows the following criteria to assess the Self Help Group:

*Norms for Functioning*

Norms generally relate to

a) Membership,

b) Meetings - time, periodicity;

c) Savings - amount, periodicity, rate of interest (return)

d) Credit - procedure for sanction, ceiling amount, purposes, rate of interest to be charged, repayment period etc.,

e) fines - in case of default in attending meetings, savings and credit repayment. Group may also levy fines for any deviant behavior etc.,

f) leadership - election or nomination of leaders, rotation of leaders etc., and

g) personal/social improvement - minimum literacy level to be achieved and social work to be done etc.

*Meetings*

The group decides the periodicity of the meetings i.e., weekly, fortnightly or monthly. They also decide on the time of the meeting. Decision on time and periodicity helps in regular conduct of meetings. The regularity in the holding of the meeting and the attendance during meeting gives an indication bout groups functioning. Therefore a Financer should see whether (1) the meetings have been held regularly, (2) the attendance in the meetings, (3) the members are punctual and stay till the end of the meeting, and (4) are there any sanctions for the delinquent members.

*Maintenance of Books*

Whether group is maintaining the basic books that will give details of its functioning and accounts of the group is an important criterion. The books show the details of number of meetings held, decisions taken in the meetings, amount of savings of the members and credit availed, the total savings of the group and repayments. Who maintains these books is another important criteria being judged.

*Verification by the Bank*

The bank will verify whether details of meetings, proceedings, and attendance are maintained, whether member-wise record of saving and credit are maintained whether the records are up to date, whether all members are kept informed of their savings and credit balances from time to time. In case of illiterate groups the system followed. Does the group verify the books maintained by NGO/outsider and whether systems have been developed to ensure safe custody of cash?

*Leadership*

Initially the opinion leaders may be the leaders and over a period of time the leadership is expected to be rotated. The group leaders are expected to

a) regularly convene and conduct the meetings,

b) help the group members in taking decisions,

c) resolve conflicts,

d) maintain books of account and

e) approach bank branch for operation of accounts.

The aspects that are to be seen by the bank includes whether the leaders have been elected and rotated, whether they help in democratic functioning of the group and whether there is a conscious attempt to groom other members to take up leadership.

*Participation and Awareness of Group Members*

Are the Members aware of the purpose of group formation, the operations and activities of the group viz. savings and the credit of the group as well as the individual member's? (1) Do they participate in group discussions and decision making , (2) Do they help solve the problem that are raised in the meetings (3) Do they work cohesively and have transparent dealings are some of the aspects to be looked into while assessing the group.

*Savings*

The group decides on the amount of savings to be collected and so also its periodicity. It has to be seen whether the saving, as decided upon, is regularly made, how the defaults are dealt with and whether the system is modified as per the requirements of the members.

*Credit*

The aspects that the bank will look into while assessing the credit function of the group are the decision making process of selecting loanees, the system followed in assessing credit requirement of individual members and the amount to be sanctioned, the system of monitoring the credit and the repayment performance of members and incidence of defaults besides the effectiveness to deal with such defaults and functioning of the concept of 'peer pressure'.

*Rating System Followed for SHGs (CRI)*

While extending finance to SHGs, assessments of SHGs are done through Critical Rating Index (CRI). The above rating system is a mandatory to be adopted. Feeling of belongingness/homogeneity/solidarity, local governance, conduct of meetings (during last six months), attendance of members in meetings, financial transactions in the group during the last six months, member awareness about all financial transactions, regularity of savings during last six months, pattern of internal lending, velocity of internal lending, repayment terms prescribed, repayment pattern, borrower quality, loan quality, maintenance of records up to date are the criteria assessed in the critical rating index. The maximum marks stipulated are 100. The rating is done basing on the marks obtained. For "A" Rating-70-100 marks to be obtained, for "B" Rating-50-70 marks and for "C" Rating-Less than 50 marks to be obtained.

*Linking SHGs with Bank Credit of Andhra Bank*

There are two ways of extending bank finance

(i) Directly to SHG and

(ii) Through bulk lending to VOs/NGOs for on lending to group.

*Quantum of Loan*

The quantum of loan directly to SHGs would be in proportion of savings mobilized by the group and can be in the ratio of savings to credit 1:1 or 1:2 initially, which has been raised to 1:4 and up to 1:10 depending on the confidence gained by the Bank. The amount of loan to the SHG can be to the tune of 1 to 4 times of its savings/corpus. Branches can consider higher ratio, if they are satisfied about the SHG's health. For availing bank finance, group will prepare a credit plan for members and submit to the Bank. With the maturity of the groups and progressive empowerment, many SHGs are inclined to take up economic activities for improving the income level. The technical feasibility and economic viability norms are adhered to determine the volume and quantum of loan requirement and eligibility of the group.

*Estimation of Credit Requirements*

The credit requirement of SHGs is estimated basing on the corpus or savings/micro-credit plan of the group. The group should be in active existence for at least six months for the first dose and the eligibility is arrived as 4 times of corpus or Rs.50,000 whichever is higher. The groups linked for the first time are also eligible for debt swapping loans arrived as

50% of eligible loan limit or extent of debt whichever is lower and additional loan of Rs.20,000 per SHG member under Indiramma. For second dose, there should at least be a gap of 12 months from the 1st dose and the earlier loan to be repaid completely. The eligibility is determined as 10 times of savings/ corpus or Rs.1.00 lakh whichever is higher for rural SHGs and 10 times of savings/ corpus or Rs.1.50 lakhs whichever is higher for Urban SHGs. Debt swapping loans for 2nd dosage are arrived as 50% of eligible loan limit or extent of debt whichever is lower and additional loan of Rs.20,000 per SHG member under Indiramma can be sanctioned alike to 1st dose. The groups become eligible for 3rd and subsequent linkages only after a gap of 18 months from the date of availing the earlier dose. The eligibility criteria for availing the third dosage is the micro credit plan (MCP) which comprises of investment, social and debt swapping needs of the group. Groups availing loans for the third time are also eligible for debt swapping to the extent of 40% of micro credit plan or extent of debt whichever is lower and additional loan of Rs.20,000 per SHG member can be sanctioned similar to 1st and 2nd dosages. The aggregate of three limits are subject to Rs.1.75 lakhs for the 1st linkage, Rs.2.50 lakhs for rural SHGs and Rs.3.25 lakhs for urban SHGs in case of 2nd linkage and Rs.5.00 lakhs for 3rd and subsequent dosages while Debt swapping is a one time measure only. The bank will disburse the loan in bulk directly to the group or to NGO for on lending.

*Security*

There is no collateral security up to the loan limits of Rs.5 lakhs. SHGs might not be in a position to offer any collateral security other than the savings under rotation within the group. Peer pressure among members is the alternative for the collaterals.

*Repayment Period*

Branches will have to prescribe appropriate repayment period in negotiation with the group. Loans from Banks are to be repaid in regular monthly installments based on local conditions, and the activities undertaken by the members.

*Monitoring of SHG Bank Linkage*

The monitoring of SHG loans are done through number and spread of Self Help Groups, amount of credit disbursed, number of loanees, deposit mobilization, repayment performance of SHG, expenditure on awareness, training programmes and cost of management.

*Bank's Encouragement to SHGs*

Some of the areas where bank is looking to encourage the programme includes every year bank is giving best SHG awards. The rate of Interest has been reduced marginally. Bank is imparting free trainings to SHG members through institutes. Also giving Best Managers awards every year who are doing very well in SHG bank linkage. Bank is conducting training programmes to Managers/Rural Development Officers who are actively participating in the linkage programme or newly joined in the branches. Some of the best Managers are being sent to abroad for further training. And conducting buyers/sellers meets of SHGs (Bancon 2006- Some of the best SHGs were invited to participate in the exhibition)

The steps being taken up by the bank to increase the lending include conducting SHG special fortnights every year i.e. first during July and second during October, conducting Training programme on micro-finance for managers and RDOs at Staff training college, Opening Micro-finance desks in 5 branches of Hyderabad, Guntur, Vijayawada and Visakhapatnam zones.

## Andhra Bank Performance

### *Region-wise overall Performance of Andhra Bank*

As evidenced from the foregoing discussion, Andhra Bank is committed and instrumental in linking the Self-help Group with banks and assisting SHGs to come out of poverty. The liberalized process and paraphernalia's are vividly discussed as well as the financial leverage criteria followed. However, the following section is giving a lucid picture of the SHG-BL activities of Andhra Bank and a thorough picture is drawn across the three regions.

The geographic spread of the regions as specified amply varies from each other and so also the coverage of groups. It is also the fact that access to banking services and especially financial support by the Self-help groups also varies across the regions. As evident from the table 4.3 there are comparatively more self-help groups accessing financial assistance from Andhra Bank from the coastal region than the other two regions. Coastal region stood as the all-time SHG-BL region of the state for Andhra Bank.

**Table 4.3**

**Year and Region-wise SHG-BL of Andhra Bank during 2001to 2007**

(Amount Rs. in lacs)

| *Year* | *Coastal* | | *Telangana* | | *Rayalseema* | | *Total* | |
|---|---|---|---|---|---|---|---|---|
| | *Accounts* | *Amt* | *Accounts* | *Amt* | *Accounts* | *Amt* | *Accounts* | *Amt* |
| 2001-02 | 16601 | 39 | 6850 | 13 | 2912 | 8 | 26363 | 60 |
| 2002-03 | 21473 | 62 | 8861 | 21 | 3766 | 12 | 34100 | 95 |
| 2003-04 | 28917 | 80 | 11932 | 27 | 5072 | 15 | 45921 | 123 |
| 2004-05 | 30130 | 117 | 12433 | 40 | 5285 | 22 | 47848 | 179 |
| 2005-06 | 32214 | 160 | 13293 | 55 | 5651 | 31 | 51158 | 246 |
| 2006-07 | 35999 | 270 | 14855 | 92 | 6314 | 52 | 57168 | 414 |
| 2007-08 | 45186 | 468 | 18646 | 160 | 7926 | 90 | 71758 | 718 |

*Source:* Compiled from Annual Progress Reports of Andhra Bank.

Figure 4.6 reveals that Andhra Bank has followed a positive step by inculcating more no of SHGs in to the base of financing. Extension of bank linkage started with a mear 26.3 thousand and is currently financing 71.7 thousand no of self-help groups in he country. The financial assistance to the no of self-help groups gradually followed an increasing trend as revealed from Fig. 4.7.

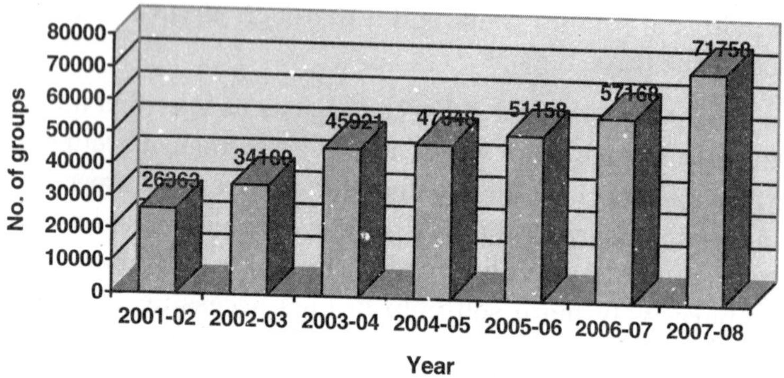


**Fig. 4.6: Year-wise Finance of No. of SHGs in the State during 2001-07**

*Source:* Compiled from Various reports of Andhra Bank.

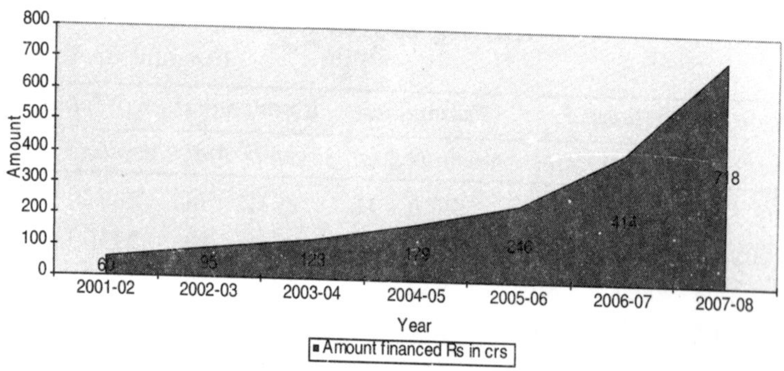


**Fig. 4.7: Year-wise SHG Financing of Andhra Bank during 2001-2007**

*Source:* Compiled from Various reports of Andhra Bank.

Figure 4.7 shows that during 2001-02 amount financed was just Rs.60 crs, which has later on increased to 718 crores during 2007. In the year 2007-08 the amount financed has been increased to Rs.414 crs. It is also revealed that there was almost a double jump in financial assistance to self-help groups in the year 2007. The inherent reason is due to the decisions taken by SLBC on Indiramma loans (housing) to the members and debt swapping loans to SHG members.

An interesting trend of Self-help group is seen from Fig. 4.8 on the regional distribution of Self-help groups. Self-help group coverage of Andhra Bank in the year 2007 exclusively reveals that there are nearly 63% of Coastal regions, 26% of Telengana region and only 11% of Rayalseema region is brought under the SHG-BL programme.

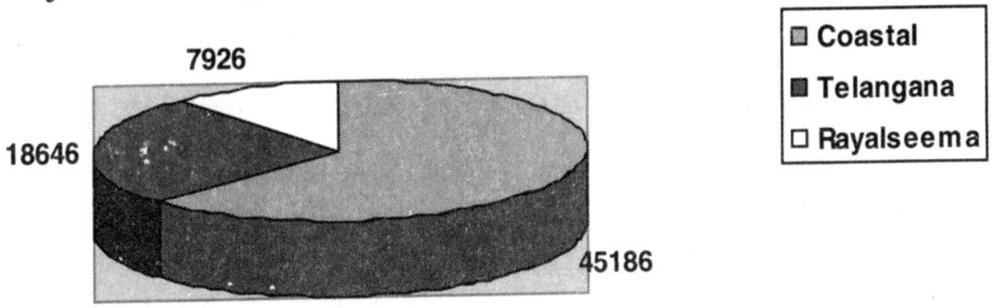


**Fig. 4.8: Region-wise SHGs Coverage of Andhra Bank in the year 2007-08**

*Source:* Compiled from Various reports of Andhra Bank.

In absolute terms, the Coastal Region dominates in share by 45186 groups followed by Telangana with 18646 groups and Rayalseema with 7926 groups. The un-skewed coverage of Self-help groups across the regions is due to positive participation of District Rural Development Agencies in coastal areas.

Figure 4.9 shows the amount financed to SHGs during 2007-08 in coastal, Telangana and Rayalseema regions of Andhra Pradesh. Coastal Region usually dominates in share amounting Rs.468 crores followed by Telangana with Rs.160 crores and Rayalseema with Rs.90 crores. However, in percentage term and relatively in correlation with group distribution coastal region accessing almost 65%, Telengana 22% and Rayalseema with 13%. It confirms to that fact that though the coverage of groups in Telengana and Rayalseema is little less in percentage terms the actual financial linkage is more.

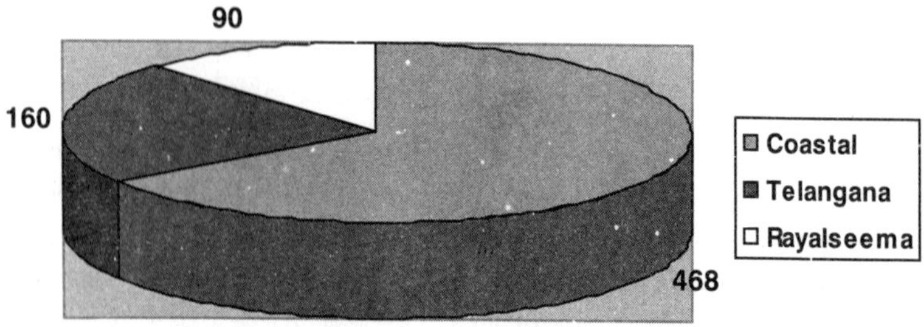


**Fig. 4.9: Region wise SHG-BL in 2007**

*Source:* Compiled from Various reports of Andhra Bank.

## *Andhra Bank's Performance in Coastal Region*

The bank is operating in the coastal region with 428 branches. The coastal region as has been clear from Table 4.4 is consisted of 9 districts and East Godavari district is toping in accessing financial assistance from Andhra Bank followed by West Godavari. On the contrary, Nellore, Prakasham and Vizianagaram districts are the lowest in terms of accessing bank linkage.

Coverage of Self-help groups in the coastal regions of the state has followed an up-ward trend over the years. Figure 4.10 reveals that SHG coverage has been increased by many folds during the period 2001-07.

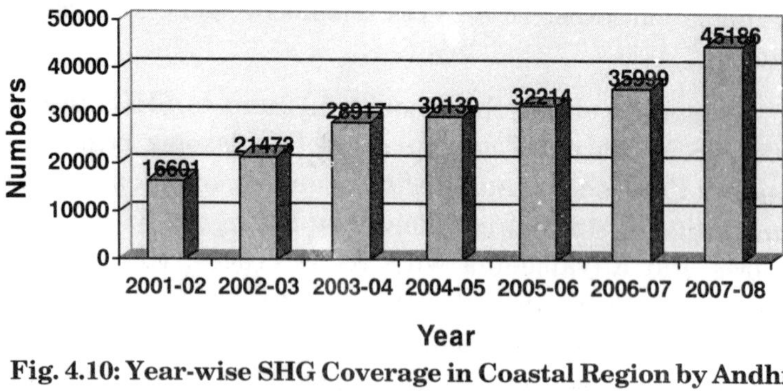


**Fig. 4.10: Year-wise SHG Coverage in Coastal Region by Andhra Bank during 2001-07**

*Source:* Data Compiled from branches of Andhra Bank operating in Coastal Region.

## Table 4.4
## Year and District-wise SHG financing in Coastal Regions of Andhra Pradesh during 2001-07

(Rs. in. crores)

| Sl. No. | District | 2001-2002 | | 2002-2003 | | 2003-04 | | 2004-05 | | 2005-06 | | 2006-07 | | 2007-08 | |
|---|---|---|---|---|---|---|---|---|---|---|---|---|---|---|---|
| | | Groups covered | Credit Accessed by the groups | Groups covered | Credit Accessed by the groups | Groups covered | Credit Accessed by the groups | Groups covered | Credit Accessed by the groups | Groups covered | Credit Accessed by the groups | Groups covered | Credit Accessed by the groups | Groups covered | Credit Accessed by the groups |
| 1 | | 2 | 3 | 4 | 5 | 6 | 7 | 8 | 9 | 10 | 11 | 12 | 13 | 14 | 15 |
| | **Coastal Regions** | | | | | | | | | | | | | | |
| 1 | Srikakulam | 922 | 2 | 1193 | 3 | 1607 | 4 | 1674 | 6 | 1790 | 8 | 2000 | 14 | 2511 | 24 |
| 2 | Visakhapatnam | 941 | 3 | 1218 | 5 | 1640 | 7 | 1708 | 9 | 1827 | 13 | 2041 | 22 | 2562 | 38 |
| 3 | Vizianagaram | 534 | 1 | 690 | 1 | 929 | 1 | 968 | 2 | 1035 | 3 | 1157 | 5 | 1452 | 8 |
| 4 | East Godavari | 4858 | 13 | 6284 | 22 | 8462 | 28 | 8817 | 42 | 9427 | 57 | 10536 | 96 | 13224 | 165 |
| 5 | Guntur | 2601 | 5 | 3365 | 8 | 4531 | 11 | 4721 | 16 | 5048 | 21 | 5641 | 36 | 7080 | 63 |
| 6 | Krishna | 2333 | 5 | 3018 | 7 | 4064 | 9 | 4235 | 13 | 4528 | 18 | 5060 | 31 | 6351 | 54 |
| 7 | Prakasam | 610 | 1 | 789 | 2 | 1063 | 2 | 1108 | 4 | 1184 | 5 | 1323 | 8 | 1661 | 14 |
| 8 | Nellore | 361 | 1 | 465 | 2 | 626 | 2 | 653 | 2 | 697 | 3 | 779 | 5 | 978 | 9 |
| 9 | West Godavari | 3441 | 8 | 4451 | 12 | 5995 | 16 | 6246 | 23 | 6678 | 32 | 7462 | 53 | 9367 | 93 |
| | **Total** | **16601** | **39** | **21473** | **62** | **28917** | **80** | **30130** | **117** | **32214** | **160** | **35999** | **270** | **45186** | **468** |

*Source:* Compiled from Various reports of Andhra Bank.

During 2001-02 in Coastal Region of nine districts have linked to 16601 groups and over years the groups were increased and during 2007-08 the groups increased to 45186. Figure 4.11 is revealing that Andhra Bank has financed Rs.39 crores during the year 2001-02 and increased to Rs.468 crores during the year 2007-08. The increase of the amount is due to involvement of AP Govt. and guidelines issues from SLBC of AP from time to time on Indiramma housing loans and debt swapping.

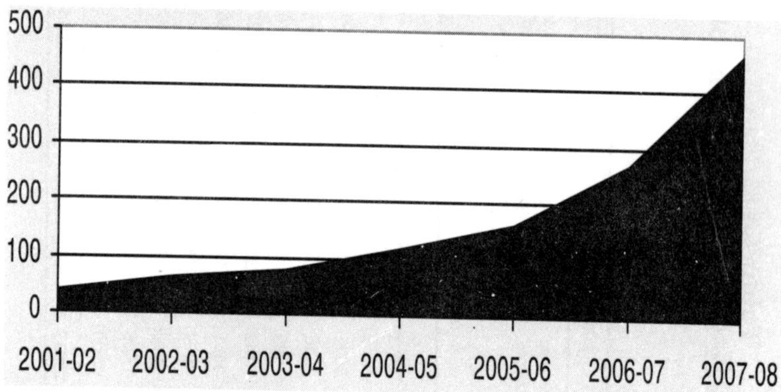


**Fig. 4.11: Year-wise SHG Finance in Coastal Regions by Andhra Bank during 2001-07**

*Source:* Data Compiled from branches of Andhra Bank operating in Coastal Region of the state of Andhra Pradesh.

### *Andhra Bank's Performance in Telanagana Region*

Telengana region of the state is constituted of 9 districts and there are 18646 self-help groups are covered by the Andhra Bank. It is the second highest region in terms of formation self-help groups as well as bank-linkage. The sample period of 2001-07 reveals that there are as less as 6850 groups are covered in 2001 and this has increased to 18646 over a period of seven years (see Table 4.5 and Fig. 4.12).

## Table 4.5
## Year and District-wise SHG Coverage of Andhra Bank in Telengana Region during 2001-07

(Amount in crores)

| Sl. No. | District | 2001-2002 | | 2002-2003 | | 2003-04 | | 2004-05 | | 2005-06 | | 2006-07 | | 2007-08 | |
|---|---|---|---|---|---|---|---|---|---|---|---|---|---|---|---|
| | | Groups covered | Credit Accessed by the groups | Groups covered | Credit Accessed by the groups | Groups covered | Credit Accessed by the groups | Groups covered | Credit Accessed by the groups | Groups covered | Credit Accessed by the groups | Groups covered | Credit Accessed by the groups | Groups covered | Credit Accessed by the groups |
| 1 | | 2 | 3 | 4 | 5 | 6 | 7 | 8 | 9 | 10 | 11 | 12 | 13 | 14 | 15 |
| | **Telengana** | | | | | | | | | | | | | | |
| 1 | Karimnagar | 1519 | 4 | 1964 | 4 | 2645 | 5 | 2755 | 8 | 2946 | 11 | 3293 | 19 | 4133 | 35 |
| 2 | Khammam | 1060 | 2 | 1372 | 3 | 1847 | 4 | 1925 | 6 | 2058 | 8 | 2300 | 13 | 2887 | 22 |
| 3 | Mahabubnagar | 203 | 1 | 262 | 1 | 353 | 1 | 368 | 2 | 393 | 3 | 439 | 5 | 551 | 8 |
| 4 | Medak | 243 | 0 | 314 | 1 | 423 | 1 | 441 | 1 | 471 | 2 | 526 | 3 | 661 | 5 |
| 5 | Nalgonda | 717 | 1 | 928 | 2 | 1250 | 3 | 1302 | 4 | 1392 | 5 | 1556 | 9 | 1953 | 15 |
| 6 | Nizamabad | 740 | 1 | 957 | 2 | 1288 | 3 | 1342 | 4 | 1435 | 6 | 1604 | 10 | 2013 | 16 |
| 7 | Rangareddy | 391 | 1 | 505 | 2 | 680 | 3 | 709 | 4 | 758 | 6 | 847 | 10 | 1063 | 17 |
| 8 | Warangal | 1340 | 2 | 1735 | 4 | 2336 | 5 | 2434 | 7 | 2603 | 9 | 2908 | 15 | 3651 | 28 |
| 9 | Adilabad | 637 | 1 | 824 | 2 | 1110 | 2 | 1157 | 4 | 1237 | 5 | 1382 | 8 | 1734 | 14 |
| **Total** | | **6850** | **13** | **8861** | **21** | **11932** | **27** | **12433** | **40** | **13293** | **55** | **14855** | **92** | **18646** | **160** |

*Source:* Compiled from Various reports of Andhra Bank.

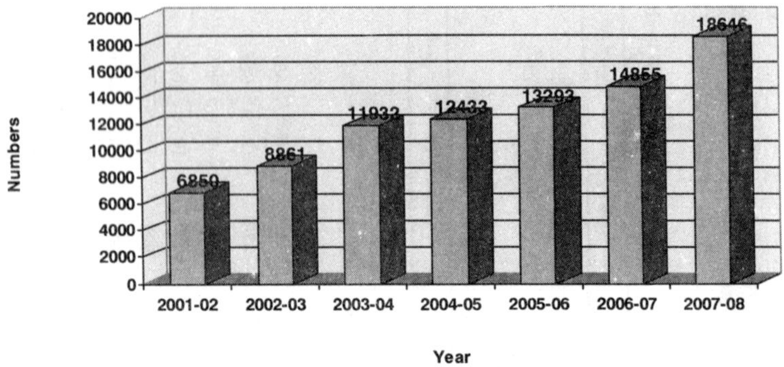


**Fig. 4.12: Year-wise SHG Coverage in Telengana Regions by Andhra Bank during 2001-07**

Figure 4.13 shows the amount financed by Andhra Bank in Telangana region from 2001-02 to 2007-08. Bank has financed Rs.13 crores during the year 2001-02 and increased to 160 crores during the year 2007-08. The jump from 2006-07 to 2007-08 is due to decisions taken at SLBC of AP in lending to Indiramma and debt swapping

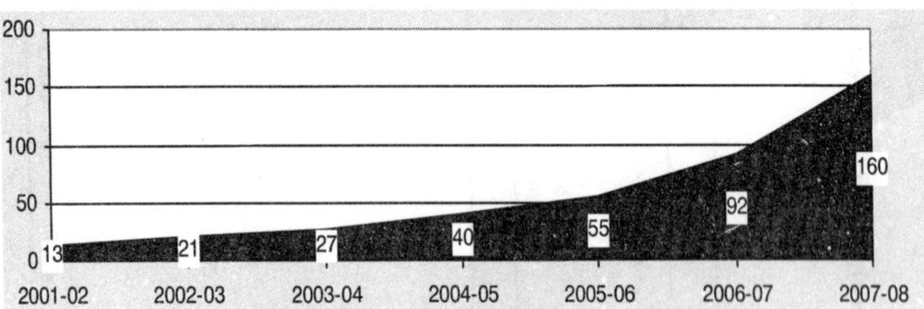


**Fig. 4.13: Year-wise SHG Finance in Telengana Regions by Andhra Bank during 2001-07**

## *Andhra Bank's Performance in Rayalseema Region*

Unlike the other two regions, Andhra Bank is operating in Rayalseema region with 65 branches. Rayalseema region is consisted of four districts i.e. Ananthapur, Chittoor, Kadapa and Kurnool. In fact, the district, SHG as well as branch network is very minimal in comparison to the other two regions of the state of Andhra Pradesh. Andhra Bank has covered a minimum of 3000 groups in 2001 and a maximum of 8000 in 2007 (see Table 4.6 and Fig. 4.14)

## Table 4.6
## Year and District-wise SHG Coverage of Andhra Bank in Rayalseema Region during 2001-07

(Amount in crores)

| Sl. No. | District | 2001-2002 | | 2002-2003 | | 2003-04 | | 2004-05 | | 2005-06 | | 2006-07 | | 2007-08 | |
|---|---|---|---|---|---|---|---|---|---|---|---|---|---|---|---|
| | | Groups covered | Credit Accessed by the groups | Groups covered | Credit Accessed by the groups | Groups covered | Credit Accessed by the groups | Groups covered | Credit Accessed by the groups | Groups covered | Credit Accessed by the groups | Groups covered | Credit Accessed by the groups | Groups covered | Credit Accessed by the groups |
| | 1 | 2 | 3 | 4 | 5 | 6 | 7 | 8 | 9 | 10 | 11 | 12 | 13 | 14 | 15 |
| | **Rayalseema** | | | | | | | | | | | | | | |
| 1 | Anantapur | 462 | 1 | 598 | 2 | 805 | 2 | 839 | 3 | 897 | 5 | 1003 | 8 | 1258 | 13 |
| 2 | Chittoor | 841 | 2 | 1088 | 4 | 1465 | 5 | 1527 | 7 | 1632 | 10 | 1824 | 17 | 2289 | 29 |
| 3 | Kadapa | 263 | 1 | 341 | 1 | 459 | 1 | 478 | 2 | 511 | 3 | 571 | 5 | 717 | 8 |
| 4 | Kurnool | 1346 | 4 | 1739 | 5 | 2343 | 7 | 2441 | 10 | 2611 | 13 | 2916 | 22 | 3662 | 40 |
| | **Total** | **2911** | **8** | **3766** | **12** | **5072** | **15** | **5285** | **22** | **5651** | **31** | **6314** | **52** | **7926** | **90** |

*Source:* Compiled from Various reports of Andhra Bank.

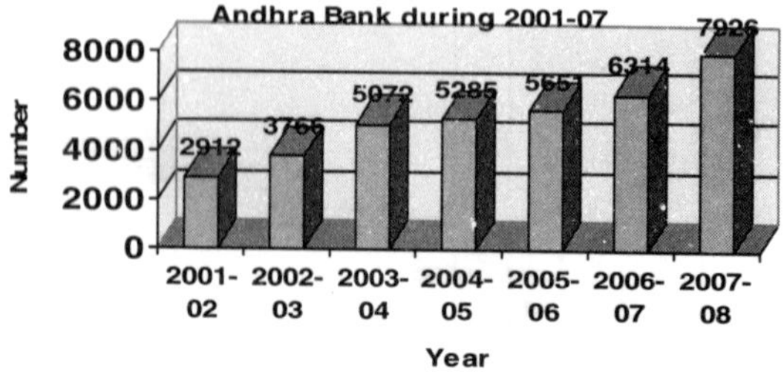


**Fig. 4.14: Year-wise Coverage in Rayalseema Regions by Andhra Bank during 2001-07**

*Source:* Data Compiled from various reports of Andhra Bank

Figure 4.14 shows the number of SHG groups linked in Rayalseema region over period of 2001-02 to 2007-08. During 2001-02 in Rayalseema Region of four districts have linked to 2912 groups and over years the groups' number was increased. During the year 2006-07 the number of groups are increased to 6314 and further increased to 7926 groups during the year 2007-08.

Figure 4.15 reveals the amount financed in Rayalseema region from 2001-02 to 2007-08. Andhra Bank has financed Rs.8 crores during the year 2001-02, which has increased to Rs. 90 crores during the year 2007-08. The substantial increase in bank financing during 2006-07 to 2007-08 is the result of the decisions taken at SLBC of AP in lending to Indiramma and debt swapping.

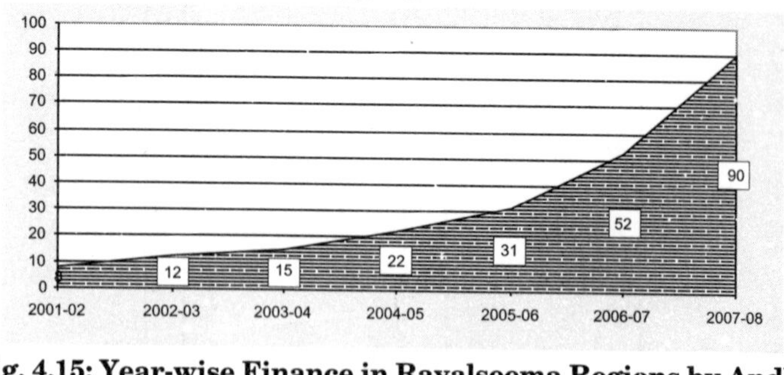


**Fig. 4.15: Year-wise Finance in Rayalseema Regions by Andhra Bank during 2001-07**

*Source:* Data compiled from all branches of Andhra Bank in Rayalseema Region.

In deed, the substantial increase in financial linkages in all the three regions under the study is primarily accredited to the favourable decision taken by the State government of Andhra Pradesh to link the financial operation of the small scale self-help groups with Andhra Bank in particular and rooting all financial operation through the Self-help Group root.

## *Swarnajayanti Gram Swarozgar Yojana (SGSY)*

The Ministry of Rural Development, Government of India has launched a new programme, "Swarnajayanti Gram Swarozgar Yojana (SGSY)" on 1st April, 1999 by restructuring the schemes namely

(1) Integrated Rural Development Programme (IRDP),

(2) Training of Rural Youth for Self Employment (TRYSEM),

(3) Development of Women and Children in Rural Areas (DWCRA),

(4) Supply of Improved Toolkits to Rural Artisans (SITRA),

(5) Ganga Kalyan Yojana (GKY) and

(6) Million Wells Scheme (MWS).

The scheme is evolved with the objective to bring the assisted poor families (*swarozgaris*) above the poverty line by ensuring appreciable sustained income over period of time. This objective is to be achieved by *inter alia* organizing the rural poor into SHGs through the process of social mobilization, their training and capacity building and provision of income generating assets. The rural poor such as those with land, landless labour, educated unemployed, rural artisans and disabled are covered under the scheme. This scheme also envisages the training, capacity building, skill and entrepreneurship development and provision of income generating assets to SHGs through bank credit and Government Subsidy.

### *Funding Pattern and Institutions Involved*

The scheme will be funded by the Centre and the States in the ratio of 75:25 and will be implemented by Commercial Banks, Regional Rural Banks and Co-operative Banks. Other financial institutions, Panchayat Raj Institutions, District Rural Development Agencies (DRDAs), and Non-Government Organizations (NGOs) Technical institutions in the district will be involved in the process of planning, implementation and monitoring of the scheme.

### *Activity Clusters, Key Activities and Lending Norm*

The focus under the scheme should be on development of activity clusters with emphasis on key activities identified in the Mandal, both for group as well as individual assistance. However, focus is generally given on 4-5 key activities, which are identified for training and micro enterprise development in a cluster approach for larger number of groups.

Key activities are identified based on the availability of local resources, aptitude and skills of the beneficiaries and also activities suited to the people. Local markets must have potential. The aim is for covering large number of *swarozgaris* with important activities having potential for marketing. Key activities cover both Farm sector and Non Farm sector. The unit cost as fixed by NABARD should be taken in to consideration for fixing the unit cost for Farm sector.

The size of the loan under the scheme would depend on the nature of the project. There is no investment ceiling other than the unit cost i.e. investment requirement worked out for the project. The loans under the scheme would be composite loan comprising of Term Loan and Working Capital. The loan component and admissible subsidy together would be equal to total project cost. Emphasis is laid on multiple dose of assistance.

# 5

# Performance Evaluation of SHGS-BL of Andhra Bank: Problems and Challenges

## Introduction

The performance of SHGs includes how the members are saving, payment of loans, action against the members in default, SHG Governance, leadership qualities rotation of leaders etc., the data from the field is collected and analyzed.

## Achievements in SHGs through SHG-Banking

With the introduction of "SHG-Banking" a highly flexible financial service structure has been made available to poor households, which allowed them to stabilize their irregular income flow and to increase their income in most cases. The SHG-System allows members to maintain a more regular financial flow in support of the family and of the micro enterprise operated by the family. The SHG system:

1. Enables the conduct of frequent transactions both for allocating small contractual saving amounts and for borrowing for a variety of self chosen purposes at irregular intervals from the SHG

2. Tunes the allocation of funds with the needs of group members at local level inside the SHG-dominated financial self help system (without formal requirements)

3. Provides a very flexible credit line from the banking system at an acceptable interest rate (mostly 9-12 per cent p.a.) at bank branch level to the SHGs and also allows small bridging loans internally by members from their SHG-fund.

4. Offers deposit facilities at the bank and at the group level that enables conduct of frequent saving transactions both individually and on group saving accounts (almost 24 hours a day);

5. Starts to offer purpose oriented savings accounts in the form of insurance with the Life Insurance Corporation of India;

The SHG-Banking is an ideal combination of the formal banking sector's "banking with the poor" and "banking by the people" through informal SHGs. This also shapes the introduction of a basic element of an informal insurance sector with gradual access to the formal insurance sector.

The good performance of the SHG-Banking Programme is due to its strategy to mobilize underused capacities of the target group. The skills and assets of low-income people - particularly women are such as they hold non-wage earning activities, they can work on own account, as self-employed person, are self-reliant, more independent, more autonomous in managing their family affairs and household budget, they do business or go into new business on one's own initiative, they think of oneself but it is also the collective wisdom of all group members which pervades the system. They are more reliable and are able to communicate much better within their self-selected groups as compared to males; they hold a poignant intelligence and are more teamwork oriented than males; they also can lead a group as cooperative or authoritarian than males.

They know how to utilize an available resource and could effectively used in multifarious livelihood promoting activities such as animal husbandry and cattle fattening, utilization of land for all kind of crops cultivation, use of water, collecting products from the forests, pulse husking, mustard oil manufacturing, betel nut and spice processing, making lime and other building materials like milestones for roads, tailoring, running tiny snack shops, petty trade, preparation of sweets and snacks with chutneys, pitching tents and organizing festive entertainments and banqueting, food-catering to schools and distribution of products through trade etc.

Male groups are involved in rickshaw or cart pulling, buffalo carting and other transport services, some are involved in crafts hide and skin preparation, shoe making, pottery making, carpentry, broom making, weaving. Their ingenuity in the endeavor to survive appears inexhaustible. Common to them is the competence to make a living from it. Their resource management skill, a fair treatment as respected bank clients, plus access to loans and financial services along with a newly established group oriented saving habit has contributed to a new conscientization of the poor (predominantly women), which allows them:

a) to overcome circumstances where nature intervenes frequently and erratically in the economic system, by building up financial resources and use them as social,

b) to start to control forces of socio-economic exploitation by landlords, moneylenders, bureaucrats, traders by using credit for extending income generating activities,

c) with additional self-employment and increase of income from investments: To overcome the gap between income flow and consumption; and

d) the socio-economic source for dependence and exploitation relationships (low wages, exorbitant interest rates for loans, bondages etc.) along with impacts of natural disasters is gradually controlled and the social process of SHG members escaping from poverty is gaining momentum. SHG Bank Linkage Programme gets through to the poor section of village India; and the SHGs have become gradually very efficient moneylenders earning good interest-income for distribution to their members at every year end.

The agencies/individuals involved in promoting SHGs are shown in two categories namely Government promoted SHGs and NGOs-promoted SHGs (see Table 5.1). Out of 429 agencies/individuals involved in 120 SHGs, 28 per cent are bank managers and animators/book keepers, each. 16, 12, 10, 6 per cent are community coordinators, NGO/Federations/ MACs, Government officials people representatives respectively. In Government-promoted SHGs community coordinators, animators/bookkeepers and bank manager played an important role with 26 per cent shares each in promotion followed by Government officials with 16 per cent share and people representative with 5 per cent share. In NGO- promoted SHGs animator/book keeper, bank and NGO/ federations/ MACs played equally important rolls in promotion with 30 per cent of shares each. To know whether there is a statistically significant difference between Government promoted SHGs and NGO promoted SHGs as to agencies/ individuals in their promotion, $X^2$ test is conducted. Since calculated $X^2$ value is more than Table value at 1 per cent level of significance, it is concluded that there is statistically significant between two groups of SHGs as to agencies / individuals involved in their proportion.

**Table 5.1**
**Government and NGO Assistance in Promotion SHGs**

| | | Promoter Agency / Individual | | | | | | |
|---|---|---|---|---|---|---|---|---|
| *Sl. No.* | *SHG Types* | *Bank Manager* | *NGO / MACs* | *Peoples Represen-tatives* | *Govt. Officials* | *Community Coordi-nators* | *Animator / Book keeper* | *Total* |
| 1. | NGO-promoted SHGs | 50 (30.67) | 50 (30.68) | 13 (7.98) | | | 50 (30.67) | 163 (100) |
| 2 | Government-promoted SHGs | 70 (26.32) | - | 13 (4.88) | 43 (16.16) | 70 (26.32) | 70 (26.32) | 266 (100) |
| 3. | All SHGs | 120 (27.97) | 50 (11.66) | 26 (6.06) | 43 (10.20) | 70 (16.32) | 120 (27.97) | 429 (100) |

Cal. $X^2$ value=153.80

** (** Significant at 1 percent level); Tab $X^2$ value at 5 def=11.07.

*Note:* Figures in the parentheses are percentage to row totals

*Source:* Field data.

## SHG-Bank Linkage Strategies

Sample SHGs are primarily micro-credit institutions organized on the principle of community-based banking. By linking SHGs to commercial banks leverage is obtained, that is, savings mobilized from SHG members are supplemented by loans from banks engaged in SHG-bank linkage programme. SHG-bank linkage is a new perspective in Indian commercial Banking system to reach the un-reached masses. A set of facilitating factors is pre-requisite in SHG-bank linkage programme: Institution agencies are catalysts in the programme. All public sector banks have been actively participating in the SHG-bank linkage.

After assessment, SHGs are linked to the banks facilitating factors in SHG-bank linkage facilitating factors are exhibited Table 5.2. 31, 29, 23, 15 and 1 per cent of facilitating factors in SHG- bank linkage are accounted for by good book-keeping, good lending and repayment, improved group quality, repeated visits and local leaders respectively. Similar pattern is obtained with regard to facilitating factors in SHGs-bank linkage programme of Government-promoted SHGs and NGO-promoted SHGs. Since calculated $X^2$ Value is less than Table value at one per cent level of significance, it can be concluded that there is no statistically difference between Government -promoted SHGs and NGO promoted SHGs as to SHG bank linkage facilitating factors. The null hypothesis is accepted.

Agencies and individuals involved in assessing SHGs for bank linkage are shown in Table 5.3 along SHG types namely Government promoted SHGs and NGO promoted SHGs. Bankers and animators account for 32 per cent of SHG assessments each followed by village organizations with 19 per cent, NGOs in 13 per cent and DRDA with four per cent. Two-thirds of SHG assessments in both the types were done by banks and animators. Village organization played significant roll in assessment in Government -promoted SHGs

**Table 5.2**

**SHG-bank Linkage: Facilitating factors by SHG Types**

| *Sl. No.* | *SHG Types* | *SHG-bank Linkage Facilitating Factors* | | | | | *Total* |
|---|---|---|---|---|---|---|---|
| | | *Improved Group Quality* | *Good Book-keeping* | *Good Lending and Repayment* | *Local Leaders* | *Repeated Visits* | |
| 1. | NGO-promcted SHGs | 38 (25.51) | 47 (31.54) | 43 (28.86) | - | 21 (14.09) | 149 (100) |
| 2. | Government-promoted SHGs | 43 (21.61) | 61 (30.65) | 58 (29.15) | 5 (2.51) | 32 (16.08) | 199 (100) |
| 3. | All SHGs | 81 (23.28) | 108 (31.03) | 101 (29.02) | 5 (1.44) | 53 (15.23) | 348 (100) |

Cal. $X^2$ value=4.54, (NS: Not Significant), Tab $X^2$ value at 5 def=9.49

*Note:* Figures in the parentheses are per centage to row totals

*Source:* Field data.

**Table 5.3**
**Assessing Agency / Individual by SHG Types in SHG-bank Linkage**

| *S. No.* | *SH G Types* | *Assisting Agency / Individual in SHG-bank Linkage* | | | | | |
|---|---|---|---|---|---|---|---|
| | | *NGO* | *Bankers* | *Animators* | *DRDA* | *Village Organization* | *Total* |
| 1 | Government promoted SHGs | - | 70 (31.25) | 70 (31.25) | 14 (6.25) | 70 (31.25) | 224 (100) |
| 2. | NGO-promoted SHGs | 50 (33.34) | 50 (33.33) | 50 (33.33) | | | 150 (100) |
| 3. | All SHGs | 50 (13.36) | 120 (32.09) | 120 (32.09) | 14 (3.74) | 70 (18.72) | 374 (100) |

Cal. $X^2$ value=131.16** (** Significant at 1 per cent level);
Tab $X^2$ value at 4 def=9.49

*Note*: Figures in the parentheses are per centage to row totals

*Source:* Field data.

with 31 per cent share. Similarly NGOs had a significant role in assessing NGO-promoted SHGs with 31 per cent share. To know whether there is statistically significant difference between government - promoted SHGs and NGO- promoted SHGs as to agencies/individuals involved in assisting SHG bank linkage, $X^2$ test is conducted.

Since calculated $X^2$ Value is more than table value at one per cent level of significance, it can be concluded that there is a statistically significant difference between two SHGs categories as to agencies / individuals involved in SHG bank linkage. The null hypothesis is rejected.

**Participants in SHG-Bank Interactions**

There are multiple sub-purposes in SHG Bank; linkage programme which are promoted by SHG leaders and members either individually or combined both in Government promoted and NGO promoted SHGs.

Participation of SHG leaders and members in SHG-bank interaction is presented in Table 5.4 purpose and promoter-wise. There are 2,015 interactions with Government - promoted SHGs. Three important purposes of SHG- Bank interaction in Government - promoted SHGs are for obtaining loans (37.52%), for repayment of loans (24.56%) and for depositing savings 24.17%). These purposes combined account for 86.25 per cent of total interactions. Of total interactions of 2,015, SHG members' participation account for 49 per cent, both SHG leader and members' participation for 38 per cent and SHG leaders' participation 14 per cent. In NGO-promoted SHGs three important purposes of SHG-bank interaction are for obtaining loans 33.35 per cent, for repayment of loans (29.00%), and for depositing savings (26.00%). These three aggregately account for 88.35 per cent of total interactions. SHG members' participation account 54 per cent of interactions, both leaders and members participation for, 33.35 per cent, SHG leaders' participation for 13 per cent of total interaction.

**Table 5.4**

**Participants in SHG-bank Interactions in Government-and NGO Promoted SHGs**

| Sl. No. | Purpose of SHG-bank Interaction | *Government-promoted SHGs (No.70) SHG Participants in Interactions* | | | | *NGO-promoted SHGs (No.50) SHG Participants in Interactions* | | | |
|---|---|---|---|---|---|---|---|---|---|
| | | *SHG Leaders* | *SHG Members* | *Both Leaders And Members* | *Total* | *SHG Leaders* | *SHG Members* | *Both Leaders And Members* | *Total* |
| *1* | *2* | *3* | *4* | *5* | *6* | *7* | *8* | *9* | *10)* |
| 1 | For depositing savings | - | 487 | - | 487 (24.17) | - | 414 | - | 414 (25.52) |
| 2 | For withdrawal of savings | 140 | - | - | 140 (6.95) | 100 | - | - | 100 (6.17) |
| 3 | For obtaining other amounts | 137 | - | - | 137 (6.80) | 100 | - | - | 100 (6.17) |
| 4 | For repayment of Loan | - | 495 | - | 495 (24.56) | - | 467 | - | 467 (28.79) |
| 5 | For obtaining Loans | - | - | 756 | 756 (37.52) | | - | 541 | 541 (33.35) |
| 6 | Total | 277 03.75) | 982 (48.73) | 756 (37.52) | 2015 (100) | 200 (12.33) | 881 (54.32) | 541 (33.35) | 1622 (100) |

*Note:* Figures in the parentheses are percentage to row totals.
*Source:* Field data.

## SHGs by Caste Categories

Caste is a relevant and significant attribute in any socio-economic analysis in Indian caste-hierarchy systems. Bank-linked sample SHGs are analyzed by categorizing them on the caste-basis. More over SHGs are promoted on exclusive principle covering members of a given social segment so as to maintain socio-economic homogeneity and group cohesiveness.

SHG caste categories cross classified by their membership size are shown in Table 5.5. The model membership size for BC , SC, ST, Minority and mixed caste SHGs are 10 and 12, 15, 14, 12 and 10 respectively. For all caste categories put together the model membership size is 10. Concentrating on the right extreme of the turtle, it can be seen that the average membership size is 12, for BC SHGs, 13 for SC, Minority and mixed caste SHGs and, 14 for ST SHGs and 13 for all SHGs clubbed together. From the proceeding analysis it can be concluded that there is no much variation in the average size of SHGs across caste categories. The average size varies quite narrowly from 12 to 14.

## Socio-demographic Profile of SHG Members' Households

Socio-demographic as well as economic profile of SHG members' households is thoroughly discussed in the following sections and tables. Among other parameters, the study has chosen parameters like population size, caste composition, land and other asset holding, education level, annual income and self-employment purposively to judge the impact of self-help groups on the live and livelihood of SHG members.

The study has analyzed the facts and figures collected from the beneficiaries of Andhra Bank assisted bank-linkage programme across the regions under the study and analyzed the findings in light of the objective of the study. Impact of

**Table 5.5**
**Caste-wise Distribution of SHG by Membership**

| *Caste Category of SHG* | *Membership Size (Members)* | | | | | | | | *Total* | *Average Size (in number)* |
|---|---|---|---|---|---|---|---|---|---|---|
| | *10* | *11* | *12* | *13* | *14* | *15* | *16* | *17* | | |
| *1* | *2* | *3* | *4* | *5* | *6* | *7* | *8* | *9* | *11* | *12* |
| Mixed-caste SHGs | 20 (21.98) | 6 (6.59) | 16 (17.58) | 9 (9.88) | 10 (10.99) | 16 (17.58) | 7 (7.70) | 7 (7.70) | 91 (100) | 13 |
| Minority SHGs | - | - | 2 (66.67) | - | - | 1 (33.33) | - | - | 3 (100) | 13 |
| S.C. SHGs | 3 (15.00) | 2 (10.00) | 2 (10.00) | 2 (10.00) | 4 (20.00) | 5 (25.00) | 2 (10.00) | - | 20 (100) | 13 |
| S.T. SHGs | - | - | - | - | 1 (100) | - | - | - | 1 (100) | 14 |
| B.C. SHGs | 2 (40.00) | - (40.00) | 2 | - (20.00) | 1 | - | - | - (100) | 5 | 12 |
| All | 25 (20.83) | 8 (6.67) | 22 (18.34) | 10 (8.33) | 17 (14.16) | 22 (18.34) | 9 (7.50) | 7 (5.83) | 120 (100) | 13 |

Note: Figures in the parentheses are percentages to row totals.

Source: Field data.

the programmes is systematically presented through the tables, figures and graphs.

Demographic profile of SHG member families in terms of house hold sizes is presented in Table 5.6. The model household size of SHG is 4 in Other Castes, Scheduled Tribes, 5 in Backward Castes, Scheduled Castes and three in minorities. The model size is 5 for all caste house holds. From Table 5.6, it can be seen that 67 per cent of the house holds are either 4 member or 5 member households. 93 per cent of the house holds are 5 member or less than 5 member households.

SHG members classified into different age groups and cross classified. The caste categories are presented in Table 5.7. Out of total 1,567 members in 120 SHGs OCs, BCs, SCs, STs and Minorities account for 33, 27, and 26,4,11 per cent respectively. Thus OCs, BCs and SCs stand first, second and third positions in terms of their shares in total membership of sample SHGs. Coming to age classification of SHG membership 53 per cent of them are above 19 and below 35 years of age. Another 44 per cent of them fall in the age group 36 to 50 years. Hardly 3 per cent of them are above 50 years. Based on the above analysis it can be observed that 70 per cent of the members is either young or middle aged.

Caste and education levels of SHG members of sample SHGs are incorporated in Table 5.8. Per centage of illiterates is highest at 41 per cent of SCs followed by 34 per cent in STs, 16 per cent in Minorities, 12 per cents BCs and 7 per cent in OCs. 86, 78, 51, 55, 73 per cent who have formal education represent OCs, BCs, SCs, STs and Minorities respectively.

All castes put together 19 per cent are illiterates 9 per cent of neo literates and 72 per cent of formal education and can in be concluded that the literacy/ education levels of SHG members are high and the status in the caste hierarchy and illiteracy level are inversely related.

**Table 5.6**
**Distribution of SHG Member Household by Caste and Size**

| Sl. No | Caste Category of SHG Families | SHG Member Household sizes | | | | | | | | | Total |
|---|---|---|---|---|---|---|---|---|---|---|---|
| | | 1 | 2 | 3 | 4 | 5 | 6 | 7 | 8 | Above 8 | |
| 1 | 2 | 3 | 4 | 5 | 6 | 7 | 8 | 9 | 10 | 11 | 12 |
| 1. | OCs. | 31 (6.04) | 37 (7.22) | 60 (11. 70) | 183 (35.67) | 174 (33.92) | 23 (4.48) | 4 (0.78) | 1 (0.19) | - | 513 (100) |
| 2. | BCs. | 26 (6.22) | 24 (5.74) | 51 (12.20) | 136 (32.54) | 141 (33.73) | 36 (8.61) | 2 (0.48) | 2 (0.48) | - | 418 (100) |
| 3. | SCs. | 36 (8.98) | 14 (3.49) | 21 (5.24) | 137 (34.16) | 181 (45.14) | 10 (2.49) | 1 (0.25) | 1 (0.25) | - | 401 (100) |
| 4. | STs. | 4 (6.25) | 13 (20.31) | 12 (18.75) | 18 (28.13) | 13 (20.31) | 3 (4.69) | 1 (1.56) | - | - | 64 (100) |
| 5. | Minorities | 12 (7.02) | 19 (11.11) | 42 (24.56) | 41 (23.98) | 32 (18.71) | 21 (12.28) | 2 (1.16) | 1 (0.58) | 1 (0.58) | 171 (100) |
| 6. | All Households | 109 (6.96) | 107 (6.83) | 186 (11.87) | 515 (32.87) | 541 (34.52) | 93 (5.93) | 10 (0.64) | 5 (0.32) | 1 (0.06) | 1567 (100) |

*Note:* Figures in the parentheses are percentages to row totals.
*Source:* Field data.

## Table 5.7
## Caste and Age-wise Distribution of SHG Members

| *Age Cate-gories (in ) years* | *Caste of SHG members* | | | | | *Total* |
|---|---|---|---|---|---|---|
| | *Minorities* | *OCs.* | *BCs* | *SCs* | *STs* | |
| *1* | *6* | *2* | *3* | *4* | *5* | *7 (2 to 6)* |
| 19 – 25 | 25<br>(12.31) | 75<br>(36.95) | 57<br>(28.08) | 34<br>(16.75) | 12<br>(5.91) | 203<br>(100)<br>[12.95] |
| 26 – 30 | 33<br>(10.96) | 87<br>(28.90) | 86<br>(28.57) | 83<br>(27.58) | 12<br>(3.99) | 301<br>(100)<br>[19.21] |
| 31 – 35 | 34<br>(10.42) | 96<br>(29.45) | 93<br>(28.53) | 84<br>(25.77) | 19<br>(5.83) | 326<br>(100)<br>[20.81] |
| 36 – 40 | 29<br>(9.06) | 97<br>(30.31) | 95<br>(29.69) | 87<br>(27.19) | 12<br>(3.75) | 320<br>(100)<br>[20.42] |
| 41 – 45 | 27<br>(13.30) | 56<br>(27.59) | 48<br>(23.64) | 68<br>(33.50) | 4<br>(1.97) | 203<br>(100)<br>[12.96] |
| 46 – 50 | 19<br>(10.92) | 92<br>(52.87) | 23<br>(13.22) | 37<br>(21.26) | 3<br>(1.73) | 174<br>(100)<br>[11.10] |
| Above 50 | 4<br>(10.00) | 10<br>(25.00) | 16<br>(40.00) | 8<br>(20.00) | 2<br>(5.00) | 40<br>(100)<br>[2.55] |
| All | 171<br>(10.91) | 513<br>(32.74) | 418<br>(26.68) | 401<br>(25.59) | 64<br>(4.08) | 1567<br>(100)<br>[100] |

*Note.* Figures in the parentheses are per centages to row totals.
Figures in the square brackets [ ] are per centages to row totals.

*Source:* Field data.

**Table 5.8**
**Caste and Education-wise Distribution of SHGs Members**

| *Caste Categories* | *Education Levels* | | | | | | |
|---|---|---|---|---|---|---|---|
| | *Neo-Literates* | *Primary* | *Upper Primary* | *Secondary* | *Higher* | *Illiterate* | *Total* |
| Minorities | 19 | 54 | 43 | 22 | 5 | 28 | 171 |
| | (11.11) | (31.58) | (25.15) | (12.87) | (2.92) | (16.37) | (100) |
| BCs. | 40 | 125 | 133 | 50 | 20 | 50 | 418 |
| | (9.57) | (29.91) | (31.81) | (11.96) | (4.79) | (11.96) | (100) |
| SCs. | 37 | 107 | 53 | 23 | 15 | 166 | 401 |
| | (9.23) | (26.68) | (13.22) | (5.74) | (3.74) | (41.39) | (100) |
| STs. | 13 | 12 | 14 | 3 | — | 22 | 64 |
| | (20.31) | (18.75) | (21.88) | (4.69) | | (34.3 7) | (100) |
| OCs. | 36 | 76 | 138 | 188 | 41 | 34 | 513 |
| | (7.02) | (14.81) | (26.90) | (36.65) | (7.99) | (6.63) | (100) |
| All Categories | 145 | 374 | 381 | 286 | 81 | 300 | 1567 |
| | (9.25) | (23.87) | (24.31) | (18.25) | (5.17) | (19.15) | (100) |

*Note:* Figures in the parentheses are per centages to row totals
*Source:* Field data

SHG member households classified with caste categories and their sizes of land holding are presented in table 5.9. All castes put together 30 per cent of house holds are landless. The incidence of landlessness varies across caste categories. Highest at 52 per cent in ST followed by 49 per cent in minorities 34 per cent in SCs, 25 per cent in OCs and 20 per cent in BCs. Among land owning SHG member households the model house holding sizes are in acre in OCs <1 acre in BCs SCs, STs , minorities and all casts put together. 50 per cent land owning SHG member house holds have 1 acre or less than 1 acre each. An inference can be deduced from the figures depicted in table 5.9 that 92 per cent of SHG member house holds belong to either marginal farmer or landless.

The housing status and types of houses of SHG households are caste in Table 5.10. All castes put together 80 per cent of the households reside in owned houses and the rest of 20 per cent in the rented houses. 82, 75, 81, 81.25, 87 of OCs, BCs, SCs, STs and Minorities respectively own their residential accommodation.

Coming to types of houses, 33, 23, 21, 10 and 7 per cent of SCs, STs, Minorities, OCs and BCs respectively reside in thatched houses. In residential ownership the incidence of pakka houses is high at 62 per cent in BCs, followed by 57 per cent in OCs, 55 per cent in minorities 54 per cent in STs and 44 per cent in SCs and 55 per cent in all castes put together respectively. From the table analysis draws the inference that four- fifths of the SHG member house holds own the houses 55 per cent of them side in owned pakka buildings and only 17 per cent of them have residence in owned thatched houses.

**Table 5.9**
**Distribution of SHG Member Household by Caste and Land Ownership**

| Sl. No. | Caste Category Of SHG Member Families | Size of Land Holdings (in acres) | | | | | | | | Total |
|---|---|---|---|---|---|---|---|---|---|---|
| | | Landless | <1 | 1 | 2 | 3 | 4 | 5 | >5 | |
| 1 | 2 | 3 | 4 | 5 | 6 | 7 | 8 | 9 | 10 | 11 |
| 1. | Minorities. | 84<br>(49.13) | 82<br>(47.95) | 3<br>(1.75) | 2<br>(1.17) | -<br>- | -<br>- | -<br>- | -<br>- | 171<br>(100) |
| 2 | DCs. | 126<br>(24.57) | 116<br>(22.61) | 118<br>(23.00) | 103<br>(20.08) | 39<br>(7.60) | 6<br>(1.17) | 3<br>(0.58) | 2<br>(0.39) | 513<br>(100) |
| 3 | BCs. | 82<br>(19.62) | 108<br>(25.84) | 94<br>(22.49) | 83<br>(19.85) | 43<br>(10.28) | 3<br>(0.72) | 4<br>(0.96) | 1<br>(0.24) | 418<br>(100) |
| 4 | SCs | 138<br>(34.41) | 209<br>(52.12) | 21<br>(5.24) | 19<br>(4.74) | 13<br>(3.24) | 1<br>(0.25) | | | 401<br>(100) |
| 5 | STs. | 33<br>(51.56) | 31<br>(48.44) | -<br>- | -<br>- | -<br>- | -<br>- | -<br>- | -<br>- | 64<br>(100) |
| 6 | All Categories | 463<br>(29.55) | 546<br>(34.84) | 236<br>(15.06) | 207<br>(13.21) | 95<br>(6.06) | 10<br>(0.64) | 7<br>(0.45) | 3<br>(0.18) | 1567<br>(100) |

*Note:* Figures in the parentheses are percentages to row totals.
*Source:* Field data.

## Table 5.10
## Distribution of SHG Member Households by Caste, Ownership and Type of House

| Sl. No. | Caste Category and Ownership | Types of Houses | | | Total |
|---|---|---|---|---|---|
| | | Tiled | Pakka (concrete) | Thatched | |
| | 1 | 2 | 3 | 4 | 5 |
| 1 | Minorities | | | | |
| | a. Owned | 35<br>(23.65) | 82<br>(55.40) | 31<br>(20.95) | 148<br>(100.00)<br>[86.55] |
| | b. Rented | 2<br>(8.70) | 11<br>(47.82) | 10<br>(43.48) | 23<br>(100.00)<br>[13.45] |
| | Sub-total | 37<br>(21.64) | 93<br>(54.38) | 41<br>(23.98) | 171<br>(100)<br>[100] |
| 2 | BCs | | | | |
| | a. Owned | 95<br>(30.45) | 194<br>(62.18) | 23<br>(7.37) | 312<br>(100.00)<br>[74.64] |
| | b. Rented | 76<br>(71.70) | 22<br>(20.75) | 8<br>(7.55) | 106<br>(100.00)<br>[25.36] |
| | Sub-total | 171<br>(40.91) | 216<br>(51.67) | 31<br>(7.42) | 418<br>(100)<br>[100] |
| 3 | SCs | | | | |
| | a. Owned | 74<br>(22.77) | 145<br>(44.62) | 106<br>(32.61) | 325<br>(100.00)<br>[81.05] |
| | b. Rented | 28<br>(36.84) | 34<br>(44.74) | 14<br>(18.42) | 76<br>(100.00)<br>[18.95] |
| | Sub-total | 102<br>(25.44) | 179<br>(44.64) | 120<br>(29.92) | 401<br>(100)<br>[100] |

*(Contd...)*

| | 1 | 2 | 3 | 4 | 5 |
|---|---|---|---|---|---|
| 4 | STs | | | | |
| | a. Owned | 12<br>(23.08) | 28<br>(53.84) | 12<br>(23.08) | 52<br>(100.00)<br>[81.25] |
| | b. Rented | 4<br>(33.33) | 8<br>(66.67) | ( - ) | 12<br>(100.00)<br>[18.75] |
| | Sub-total | 16<br>(25.00) | 36<br>(56.25) | 12<br>(18.75) | 64<br>(100)<br>[100] |
| 5 | OCs. | | | | |
| | a. Owned | 139<br>(32.86) | 241<br>(56.97) | 43<br>(10.17) | 423<br>(100.00)<br>[82.46] |
| | b. Rented | 35<br>(38.89) | 36<br>(40.00) | 19<br>(21.11 ) | 90<br>(100.00)<br>[17.54] |
| | Sub-total | 174<br>(33.91) | 277<br>(54.00) | 62<br>(12.09) | 513<br>(100)<br>[100] |
| 6 | All Categories | | | | |
| | 3. Owned | 355<br>(28.18) | 690<br>(54.76) | 215<br>(17.06) | 1260<br>(100.00)<br>[80.41] |
| | b. Rented | 145<br>(47.23) | 111<br>(36.16) | 51<br>(16.61) | 307<br>(100.00)<br>[19.59] |
| | Sub-total | 500<br>(31.91) | 801<br>(51.12) | 266<br>(16.97) | 1567<br>(100)<br>[100] |

*Note:* Figures in the parentheses () are per centages to row totals
Figures in the parentheses [ ] are per centages to row totals

*Source:* Field data

Annual incomes of SHG members are shown along with their landholding sizes in Table 5.11. Majority of members are in annual income range of Rs. 11,000-13,000 in landless and less than one acre households, Rs.13,000-15,000 in 2 acres, three acre households, more than Rs.15,000 in 4 acre,

5 acre and more than 5 acre house holds. It can be seen from Table 5.11 that 92 per cent of SHG members have an annual income exceeding Rs.9,000. Figure 5.1 shows the household spread of Self-help group members by Annual Income. It is also revealed that a positive correlation is established between the level of income and stand of living of self-help group members.

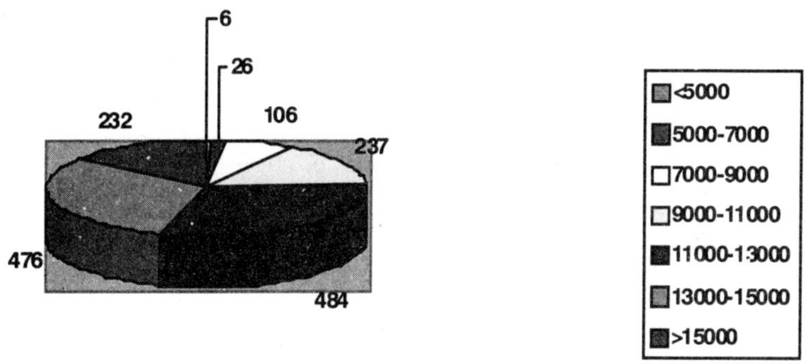


**Fig. 5.1: Annual Income of SHG Members**

## SHG-member Turnover

Self-help group like any other group operates under group dynamics. There are attractions and repulsions in being members of the group. Detracted of SHG operations, people quit SHGs, which can be captured by a measure of SHG-member turnover. In other words it is member out-flows from the SHGs.

SHG membership dynamics are shown in Table 5.12. Total membership in SHGs was 1,592 at the beginning and 1567 at the present, which means a loss of 25 members over a period of time after taking into account intake of new members and members replacing those who quit the SHGs. Member drop-outs were more in mixed caste SHGs (32 members) and SC SHGs (14 members). SHG membership turnover under separation method is 13 per cent in ST SHGs

## Table 5.11
## Distribution of SHG Member Households by Size of Land-holdings and Annual Income in 2006-07

| Sl. No. | SHG Member Household Land Holding sizes (in acres) | Annual Income (in rupees) | | | | | | | Total |
|---|---|---|---|---|---|---|---|---|---|
| | | < 5000 | 5000 - 7000 | 7000 - 9000 | 9000 - 11000 | 11000 - 13000 | 13000 - 15000 | > 15000 . | |
| 1 | 2 | 3 | 4 | 5 | 6 | 7 | 8 | 9 | 10 |
| 1 | Land less | 3 (0.65) | 12 (2.59) | 36 (7.78) | 73 (15.77) | 153 (33.05) | 143 (30.88) | 43 (9.28) | 463 (100) |
| 2 | < 1 | 2 (0.37) | 11 (2.02) | 48 (8.79) | 96 (17.58) | 188 (34.43) | 156 (28.57) | 45 (8.24) | 546 (100) |
| 3 | 1 | 1 (0.42) | 3 (1.27) | 11 (4.66) | 29 (12.29) | 73 (30.93) | 68 (28.82) | 51 (21.61) | 236 (100) |
| 4 | 2 | - | - | 9 (4.35) | 31 (14.98) | 49 (23.67) | 64 (30.91) | 54 (26.09) | 207 (100) |
| 5 | 3 | - | - | 2 (2.1 0) | 8 (8.42) | 18 (18.95) | 38 (40.00) | 29 (30.53) | 95 (100) |
| 6 | 4 | - | - | - | - | 1 (10.00) | 4 (40.00) | 5 (50.00) | 10 (100) |

(Contd...)

| | | | | | | | | | |
|---|---|---|---|---|---|---|---|---|---|
| 7 | 5 | - | - | - | - | 2<br>(28.57) | 2<br>(28.57) | 3<br>(42.86) | 7<br>(100) |
| 8 | > 5 | - | - | - | - | - | 1<br>(33.33) | 2<br>(66.67) | 3<br>(100) |
| 9 | All Households | 6<br>(0.38) | 26<br>(1.66) | 106<br>(6.76) | 237<br>(15.12) | 484<br>(30.89) | 476<br>(30.38) | 232<br>(14.81) | 1567<br>(100) |

*Note:* Figures in the parentheses are percentages to row totals.
*Source:* Field data.

followed by 5 per cent in SC and Minority SHGs and 3 per cent in BC, Mixed-caste, and all SHGs clubbed together. Under flex method membership turnover which takes in account separations and replacements, the membership turnover rates are 13 per cent in ST SHGs, 6 per cent in SC SHGs, 5 per cent in BC and minority SHGs. 4 per cent in all SHGs and 3 per cent in Mixed-caste SHGs. The analysis reveals that the membership turnover rates and status in caste hierarchy are inversely related.

**Table 5.12**
**SHG Membership Changes by SHG Caste Categories**

| *Sl. No.* | *Dimension* | *SHG Caste Categories* | | | | | *All SHGs* |
|---|---|---|---|---|---|---|---|
| | | *Mixed-caste SHGs* | *Minority SHGs* | *BC SHGs* | *SC SHGs* | *ST SHGs* | |
| *1* | *2* | *3* | *4* | *5* | *6* | *7* | *8* |
| 1 | Initial Membership | 1,201 | 41 | 58 | 276 | 16 | 1,592 |
| 2 | Dropout Members or Separations | 32 | 2 | 2 | 14 | 2 | 52 |
| 3 | Replacement of Members | 9 | - | 1 | 2 | - | 12 |
| 4 | New Member Admissions | 13 | - | 1 | 1 | - | 15 |
| 5 | Present Membership [1 (-2+3+4)] | 1,191 | 39 | 58 | 265 | 14 | 1,567 |
| 6 | Average Membership (average of SHGs Membership at the Initial and the final) | 1,196 | 40 | 58 | 271 | 15 | 1,580 |

*(Contd...)*

| *1* | *2* | *3* | *4* | *5* | *6* | *7* | *8* |
|---|---|---|---|---|---|---|---|
| 7 | SHG Membership Turnover : Separation Method (in%ge) | 3 | 5 | 3 | 5 | 13 | 3 |
| 8 | SHG Membership Turnover: Replacement Method (in % age) | 1 | - | 2 | 1 | - | 1 |
| 9 | SHG Membership Turnover : Flex Method (in % age) | 3 | 5 | 5 | 6 | 13 | 4 |
| 10 | SHG Turnover | 1 | - | 2 | 0 | - | 1 |

*Source:* field data.

Table 5.13 reveals the reasons for SHG members' drop-outs by SHG caste category. Highlighted data in the last row of the table reveals that out of total 52 number dropouts, the major reasons were non-payment of loan (27% of the total), misuse of group funds (13%), migration (12%), irregular payments and death (10 per cent each).

## SHGs Savings Behaviour

Savings by Self-Help Group members are fulcrum of micro-credit through SHG- bank linkage programme. Savings inculcate the habit of thrift pooling of savings and distribution of them according to the needs of the members are the basic tenets underlying their operations. Savings are the major component of corpus fund which is used for lending to the members of SHGs. Growth in the monthly volume of savings by SHG members is one of the valid measures of healthy micro-credit institutions such as SHGs. Without savings, SHGs wither and perish, thus savings is a central aspect of SHG existence and operations.

**Table 5.13**
**Reason for Drop-outs by Caste-wise SHGs**

| *Sl. No.* | *Caste-wise SHGs* | *Reasons for Drop-outs* | | | | | | | | | | *All* |
|---|---|---|---|---|---|---|---|---|---|---|---|---|
| | | *1* | *2* | *3* | *4* | *5* | *6* | *7* | *8* | *9* | *10* | |
| *1* | *2* | *3* | *4* | *5* | *6* | *7* | *8* | *9* | *10* | *11* | *12* | *13* |
| 1. | Minority SHGs(2) | | | 1 (50.00) | 1 (50.00) | | | | | | | 2 (100) |
| 2. | Mixed caste SHGs(32) | 3 (9.37) | 3 (9.37) | 2 (6.25) | 2 (6.25) | 9 (28.13) | 5 (15.63) | 2 (6.25) | 3 (9.37) | | 3 (9.38) | 32 (100) |
| 3 | BC SHGs (2) | | | | 1 (50.00) | 1 (50.00) | | | | | | 2 (100) |
| 4 | SC SHGs (14) | 2 (14.29) | 2 (14.28) | 2 (14.28) | 1 (7.14) | 4 (28.58) | 2 (14.29) | - | . | 1 (7.14) | - | 14 (100) |
| 5 | ST SHGs (2) | | | | 1 (50.00) | | | | | 1 (50.00 | | 2 (100) |
| 6. | All SHGs (52) | 5 (9.62) | 5 (9.62) | 5 (9.62) | 6 (11.53) | 14 (26.92) | 7 ( 13 .46) | 2 (3.85) | 3 (5.77) | 2 (3.84) | 3 (5.77) | 52 (100) |

Note: 1. Low saving capacity, 2. Group conflicts, 3. Irregular payments, 4. Marriage, 5. Death, 6. Migration, 7. Recovery of old loan, 8. Misuse of group funds, 9. High interest rates.

Self-help groups are generally known for its multiple contributions and saving (financial) contribution is one among parameters to judge the level of commitment of the group. Moving beyond, the group coherence as well as credit worthiness is also measured from the level of financial contributions. Not only the bank but also government initiated programmes/projects for women empowerment following the self-help group root do look at the financial soundness of the group as well as the transactions done by the groups. Hence, self-help groups without adequate saving is just considered as mere group of people congregated to address some issues at will without commitment.

Looking at the tenet and objectivity as well as the value of SHGs in alleviating poverty following the populist mode of project/programme execution, the study is attempting to study holistically the saving pattern of the SHGs and frequency of savings etc.

The caste and category-wise volume of initial and current monthly savings of SHGs is shown in Table 5.14 as well as in fig 5.2. As evidenced from the Table 5.14, that there is an increase in current monthly volume of savings across SHG caste categories, except the SHGs of Scheduled Tribe. In per centage terms the increase in savings is highest at 71.17 in BC SHGs followed by 68.29 in minority SHGs, 41.25 in mixed-caste SHGs, 20.29 in SC SHGs, and 12.5 in ST SHG.

All SHGs put together revealed a 39.47 per centage increase in savings. The per centage increase in savings reflects the economic status of caste hierarchy in the sample SHGs under the study. ***y*** value is calculated between initial year and current year savings across SHG caste categories. Since **y** value is 0.99, it can safely be concluded that there is high positive correlation between savings of initial year and current year for all SHG-caste categories.

**Table 5.14**

**Caste Category of SHGs by Volume of Annual Savings**

| *Sl. No.* | *Caste Category of SHGs* | *Initial Volume of Yearly Savings* | *Current Volume of Yearly Savings* | *Absolute Increase* | *% increase* |
|---|---|---|---|---|---|
| *1* | *2* | *3* | *4* | *5 (4–3)* | *6* |
| 1 | Minority SHGs (3) | 14,760 | 24,840 | 10,080 | 68.29 |
| 2 | Mixed-caste SHGs (91) | 6,14,160 | 8,67,480 | 2,53,320 | 41.25 |
| 3 | B.C. SHGs (5) | 26,640 | 45,600 | 18,960 | 71.17 |
| 4 | S.C. SHGs (20). | 1,07,640 | 1,29,480 | 21,840 | 20.29 |
| 5 | S.T. SHG (1) | 5,760 | 5,040 | -720 | -12.50 |
| 6 | All SHGs (120) | 7,68,960 | 10,72,440 | 3,03,480 | 39.47 |

**r (3,4)=0.99**

*Notes:* Figures in the parentheses in column 2 are number of SHGs

Figures in the parentheses in column 3 and 4 are average savings per SHG.

Figures in column 6 are per cent increases of current monthly savings over initial monthly Savings.

*Source:* Field data.

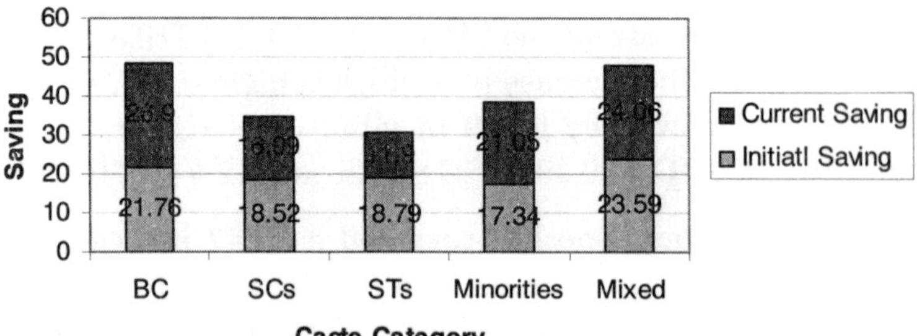


**Fig 5.2: Caste-wise per SHG Savings in Initial and current years**

Table 5.15 portrays distribution of sample SHGs by their initial monthly volume of savings cross-classified by current volume of monthly savings. Majority SHGs falling in the class intervals of initial monthly savings namely Rs.350-400,

**Table 5.15**

**Distribution of SHGs by SHG Monthly Average Initial and Current Volume of Savings**

| *Volume of SHG Initial Monthly Savings (in Rs.)* | *Current Volume of SHG Monthly Savings (in Rs.)* | | | | | | | *Total SHGs* |
|---|---|---|---|---|---|---|---|---|
| | *300-350* | *350-400* | *400-450* | *450-500* | *500-550* | *550-600* | *> 600* | |
| *1* | *2* | *3* | *4* | *5* | *6* | *7* | *8* | *9 (2 to 8)* |
| 300-350 | 10<br>(62.50) | 1<br>(6.25) | 2<br>(12.50) | - | - | - | 3<br>(18.75) | 16<br>(100) |
| 350-400 | - | 5<br>(25.00) | 2<br>(10.00) | 3<br>(15.00) | - | - | 10<br>(50.00) | 20<br>(100) |
| 400-450 | - | 1<br>(3.57) | 3<br>(10.72) | 4<br>(14.29) | 1<br>(3.57) | 3<br>(10.71) | 16<br>(57.14) | 28<br>(100) |
| 450-500 | - | - | 2<br>(33.33) | - | - | 1<br>(16.67) | 3<br>(50.00) | 6<br>(100) |
| 500-550 | - | - | - | - | 3<br>(20.00) | 4<br>(26.67) | 8<br>(53.33) | 15<br>(100) |
| 550-600 | - | - | - | - | - | 3<br>(50.00) | 3<br>(50.00) | 6<br>(100) |
| 600, and above | - | - | - | 1<br>(3.45) | 2<br>(6.90) | 2<br>(6.90) | 24<br>(82.75) | 29<br>(100) |
| Total | 10<br>(8.33) | 7<br>(5.84) | 9<br>(7.50) | 8<br>(6.67) | 6<br>(5.00) | 13<br>(10.83) | 67<br>(55.83) | 120<br>(100) |

*Note:* Figures in the Parentheses are percentages to row totals.
*Source:* Field data.

Rs.400-450, Rs.450-500 and Rs.500-550 registered improvement in the current monthly savings. Majority of SHGs classified in class intervals Rs.300-350 and Rs.600 and above either stagnated or regressed. Fifty per cent of SHGs in class interval 550-600 stagnated in their current monthly savings and other 50 per cent registered growth. From the table (Table 5.15) it can be inferred that majority of sample SHGs progressed in their current monthly savings as compared to their initial monthly savings.

Formation of self-help group is less immaterial to be noticed than of the functionality. It is also noticed during the interview with the respondents that functionality of many groups takes up on line with community development activities and primarily of non-financial in nature. However, survival, prosperity and becoming a means of income generation and sustenance of any self-help group is mostly regulated by the volume and time of financial transaction carried out since its inception. The study therefore put persistent effort to look at the financial transactions capability of different categories of self-help groups as well as by different community groups.

The facts collected are presented in Table 5.16. from the table it can be noticed that average per SHG annual deposits into banks is highest at Rs. 10,157 by mixed-caste SHGs, and was lowest at Rs. 5,328 by ST SHGs. Coming to withdrawals banks, annual per SHG withdrawals was highest at Rs. 9,599 by mixed-caste SHGs, and lowest at Rs.4,828 by ST SHGs.

Since Y values are of high magnitude at 0.99 between deposits and withdrawals by NGO-promoted SHGs, it can be concluded that there is high positive correlation between these two variables. The SHGs promoted by NGOs therefore are more vibrant and functionally better of than SHGs formulated by the Government. This may also be safely concluded that the procedure followed for formation of self-help groups by NGOs is little tough but teaches the ways of sustenance and therefore survive for long.

**Table 5.16**

**Caste-wise Distribution of NGO-promoted SHGs by the Amount Deposited and Withdrawn during 2002-03 to 2006-07**

| *Sl. No.* | *Caste Category of SHGs* | *Deposits* | | | *Withdrawals* | | | *Difference between SHG Annual Average Deposit and withdrawal* |
|---|---|---|---|---|---|---|---|---|
| | | *SHGs 5-year Total* | *SHGs 5-year Annual Average* | *Per SHG Annual Average* | *SHGs 5-year Total* | *SHGs 5-year Annual Average* | *Per SHG Annual Average* | |
| *1* | *2* | *3* | *4* | *5* | *6* | *7* | *8* | *9* (5–8) |
| 1 | Minority SHGs (1) | 35,280 | 35,280 | 7,056 | 32,280 | 32,280 | 6,456 | 600 |
| 2 | Mixed-caste SHGs (31) | 15,74,400 | 50,787 | 10,157 | 14,87,900 | 47,997 | 9,599 | 558 |
| 3 | B.C SHGs (2) | 87,120 | 43,560 | 8,712 | 81,120 | 40,560 | 8,112 | 600 |
| 4 | S.C SHGs (15) | 4,59,000 | 30,600 | 6,120 | 4,20,300 | 28,020 | 5,604 | 516 |
| 5 | S.T SHG (1) | 26,640 | 26,640 | 5,328 | 24,140 | 24,140 | 4,828 | 500 |
| 6 | All SHGs (50) | 21,82,440 | 43,649 | 8,730 | 20,45,740 | 40,917 | 8,183 | 547 |

r (3,6) =0.99
r (4,7) =0.99
r (5,8) =0.99

*Source:* field data

Deposits into and withdrawals from the bank account of SHGs across caste categories is shown in Table 5.17. Per SHG annual average deposits is highest at Rs.9,431 in mixed-caste SHGs followed by Rs.7,373 in BCs, SHGs, Rs.6,888 in minority SHGs, Rs.6,152 in SC SHGs and Rs.5,328 in ST SHGs. Similar pattern exist with regard to withdrawals. The highest amount per SHG annual average withdrawals is highest at Rs.8, 922 in mixed-caste SHGs followed Rs.6, 803 in BC SHGs, Rs.6, 388 in minority SHGs, Rs.5, 690 in SC SHGs and Rs 4,828 in ST SHGs. From the foregoing analysis it is clear that per SHG volume of deposits and withdrawals reflects the economic status of caste categories in the hierarchy of Indian society. Since Y values between deposits and withdrawals by all SHGs are of high magnitude, it can be deduced that there is high positive correlation between these two variables.

Deposits and withdrawals of Government-promoted SHGs and NGO-promoted SHGs across the caste-category are shown in Table 5.17 and Table 5.16 respectively. Analysis of information in both the tables shows that that NGO-promoted sample SHGs had higher amounts per SHG Annual Average Deposits and withdrawals as compared to Government-promoted SHGs, in all SHG caste categories.

SHGs classified into stagnating and growing SHGs on the parameters of per member savings behavior between inception and as on date are shown along caste categories in Table 5.18. All SHGs performance combined together reveals that per member savings are stagnant in 42.5 per cent of sample SHGs and growing in remaining 57.5 per cent of sample SHGs. Savings stagnating SHGs are 100 per cent in STs, 55 per cent in SCs 40.66 per cent in mixed- caste SHGs and 40 per cent in BC SHGs.

**Table 5.17**

**Caste-wise Distribution of SHGs by the Amount Deposited into, and Withdrawn From, the Banks: 2002-03 to 2006-07**

| *Sl. No.* | *Caste Category of SHGs* | *Deposits* | | | *Withdrawals* | | | *Difference between SHG Annual Average Deposit and withdrawal* |
|---|---|---|---|---|---|---|---|---|
| | | *SHGs 5-year . Total* | *SHGs 5-year Annual Average* | *Per SHG Annual Average* | *SHGs 5-year total* | *SHGs 5-year Annual Average* | *Per SHG Annual Average* | |
| *1* | *2* | *3* | *4* | *5* | *6* | *7* | *8* | *9 (5-8)* |
| 1 | Minority SHGs (3) | 1,03,320 | 34,440 | 6,888 | 95,820 | 31,940 | 6,388 | 500 |
| 2 | Mixed-caste SHGs (91) | 42,91,200 | 47,156 | 9,431 | 40,59,700 | 44,612 | 8,922 | 509 |
| 3 | B.C SHGs (5) | 1,84,320 | 36,864 | 7,373 | 1,70,070 | 34,014 | 6,803 | 570 |
| 4 | S.C SHGs (20) | 6,15,240 | 30,762 | 6,152 | 5,69,040 | 28,452 | 5,690 | 462 |
| 5 | S.T SHG (1) | 26,640 | 26,640 | 5,328 | 24,140 | 24,140 | 4,828 | 500 |
| 6 | All SHGs (120) | 52,20,720 | 43,506 | 8,701 | 49,18,770 | 40,990 | 8,198 | 503 |

r (3,6) =1.00.
r (4,7) =0.99.
r (5,8) =0.99.

*Source:* Field Data.

**Table 5.18**
**Per Member Monthly Savings since Inception by Caste**

| *Sl. No.* | *Caste Category of SHGs* | *Compared to Their Original Savings* | | |
|---|---|---|---|---|
| | | *Savings Stagnating SHGs* | *Savings Growing SHGs* | *Total* |
| 1 | Minority SHGs (3) | | 3<br>(100) | 3<br>(100) |
| 2 | Mixed-caste SHG (91) | 37<br>(40.66) | 54<br>(59.34) | 91<br>(100) |
| 3 | BC SHGs ('5) | 2<br>(40.00) | 3<br>(60.00) | 5<br>( 100) |
| 4 | S.C SHGs (20) | 11<br>(55.00) | 9<br>(45.00) | 20<br>(100) |
| 5 | S.T SHGs (I) | 1<br>(100) | - | 1<br>(100) |
| 6 | All SHGs (120) | 51<br>(42.50) | 69<br>(57.50) | 120<br>(100) |

cal. $X^2$ value=4.99$^{NS}$ (NS: Not Significant).
tab $X^2$ value at 4 def=9.49.

*Note:* Figures in the parentheses are per centage to row totals.

*Source:* Field data.

From the preceding analysis it can be informed that majority of SHGs in all caste categories experienced growthin per member savings, the only exception being SC SHGs. Since calculated $X^2$ Value is less than tabulated $X^2$ value, it can be analyzed that there is statistically no difference between SHG caste categories as to proportion of SHGs falling in savings growing category and savings stagnating category. The null hypothesis is accepted.

Regularity in payment is being chosen as a parameter of utmost importance to the functionality of self-help groups. The study attempted to capture the saving trend of SHG members and hence, gathered information in line with regular savers and intermittent saver by caste group. The table 5.19 shows the saving trend by different caste groups.

Concentrating on extreme bottom of the Table 5.19, it can be observed 94 per cent of SHG members of all caste categories are continuous savers and only 6 per cent are intermittent savers in the case of Government-promoted SHGs. In the case of NGOs-promoted SHGs the same pattern exists as 94 and 6 per cent of members of all caste categories are continues and intermittent respectively. It is heartening to note that across caste categories more than 90 per cent of SHG members are continues savers both in Government - promoted and NGOs-promoted SHGs. Since calculated $X^2$ Value is less than table $X^2$ value, for all SHG caste categories as to number of SHGs falling under continues saving category and intermittent category, it can be inference that there is statistically no significant difference between SHG caste categories as to proportion of SHGs falling in continues savings category and intermittent savings stagnating category. The null hypothesis is accepted.

The study also intended to capture information on per member monthly current savings across SHG caste categories and the finding is capitulated in Table 5.20. Lowest and highest per member monthly savings are Rs.30 in ST SHGs, Rs.30 and Rs.50 in SC SHGs, Rs.30 and Rs.100 in BC SHGs, Rs.50 and Rs.60 in Minority SHGs, Rs.30 and more than Rs.100 in mixed caste SHGs and all caste categories SHGs clubbed together.

Per member weighted average current monthly savings are highest at Rs.66 in BC SHGs, followed by 60.11 in mixed-

**Table 5.19**
**Distribution of SHG Members by Promoters and Savings Intensity**

| Sl. No. | Members | NGO-promoted SHGs | | | Government-promoted SHGs | | |
|---|---|---|---|---|---|---|---|
| | | Continuous Savers | Intermittent Savers | Total | Continuous Savers | Intermittent Savers | Total |
| 1 | Minority SHGs members (39) | 11 (100) | - | 11 (100) | 26 (92.86) | 2 (7.14) | 28 (100) |
| 2 | Mixed-caste SHGs Members (1191) | 388 (94.40) | 23 (5.59) | 411 (100) | 732 (93.85) | 48 (6.15) | 780 (100) |
| 3 | B.C SHGs Members (58) | 22 (91.67) | 2 (8.33) | 24 (100) | 31 (91.18) | 3 (8.82) | 34 (100) |
| 4 | S.G SHGs Members (265) | 182 (94.30) | 11 (5.70) | 193 (100) | 68 (94.44) | 4 (5.56) | 72 (100) |
| 5 | S.T SHGs Members (14) | 13 (92.86) | 1 (7.14) | 14 (100) | - | - | - |
| 6 | All SHGs members (1567) | 616 (94.33) | 37 (5.66) | 653 (100) | 857 (93.76) | 57 (6.24) | 914 (100) |
| | | **cal. $X^2$ value=1.04$^{NS}$ (NS: Not Significant.) tab $X^2$ value at 4 def=9.49** | | | **cal. $X^2$ value=0.49$^{NS}$ (NS: Not Significant) tab $X^2$ value at 4 def=9.49** | | |

*Note:* Figures in the parentheses are per centages to row totals

*Source:* Field data.

## Table 5.20
## Distribution of SHGs by Caste Categories and the Volume of Monthly Current Savings per Member (Nos.)

| *Sl. No.* | *Caste Category of SHGs* | *Volume of Monthly Savings per Member (in Rs.)* | | | | | | | *Total* | *Per Member Waited Average Current Monthly Savings* |
|---|---|---|---|---|---|---|---|---|---|---|
| | | *30* | *40* | *50* | *60* | *70* | *100* | *>100** | | |
| *1* | *2* | *3* | *4* | *5* | *6* | *7* | *8* | *9* | *10* (3 to 9) | *11* |
| 1 | Minority SHGs | - | - | 2 (66.67) | 1 (33.33) | - | - | - | 3 (100) | 53.33 |
| 2 | Mixed-caste SHGs | 20 (21.98) | 4 (4.40) | 36 (39.56) | 4 (4.39) | 4 (4.40) | 18 (19.78) | 5 (5.49) | 91 (100) | 60.11 |
| 3 | B.C SHGs | 1 (20.00) | - | 2 (40.00) | | | 2 (40.00) | | 5 (100) | 66.00 |
| 4 | SC SHGs | 7 (35.00) | 5 (25.00) | 8 (40.00) | - | - | - | - | 20 (100) | 40.50 |
| 5 | S.T SHGs | 1 - | - | - | - | - | - | (100) | 1 (100) | 30.00 |
| 6 | All SHGs | 29 (24.17) | 9 (7.50) | 48 (40.00) | 5 (4.17) | 4 (3.33) | 20 (16.66) | 5 (4.17) | 120 (100) | 56.67 |

*Note:* * Five SHGs have per member current monthly savings of Rs.130, Rs. 120, Rs.120, Rs.110, Rs, 110 in that order.
Figures in the Parentheses are percentages to row totals.

*Source:* Field data.

## Table 5.21
## Growth of Per Member Monthly Savings since Inception Mixed-caste SHGs

| Sl. No. | Per Member Initial Monthly Savings (in Rs.) | SHGs with Subsequent Growth in Per Member Monthly Savings (in Rs.) | | | | | | | Total |
|---|---|---|---|---|---|---|---|---|---|
| | | 30 | 40 | 50 | 60 | 70 | 100 | >100 | |
| 1 | 2 | 3 | 4 | 5 | 6 | 7 | 8 | 9 | 10 (3 to 9) |
| 1 | 30 | 20<br>(37.74) | 3<br>(5.66) | 25<br>(47.17) | 3<br>(5.66) | - | 2<br>(3.77) | - | 53<br>(100) |
| 2 | 40 | - | 1<br>(100) | - | - | - | - | - | 1<br>(100) |
| 3 | 50 | - | - | 11<br>(44.00) | - | 2<br>(8.00) | 12<br>(48.00) | - | 25<br>(100) |
| 4 | 60 | - | - | - | 1<br>(50.00) | - | 1<br>(50.00) | - | 2<br>(100) |
| 5 | 70 | - | - | - | - | 2<br>(66.67) | 1<br>(33.33) | - | 3<br>(100) |
| 6 | 100 | - | - | - | - | - | 2<br>(28.57) | 5<br>(71.43) | 7<br>(100) |

*Note:* Figures in the parentheses are percentages to row totals.
*Source:* Field data.

caste SHGs, Rs.53.33 in minority SHG, Rs.40.50 in SC SHGs, and Rs.30 in ST SHGs all caste put together the weighted average current savings are Rs.56.67. Taking into account above analysis it can be observed that per member weighted average savings are higher in BC-SHGs and mixed caste SHGs than overall average, and lower in minority, SC, ST, SHGs than overall average.

Table 5.21 presents improvement in per member savings as compared to per member initial monthly savings for mixed-castes SHGs. In 53 SHGs whose per member initial monthly savings were Rs. 30, 62 per cent of them witnessed growth in per member monthly savings. One SHG whose per member initial monthly savings was Rs. 40 did not show any growth in per member monthly savings. In 25 SHGs whose per member monthly initial savings was Rs.50, 56 per cent of them noticed growth in savings. Fifty, 33 and 71 per cent of sample SHGs in Rs.60, Rs.70 and Rs.100 initial per member savings groups respectively experienced subsequent growth in savings.

From the preceding analysis it can be concluded that majority of the SHGs with the initial per member monthly savings of Rs.30, Rs.50, Rs.60 and Rs.100 experienced growth in subsequent saving, the exceptions being SHGs with per member monthly initial savings Rs.50 and Rs.70.

Growth of per member monthly savings in SC SHGs is shown in Table 5.22. In 16 SHGs having per member initial monthly savings is Rs.30, 9 SHGs (53%) of them experienced growth in savings. All other SHGs numbering 11 (47%) had stagnated in per member monthly savings. Based on above analysis it can be inference that majority of the SC SHGs witnessed growth in per monthly savings.

**Table 5.22**
**Per Member Monthly Savings since Inception: SC SHGs**

| *Sl. No.* | *Per Member Initial Monthly Savings* | *Growth in Per Members Monthly Savings* | | | |
|---|---|---|---|---|---|
| | | *30* | *40* | *50* | *Total* |
| 1 | 30 | 7(43.75) | 2(12.50) | 7(43.75) | 16(100) |
| 2 | 40 | - | 3(100) | - | 3(100) |
| 3 | 50 | - | - | 1(100) | 1(100) |

*Note:* Figures in the parentheses are per centages to row totals.
*Source:* Field data.

## SHG-Bank Loans

Group-based lending by banks linking SHGs is characteristic feature of SHG-bank linkage programme. Guided by effective financial management banks come forward to lend loans to SHGs on group basis and group norms are operative in loan repayment to the lending banks. In order to be eligible to access loan, the SHGs should mobilize the savings from their members and deposit them with the linked banks so as to avail higher volumes of loans. Government in the past so as to help the rural poor gain access to bank loans initiated revolving fund scheme under which SHGs of economically poorer social segments were granted amounts which, in truth, served the seed capital or savings of the SHGs using SHGs gained access to bank loans.

With the introduction of three per cent interest loan scheme by Government of Andhra Pradesh the revolving fund scheme operation came to a halt. Growth of loan amounts to SHGs is one of the indicators of financial health of SHG operations. It is summed up that higher is the loan velocity better is the financial performance of SHGs.

Table 5.23 indicates that the decision - making regarding SHG loans and pattern of lending in SHGs caste category - wise. Across SHG caste categories majority of loan sanctions decisions were made by leaders and members collectively. For all castes put together their mode of decision- making was as high as 80 per cent. As can be seen from the Table 5.23 that there are two broad patterns of lending were noticed across SHG caste categories. All SHGs combined together in 41 per cent of the SHGs loans were equally distributed among needy members, followed by 30 per cent of SHGs in which loans were equally distributed irrespective needs of their members, and 29 per cent of SHGs in which loan amounts were distributed based on members' needs.

Revolving fund was given by the Government during the early years to improve the corpus fund of the SHGs. The revolving support was extended according to their membership size. Table 5.24 gives details revolving fund given to SHGs of different caste groups by promoters. The average revolving fund per SHG in Government-promoted SHGs was Rs.11,262 as compared to that of Rs.11,057 in NGO-promoted SHGs. The average revolving fund is higher in BC and SC SHGs and lower in minority and mixed-caste SHGs as compared to overall average in the Government-promoted SHG categories. In NGO-promoted SHG categories the average revolving fund is lower than overall average amount in all SHG caste-categories, the only exception being revealed in the mixed-caste SHGs.

Caste as well as promoter wise accessibility of loan by the SHGs are captured in Table 5.25. Paying attention on the bottom extreme of the Table 5.25 it can be seen that 49 per cent of all caste category sample SHGs have availed two repeat loans followed by 20 per cent availing one repeat loan. Similarly, there are 11 per cent availed three repeat loans and equal per cent have also been accessed four repeat loans. There are only 5 per cent sample SHGs availed five repeat loans.

## Table 5.23
## SHGs Loan Lending Procedures by Caste

| Sl. No. | Dimension | SHG Categories | | | | | |
|---|---|---|---|---|---|---|---|
| | | BC SHGs | SC SHGs | ST SHGs | Minority SHGs | Mixed-caste SHGs | All SHGs |
| *1* | *2* | *3* | *4* | *5* | *6* | *7* | *8* |
| 1 | Decision-makers in Loan Sanctions at SHG Level | | | | | | |
| a | Leaders Only | - | 4 (20.00) | - | - | 4 (4.40) | 8 (6.67) |
| b | Members Collectively | 1 (20.00) | 3 (15.00) | - | 1 (33.33) | 11 (12.09) | 16 (13.33) |
| c | Leaders and Members Collectively | 4 (80.00) | 13 (65.00) | 1 (100) | 2 (66.67) | 76 (83.52) | 96 (80.00) |
| c | Sub-total (a+b+c) | 5 (100) | 20 (100) | 1 (100) | 3 (100) | 91 (100) | 120 (100) |
| 2 | Pattern of Lending of the Latest Loan | | | | | | |
| a | Equal Distribution Among Members | 2 (40.00) | 4 (20.00) | 1 (100) | 1 (33.33) | 28 (30.77) | 36 (30.00) |
| b | Equal Distribution Among Those Members who Needed Loans | 2 (40.00) | 7 (35.00) | - | 1 (33.33) | 39 (42.86) | 49 (40.83) |
| c | Lending Based on Members Needs | 1 (20.00) | 9 (45.00) | - | 1 (33.34) | 24 (26.37) | 35 (29.17) |
| d | Sub-total (a+b+c) | 5 (100) | 20 (100) | 1 (100) | 3 (100) | 91 (100) | 120 (100) |

*Note:* Figures is parentheses are percentages to column sub-totals.
*Sources:* Field Data.

## Table 5.24
## Revolving Fund Availed by SHGs by Caste Categories and Promoting Agencies

(in Rs.)

| *Sl. No.* | *Caste Category of SHGs* | *Government-promoted SHGs* | | *N GO-promoted SHGs* | | *Deference Between 4 and 6* |
|---|---|---|---|---|---|---|
| | | *Amount* | *Average* | *Amount* | *Average* | |
| *1* | *2* | *3* | *4* | *5* | *6* | *7* |
| 1 | Minority SHGs | 20,000 (2) | 10,000 | 10,000 (1) | 10,000 | |
| 2 | Mixed-caste SHGs | 4,61,841 (42) | 10,996.21 | 2,29,000 (20) | 11,450 | 453.79 |
| 3 | B.C SHGs | 25,000 (2) | 12,500 | 10,000 (1) | 10,000 | 2,500 |
| 4 | S.C SHGs | 45,000 (3) | 15,000 | 1,28,000 (12) | 10,666.67 | 4,333.33 |
| 5 | S.T SHGs | - | - | 10,000 (1) | 10,000 | 10,000 |
| 6 | All SHGs | 5,51,841 (49) | 11,262.06 | 3,87,000 (35) | 11,057.14 | 204.92 |

*Notes:* 1. Out of sample 70 Government-promoted SHGs and 50 NGO-promoted SHGs, 49 in the formal and 35 in the latter categories availed revolving facility.

2. Figures in the parentheses are number of SHGs that availed revolving fund facility.

*Source:* Field data.

From the above analysis it can be concluded that 80 per cent of NGO-promoted all caste category SHGs took one or two repeat loans where as it was limited to 61 per cent of Government-promoted all caste category SHGs. It can also be seen from the above table that only mixed-caste SHGs promoted by Government and NGOs took fourth repeat loans and fifth repeat loans with exception of one SHG each under BC and minority SHG categories.

**Table 5.25**
**Caste and Promoter-wise Distribution of SHGs by Number of Loans Taken from SHG-linked Banks Since inception**

| *Sl. No.* | *Caste Category of SHG and Promotes* | | *Repeat Loans* | | | | | |
|---|---|---|---|---|---|---|---|---|
| | | | *1st* | *2nd* | *3rd* | *4th* | *5th* | *Total* |
| *1* | *2* | *3* | *4* | *5* | *6* | *7* | *8(3 to 7)* | |
| 1 | Minority SHGs | (3) | - | - | 2 (66.67) | - | 1 (33.33) | 3(1 00) |
| | a. Govt-promoted | (2) | - | - | 1 (50.00) | - | 1 (50.00) | 2(00) |
| | b. NGO-promoted | (1) | - | - | 1 (100.00) | - | - | 1 (100) |
| 2 | Mixed caste SHGs | (91) | 15 (6.48) | 45 (49.46) | 14(5.38) | 12(3.19) | 5 (5.49) | 91 (100) |
| | a. Government -promoted | (60) | 9 (15.00) | 27 (45.00) | 9(5.00) | 10(6.67) | 5 (8.33) | 60 (100) |
| | b. NGO-promoted | (31) | 6 (19.35) | 18 (58.06) | 5(6.13) | 2 (6.45) | - | 31 (100) |
| 3 | B.C SHGs | (5) | - | 3 (60.00) | 1 (20.00) | 1 (20.00) | - | 5 (100) |
| | a. Govt-promoted | (3) | - | 2 (66.67) | - | 1 (33.33) | - | 3(00) |
| | b. NGO-promoted | (2) | - | 1 (50.00) | 1 (50.00) | - | - | 2(100) |
| 4 | SC SHGs | (20) | 9 (45.00) | 10 (50.00) | 1 (5.00) | - | - | 20 (100) |
| | a. Government -promoted | (5) | 3 (60.00) | 2 (40.00) | - | - | - | 5 (100) |
| | b. NGO-promoted | (15) | 6 (40.00) | 8 (53.33) | 1 (6.67) | - | - | 15 (100) |

(Contd...)

| | | | | | | | | |
|---|---|---|---|---|---|---|---|---|
| 5 | ST SHGs | (0) | - | 1 (100.00) | - | - | - | 1 (100) |
| | a. Government –promoted | (-) | - | - | - | - | - | - |
| | b. NGO-promoted | (1) | - | 1 (100.00) | - | - | - | 1 (100) |
| 6. | All SHGs | (120) | 24 (20.00) | 59 (49.17) | 18(15.00) | 13 (10.83) | 6. (5.00) | 120 (100) |
| | a. Govt-promoted | (70) | 12 (17.14) | 31 (44.28) | 10(4.29) | 11 (5.71) | 6 (8.58) | 70 000) |
| | b. NGO-promoted | (50) | 12 (24.00) | 28 (56.00) | 8 (16.00) | 2 (4.00) | - | 50 (100) |

*Note:* Figures in parentheses are percentages to row totals.
*Sources:* Field data.

Table 5.26 gives details of time taken for obtaining repeat loans after repayment of the preceding loans. All together 278 repeat loans were taken by 120 sample SHGs averaging 2 loans per SHG. Out of total 278 repeat loans 43, 35, 13, seven and two per cent are first, second, third, fourth and fifth repeat loans respectively. Eighty eight, 82, 84, 90, 100 per cent of first, second, third, fourth and fifth repeat loans were taken respectively within four months after payment of preceding loans. In the rest of the minority of the cases time taken for getting repeat loans ranged from the minimum of five months to the maximum of 30 months and above.

Loan amounts requested and sanctioned and difference between them are shown in Table 5.27 for SHG caste-categories promoter wise. Average difference between requested and sanctioned loan amounts is highest at Rs.40,000 in BC SHGs followed by Rs.38,500 in minority SHGs, Rs.32,917 in mixed-caste SHGs and Rs.21,000 in SC SHGs in Government-promoted SHG categories. Overall average difference of all SHG caste categories put together is Rs.32,529.

In NGO promoted SHGs the average difference is highest at Rs.62,500 in BC SHGs followed by Rs.31,839 in mixed caste SHGs, Rs.30,000 in ST SHGs, Rs.25,000 in minority SHGs and Rs.23,000 in SC SHGs. For all SHG caste categories put together the average difference Rs.30,240.

Table 5.28 displays range of interest rates and loan repayment periods SHG caste category-wise cross classified by SHG promoters. Across SHG caste categories the minimum interests on loans to Government–promoted SHGs and NGO-promoted are same, but variations can be noticed in maximum rates of interests on loans. The maximum rates of interests on loans in Government promoted SHGs are 18, 24 and 30 per cent in minority, BC, and SC and mixed caste SHGs respectively. Maximum interest rates on loans are on higher side in NGO-promoted SHGs than those in Government-promoted SHGs. The maximum rates of interest on loans to NGO-promoted SHGs are 18,30,33 and 36 per cent in ST, minority, BC and SC and mixed caste SHGs in that order with regard to loan repayment period in both Government and NGO-promoted SHGs the minimum period is 10 months which is same across SHG caste categories. The maximum loan repayment period in Government -promoted SHGs was 24 months in BC, SC and minority SHGs and 36 months in mixed caste SHGs respectively.

Panel A of Table 5.29 shows the different types of average opportunity costs incurred in obtaining latest bank loans by SHG caste categories. Focusing on right extreme of the table it can be noticed that for all SHG caste categories put together the major components of average opportunity costs were: grease money (30% of average total cost) followed by records/stationary (16%), travel cost (16%), and expendi-ture on food in visits to banks (12%). These four cost components put together account for 74 per cent of average total opportunity cost of latest bank loan to all SHGs put together. The same pattern exists across SHG caste categories as to the major components of total average opportunity cost of bank loans.

Panel B of Table 5.29 shows the opportunity cost as per centage of the loan for all SHG caste categories. It was highest at 3.65 per cent in SC SHGs followed by 2.99 per cent in mixed-caste SHGs, 2.85 per cent in all SHG caste categories, 1.55 per cent in OC SHGs, 1.17 in ST SHGs and 0.97 per cent in minority caste SHGs.

Coming to on time of savings in sample SHGs, it can be said that in 53, 29, 12 and 8 per cent of SHGs savings payments were made on time to the extent of 100 per cent, ≥ 90 but less than 100 per cent, 70 to 89 per cent, and less than 70 per cent respectively.

**Table 5.26**
**Distribution of SHGs by Time Taken for Obtaining Repeat Loans after Repayment of the Preceding Loans**

| *No. of Repeat Loans* | | *Time Taken (in Months)* 1 | 2 | 3 | 4 | 5 | 6 | 6-12 | 12-18 | 18-24 | 24-30 | 30 and Above | *Total* |
|---|---|---|---|---|---|---|---|---|---|---|---|---|---|
| *1* | *2* | *3* | *4* | *5* | *6* | *7* | *8* | *9* | *10* | *11* | *12* | | *13* |
| 1st | (120) | 41<br>(34.17) | 36<br>(30.00) | 21<br>(17.50) | 7<br>(5.83) | 3<br>(2.50) | 4<br>(3.33) | 3<br>(2.50) | - | 2<br>(1.67) | 1<br>(0.83) | 2<br>(1.67) | 120<br>[43.17]<br>(100) |
| 2nd | (96) | 24<br>(25.00) | 29<br>(30.21) | 13<br>(13.54) | 12<br>(12.50) | 14<br>(14.59) | 1<br>- | (1.04) | 2<br>- | (2.08) | - | 1<br>(1.04) | 96<br>[34.53]<br>(100) |
| 3rd | (37) | -<br>- | 7<br>(18.92) | 16<br>(43.24) | 8<br>(21.62) | - | 1<br>(2.70) | 3<br>(8.12) | 1<br>(2.70) | - | - | 1<br>(2.70) | 37<br>[13.31]<br>(100) |
| 4th | (19) | -<br>- | 4<br>(21.05) | 13<br>(68.43) | - | 1<br>(5.26) | 1<br>(5.26) | - | - | - | - | - | 19<br>[6.83]<br>(100) |

| | | | | | | | | | | | | | |
|---|---|---|---|---|---|---|---|---|---|---|---|---|---|
| 5th | (6) | - | 2 | 3 | 1 | | | | | | | - | 6 |
| | | - | (33.33) | (50.00) | (16.67) | - | - | - | - | - | - | - | [2.16] |
| | | | | | | | | | | | | | (100) |
| Total | | 65 | 78 | 66 | 28 | 18 | 6 | 7 | 1 | 4 | 1 | 4 | 278 |
| | | (23.38) | (28.06) | (23.74) | (10.07) | (6.47) | (2.16) | (2.52) | (0.36) | (1.44) | (0.36) | (1.44) | [100] |
| | | | | | | | | | | | | | (100) |

*Notes:*

1. Figures in parentheses ( ) are percentages to row totals.
2. Figures in square brackets [ ] are percentages to column totals.

*Sources:* Field data.

**Table 5.27**
**Status of Loan Requested and Sanctioned by Caste, Category and Promoter-wise**

| *Sl. No.* | *Caste-Category of SHGs* | *Government-promoted SHGs* | | | *NGO-promoted SHGs* | | |
|---|---|---|---|---|---|---|---|
| | | *Request Loan Amount* | *Sanctioned Loan Amount* | *Difference* | *Request Loan Amount* | *Sanctioned Loan Amount* | *Difference* |
| *1* | *2* | *3* | *4* | *5 (3-4)* | *6* | *7* | *8 (6-7)* |
| 1 | Minority SHGs | 3,20,000<br>(2)<br>[1,60,000] | 2.43.000<br>(2)<br>[1,21,500] | 77,000<br><br>[38,500] | 1,00,000<br>(1)<br>[1,00,000] | 75,000<br>(1)<br>[75,000] | 25,000<br><br>[25,000] |
| 2 | Mixed caste SHGs | 53,35,500<br>(60)<br>[88,925] | 33.60.500<br>(60)<br>[56,008] | 19,75,000<br><br>[32,917] | 24,72,000<br>(31)<br>[79,742] | 14,85,000<br>(31)<br>[47,903] | 9,87,000<br><br>[31,839] |
| 3 | B.C. SHGs | 3,60,000<br>(3)<br>[1,20,000] | 2.40.000<br>(3)<br>[80,000] | 1,20,000<br><br>[40,000] | 3,00,000<br>(2)<br>[1,50,000] | 1,75,000<br>(2)<br>[87,500] | 1,25,000<br><br>[62,500] |
| 4 | SC SHGs | 2,95,000<br>(5)<br>[59,000] | 1.90.000<br>(5)<br>[38,000] | 1,05,000<br><br>[21,000] | 8,36,000<br>(15)<br>[55,733] | 4,91,000<br>(15)<br>[32,733] | 3,45,000<br><br>[23,000] |
| 5 | ST SHGs | - | - | - | 1,00,000<br>(1)<br>[1,00,000] | 70,000<br>(1)<br>[70,000] | 30,000<br><br>[30,000] |
| 6 | All SHGs | 63,10,500<br>(70)<br>[90,150] | 40.33.500<br>(70)<br>[57,621] | 22,77,000<br><br>[32,529] | 38,08,000<br>(50)<br>[76,160] | 22,96,000<br>(50)<br>[45,920] | 15,12,000<br><br>[30,240] |

*Notes:* 1. Figures in the parentheses ( ) are number of SHGs that requested for and were sanctioned loans by banks.
2. Figures in the square brackets [ ] are average amount of loan

*Sources:* Field Data.

**Table 5.28**

**Range of Interest Rates and Repayment period by Caste**

| *Sl. No* | *Caste-wise SHG Category* | *Range of Interest Rates (per cent)* | | *Range of Repayment eriod (in months)* | |
|---|---|---|---|---|---|
| | | *Government - Promoted SHGs* | *NGO-promoted SHGs* | *Government - Promoted SHGs* | *NGO-promoted SHGs* |
| *1* | *2* | *3* | *4* | *5* | *6* |
| 1 | Minority SHGs | 12-18 | 12-30 | 10-24 | 10-24 |
| 2 | Mixed-caste CategorySHGs | 12-30 | 12-36 | 10-30 | 10-36 |
| 3 | BC SHGs | 12-24 | 12-33 | 10-24 | 10-18 |
| 4 | SC SHGs | 12-30 | 12-36 | 10-24 | 10-24 |
| 5 | ST SHGs | - | 12-18 | - | 10-12 |
| 6 | All SHGs | 12-30 | 12-36 | 10-30 | 10-36 |

*Sources:* Field data

**Table 5.29**
**Average Opportunity Costs for Obtaining Loan by SHG in Caste Category-wise**

| *Sl. No.* | *Components of Average Opportunity cost* | *BC SHGs* | *SC SHGs* | *ST SHGs* | *Minority SHGs* | *Mixed-caste SHGs* | *All SHGs* |
|---|---|---|---|---|---|---|---|
| | *1* | *2* | *3* | *4* | *5* | *6* | *7* |
| | **Panel- A** | | | | | | |
| 1 | Travel cost | 235 (18.23) | 238 (19.15) | 174 (21.19) | 175 (17.00) | 246 (15.43) | 242 (16.10) |
| 2 | Expenditure on Food in Visits to Banks | 174 (13.50) | 160 (12.87) | 130 (15.83) | 115 (11 18) | 180 (11.29) | 174 (11.57) |
| 3 | Daily Wages/Other Incomes Foregone During the Days of Visit | 80 (6.21) | 40 (3.22) | - | 75 (7.29) | 65 (4.08) | 61 (4.06) |
| 4 | Bribes | 300 (23.27) | 300 (24.13) | 200 (24.36) | 245 (23.81) | 550 (34.50) | 487 (32.40) |
| 5 | Loan Documentation | 25 (1.94) | 30 (2.41) | 27 (3.29) | 29 (2.82) | 27 (1.69) | 29 (1.93) |
| 6 | Payments to Book-keeper, Animator | 50 (3.88) | 65 (5.23) | 60 (7.31) | 50 (4.86) | 65 (4.08) | 64 (4.26) |

| | | | | | | | |
|---|---|---|---|---|---|---|---|
| 7 | Records/ Stationery | 225<br>(17.46) | 234<br>(18.83) | 230<br>(28.02) | 220<br>(21.38) | 236<br>(14.81) | 235<br>(15.64) |
| 8 | Service Charges (NGOs) | 150<br>(11.63) | 136<br>(10.94) | - | 120<br>(11.66) | 140<br>(8.79) | 138<br>(9.18) |
| 9 | Any Other Processing Charges | 50<br>(3.88) | 40<br>(3.22) | - | - | 85<br>(5.33) | 73<br>(4.86) |
| 10 | Total Average Opportunity Cost | 1289<br>(100) | 1243<br>(100) | 821<br>(100) | 1029<br>(100) | 1594<br>(100) | 1503<br>(100) |
| | **Panel B** | | | | | | |
| 11 | Total Latest Loan Amount (in Rs.) | 415,000 | 681,000 | 70,000 | 318,000 | 4,845,500 | 6,329,500 |
| 12 | Total Opportunity Cost (in Rs.) | 6,445 | 24,860 | 821 | 3,087 | 145,054 | 180,360 |
| 13 | Opportunity Cost as % age of the Latest Loan Amount(12+11 × 100) | (1.55) | (3.65) | (1.17) | (0.97) | (2.99) | (2.85) |

*Note:* Figures in the parentheses are percentages to column totals in panel-A.
*Sources:* Field data

Table 5.30 gives information on the end-uses of bank loans by SHG members' caste category-wise. Paying attention to the last column of the table it can be inferred that 52, 22 and 26 per cent of members of sample SHGs used their loans for production, consumption and other purposes respectively. It is worth noticing that almost 22 per cent beneficiaries intending to avail loans for consumptive purposes (day-to-day requirements), followed by 18 per cent requiring the loan for 'purchase of milk cow for starting small enterprise and business'. Category-wise disintegration of the collected statistics reveals that a significant proportion of scheduled caste community self-help groups requires loan for consumption purposes followed by the minorities and SCs.

Loan repayment is another category of parameters to measure the efficiency of self-help groups. The loan repayment practice as well as behaviour of sample SHG beneficiaries from the selected regions is captured in Table 5.31. It can be observed from the table that the loan repayment period of the latest loan for 49 per cent of sample SHGs is 15 months followed by 20,15,12, and 5 per cent SHGs reported of loan repayment periods 12, 20, 24, and 30 months respectively. The defaulting groups are more in mixed groups followed by SC groups. It is further observed that the more repayments are being done within the period of 20 months.

Table 5.32 exhibits drop-out members caste category-wise cross-classified by defaulted and non-defaulted categories. Paying attention, to the margins of the table it can be observed that drop-outs from mixed caste SHG groups accounted for 62 per cent of total drop-outs followed by these from SC SHG groups for 27 per cent. Of total dropout members 85 per cent of them were defaulted members and the remaining 15 per cent were non-defaulted members. In 21 per cent of drop-out members their savings exceeded loan out-standings were as in 79 per cent of drop-out membership loan outstanding exceeded their savings.

Since calculated $\mathbf{X}^2$ value is less than Table $\mathbf{X}^2$value, it can be concluded that difference between caste categories as to number of SHGs drop-out numbers falling in savings more than loan outstanding category and loan outstanding more than saving category. Since calculated $\mathbf{X}^2$ Value is less than Table value , it can be concluded that the difference between caste categories as to number of SHGs dropout numbers falling in savings more than loan outstanding category and loan outstanding more than savings category.

Table 5.33 illustrates actions taken for recovering loans from defaulted SHG members' caste category - wise and impact of delayed / outstanding payments. Focusing on right extreme of the Table it can be seen that peer pressure (34%), no action (27%) and non-eligibility for further loans until the outstanding loan is cleared (19%) are the three major measures for recovery of loans. It is noticed from the table that the loan recovery strategy is stringent in case of Mixed-caste SHGs. Interesting all the loan recovery measures are being tried and tested. The ST and BC community are sincere in payment and hence, very minimal application of loan recovery measures are reported off.

Coming to the impact, 61 and 33 per cent of the defaulted members felt repeat loans were delayed and denied respectively. Seventy Three defaulted members delayed but paid the latest loans and from 27 members the loans are still outstanding. It is a fact to be noticed that the SHG beneficiaries across the caste groups are aware of the delayed and non-approval of the second dose of loan from Andhra Bank.

Table 5.34 sets out procedures and end-use of bank loans to SHGs caste- wise. Highlighting the data in the last column

**Table 5.30**
**Caste and Categories-wise Loan Purposes by SHG Members**

| *Sl. No.* | *Loans purposes (N =1567 SHG Members)* | *Caste Categories* | | | | | |
|---|---|---|---|---|---|---|---|
| | | *Minorities* | *BCs.* | *SCs.* | *STs.* | *OCs.* | *Total Members* |
| *1* | *2* | *3* | *4* | *5* | *6* | *7* | *8* |
| 1 | Production Purposes | 2 (1.17) | 13 (3.11) | 7 (1.74) | - | 20 (3.90) | 42 (2.68) |
| 2 | Drilling bore wells/ digging wells | 2 (1.17) | 11 (2.63) | 4 (1.00) | 1 (1.56) | 13 (2.53) | 31 (1.98) |
| 3 | Seeds, fertilizers, pesticides | 16 (9.36) | 64 (15.31) | 43 (10.72) | 2 (3.13) | 69 (13.45) | 194 (12.38) |
| 4 | Other working expenses in relation to cultivation | 20 (11.69) | 67 (16.03) | 46 (11.47) | 4 (6.25) | 76 (14.82) | 213 (13.59) |
| 5 | Purchases of milk cow for starting small Enterprise / business | 40 (23.39) | 79 (18.90) | 54 (13.46) | 12 (18.75) | 94 (18.32) | 279 (17.81) |
| 6 | House Construction | 12 (7.02) | 8 (1.92) | 3 (0.75) | 5 (7.81) | 13 (2.54) | 41 (2.62) |

| | | | | | | | |
|---|---|---|---|---|---|---|---|
| 7 | Day-to-Day Consumption | 44<br>(25.73) | 75<br>(17.94) | 120<br>(29.93) | 16<br>(25.00) | 84<br>(16.37) | 339<br>(21.63) |
| 8 | Ceremonies/festivals | 6<br>(3.51) | 10<br>(2.39) | 5<br>(1.25) | 2<br>(3.13) | 23<br>(4.48) | 46<br>(2.94) |
| 9 | Medical | 10<br>(5.85) | 25<br>(5.98) | 47<br>(11.72) | 4<br>(6.25) | 46<br>(8.97) | 132<br>(8.42) |
| 10 | Education | 14<br>(8.19) | 31<br>(7.42) | 23<br>(5.74) | 6<br>(9.37) | 39<br>(7.60) | 113<br>(7.21) |
| 11 | Others | 5<br>(2.92) | 35<br>(8.37) | 49<br>(12.22) | 12<br>(18.75) | 36<br>(7.02) | 137<br>(8.74) |
| 12 | Total (1 to 11) | 171<br>(100) | 418<br>(100) | 401<br>(100) | 64<br>(100) | 513<br>(100) | 1567<br>(100) |

*Note:* Figures in parentheses are percentages tc column totals.
*Sources:* Field Data.

**Table 5.31**
**Current Loan Repayment Periods and Practices by SHG Caste-categories**

| *Sl. No.* | *Particulars* | *SHG Categories* | | | | | |
|---|---|---|---|---|---|---|---|
| | | *Minority SHGs* | *Mixed caste SHGs* | *BC SHGs* | *SC SHGs* | *ST SHGs* | *All SHGs* |
| *1* | *2* | *3* | *4* | *5* | *6* | *7* | *8* |
| 1 | Repayment period of the latest loan (in months) | | | | | | |
| | a 12 | - | 15<br>(16.48) | - | 9<br>(45.00) | - | 24<br>(20.00) |
| | b 15 | - | 45<br>(49.45) | 3<br>(60.00) | 10<br>(50.00) | 1<br>(100) | 59<br>(49.17) |
| | c 20 | 2<br>(66.67) | 14<br>(15.38) | 1<br>(20.00) | 1<br>(5.00) | - | 18<br>(15.00) |
| | d 24 | - | 12<br>(13.19) | 1<br>(20.00) | - | - | 13<br>(10.83) |
| | e 36 | 1<br>(33.33) | 5<br>(5.50) | - | - | - | 6<br>(5.00) |
| | Sub total (a to f) | 3<br>(100) | 91<br>(100) | 5<br>(100) | 20<br>(100) | 1<br>(100) | 120<br>(100) |

| | | | | | | |
|---|---|---|---|---|---|---|
| 2 | Number of | | | | | | |
| | a Non- defaulting members | 35 (89.74) | 1135 (95.30) | 54 (93.10) | 245 (92.45) | 12 (85.71) | 1481 (94.51) |
| | b Defaulting members | 4 (10.26) | 56 (4.70) | 4 (6.90) | 20 (7.55) | 2 (14.29) | 86 (5.49) |
| | Sub Total (a to b) | 39 (100) | 1191 (100) | 58 (100) | 265 (100) | 14 (100) | 1567 (100) |

*Note:* Figures in the parentheses are percentages to column totals.
*Source:* Field data.

**Table 5.32**
**Caste-wise SHGs According to Defaulting and Non-defaulting Status of Drop-out Members**

| *Sl. No.* | *Caste-wise SHG Category* | *Drop-outs* | | | |
|---|---|---|---|---|---|
| | | *Defaulted Members Whose* | | *Non-Defaulted Members Whose* | |
| | | *Savings / Loan Outstanding* | *Loan Outstandings / Savings* | *Savings / Loan Outstandings* | *Loan Outstanding / Savings* |
| *1* | *2* | *3* | *4* | *5* | *6* |
| 1 | Minority SHGs | 1 (16.67) | 1 (2.63) | | |
| 2 | Mixed-caste Category SHGs | 3 (50.00) | 26 (68.42) | 2 (40.00) | 1 (33.33) |
| 3 | BC SHGs | - | - | 2 (40.00) | |
| 4 | SC SHGs | 2(33.33) | 9 (23.69) | 1 (20.00) | I 2 (66.67) |
| 5 | ST SHGs | - | 2 (5.26) | - | - |
| 6 | All SHGs | 6 (100) | 38 (100) | 5 (100) | 3 (100) |
| | | [11.54] | [73.08] | [9.61] | [5.77] |

cal. $X_2^2$ value=3.02$^{NS}$
tab $X^2$ value at 4 def=9.49
NS: Not Significant.

*Notes:* 1. Figures in the parentheses ( ) are percentages to column totals.
2. Figures in the square brackets [ ] are percentages to row totals
*Source:* Field data.

**Table 5.33**

**Actions to Recover Latest Loans and Impact on Non-payment by Caste-wise SHGs**

| *Sl. No.* | *Dimension* | *SHG Categories* | | | | | *All SHGs* |
|---|---|---|---|---|---|---|---|
| | | *BC SHGs* | *SC SHGs* | *ST SHGs* | *Minority SHGs* | *Mixed-caste SHGs* | |
| *1* | *2* | *3* | *4* | *5* | *6* | *7* | *8* |
| 1 | Measures to Recover Loans | | | | | | |
| | A No action | 2 | 6 | - | 2 | 13 | 23 |
| | | (50.00) | (30.00) | | (50.00) | (23.21) | (26.74) |
| | B Sale of security | - | - | - | - | 6 | 6 |
| | | | | | | (10.72) | (6.98) |
| | C Proceeded against surety | - | - | - | 1 | 3 | 4 |
| | | | | | (25.00) | (5.36) | (4.65) |
| | D Recovery from surety | - | - | - | - | 2 | 2 |
| | | | | | | (3.57) | (2.33) |
| | E Removal from Membership | - | 3 | - | - | 2 | 5 |
| | | | (15.00) | | | (3.57) | (5.81) |
| | F Non-eligibility for further loans until outstanding loan is repaid | - | 3 | I | - | 13 | 17 |
| | | | (15.00) | (50.00) | - | (23.21) | (19.77) |
| | G Peer pressure | 2 | 8 | I | 1 | 17 | 29 |
| | | (50.00) | (40.00) | (50.00) | (25.00) | 30.36) | (33.72) |
| | Sub-total (a to g) | 4 | 20 | 2 | 4 | 56 | 86 |
| | | (100) | (100) | (100) | (100) | (100) | (100) |

*(Contd...)*

| *1* | *2* | *3* | *4* | *5* | *6* | *7* | *8* |
|---|---|---|---|---|---|---|---|
| 2 | Impact of non-payment of loans On SHGs | | | | | | |
| | A Repeat loans Delayed | 3 (75.00) | 14 (70.00) | 1 (50.00) | 2 (50.00) | 38 (67.86) | 58 (67.44) |
| | B Penal of repeat loans | 1 (25.00) | 6 (30.00) | 1 (50.00) | 2 (50.00) | 18 (32.14) | 28 (32.56) |
| | Sub-total (a+b) | 4 (100) | 20 (100) | 2 (100) | 4 (100) | 56 (100) | 86 (100) |
| 3 | Repayment to the Bank | | | | | | |
| | (i) Delayed, but paid | 2 (50.00) | 11 (55.00) | 1 (50.00) | 3 (75.00) | 46 (82.14) | 63 (73.26) |
| | (ii) Outstanding | 2 (50.00) | 9 (45.00) | 1 (50.00) | 1 (25.00) | 10 (17.86) | 23 (26.74) |
| | Sub-total (i+ii) | 4 (100) | 20 (100) | 2 (100) | 4 (100) | 56 (100) | 86 (100) |

*Note:* Figures in the parentheses are percentages to column sub total.

*Source:* Field data

**Table 5. 34**

**Loan Procedures and Purposes by Caste-wise SHGs**

| Sl. No. | Dimension | SHG Categories | | | | | All SHGs |
|---|---|---|---|---|---|---|---|
| | | BC SHGs | SC SHGs | ST SHGs | Minority SHGs | Mixed-caste SHGs | |
| 1 | 2 | 3 | 4 | 5 | 6 | 7 | 8 |
| 1. | Mode of Fund Collection and Financial Decision Making (N=120) | 3 (60.00) | 13 (65.00) | 1 (100) | 1 (33.33) | 49 (53.85) | 67 (55.83) |
| A | In the Meetings | | | | | | |
| B | Decisions in the Meetings but from Disbursements Outside | I (20.00) | 3 3 (15.00) | - | - | 26 (28.57) | 30 (25.00) |
| C | Fund Collections Outside the Meetings but the Loan Decisions Made in the Meetings | 1 (20.00) | 3 (15.00) | - - | 1 (33.33) | 9 (9.89) | 14 (11.67) |
| D | Fund Collections and Financial Decisions Outside | - | 1 (5.00) | - | 1 (33.34) | 7 (7.69) | 9 (7.50) |
| | Sub-total (a to d) | 5 (100) | 20 20 000) | 1 (100) | 3 (100) | 91 (100) | 120 (100) |

(Contd...)

| *1* | *2* | *3* | *4* | *5* | *6* | *7* | *8* |
|---|---|---|---|---|---|---|---|
| 2 | SHG Members Awareness of Financial Transactions (N= 20) | | | | | | |
| A | 100% Awareness | 2 (40.00) | 5 (25.00) | - | - | 26 (28.57) | 33 (27.5) |
| B | > 75% Awareness | 2 (40.00) | 11 11 (55.00) | 1 (100) | 2 (66.67) | 47 (51.65) | 63 (52.5) |
| C | Only Few are Aware | 1 (20.00) | 2 (20.00) | - - | 1 (33.33) | 13 (4.29) | 17 (4.17) |
| D | None are aware | - | 2 (10.00) | - | - | 5 (5.49) | 7 (5.83) |
| | Sub-total (a to d) | 5 (100) | 20 (100) | 1 (100) | 3 (100) | 91 (100) | 120 (100) |
| 3 | Level of on-time Payment of Savings Made by the Members (N = 120) | | | | | | |
| A | 100% | 3 (60.00) | 10 10 (50.00) | - | 2 (66.61) | 48 (52.75) | 63 (52.5) |

| | | | | | | |
|---|---|---|---|---|---|---|
| B > 90 %<100% | 1<br>(20.00) | 5<br>(25.00) | 1<br>(100) | 1<br>(33.33) | 27<br>(29.67) | 35<br>(29.17) |
| C 70 to 89% | 1<br>(20.00) | 5<br>(25.00) | - | - | 9<br>(9.89) | 15<br>(2.50 |
| D <70% | - | - | - | - | 7<br>(7.69) | 7<br>(5.83) |
| Sub-total (a to d) | 5<br>(100) | 20<br>(100) | 1<br>(100) | 3<br>(100) | 91<br>(100) | 120<br>(100) |

*Note:* Figures in the parentheses are percentages to column sub-totals.
*Source:* Field data.

of the table, it can be observed that fund collection and financial decisions were made in the meeting, followed by another 25 per cent of SHGs in which loan decisions were made in the meetings but disbursements outside, and yet in another 12 per cent of SHGs fund collections were made outside but loans decisions inside the meetings.

Focusing in the last column of the table as to different levels of members' awareness of financial transactions in sample SHGs, it can be seen that in 27, 53, 14 and 6 per cent of sample SHGs the levels of members' awareness were 100, >75, only few were aware and none were aware respectively.

Pattern of fund use is of paramount importance to the development of the SHG and the individual. The study has attempted to understand the lending pattern of loan (a few or many) following the procedure of end use of bank-loan. The Lending pattern in SHGs by caste-category wise and promotion wise is shown in Table 5.35. In the last row of the table it can be observed that in 38 per cent of sample SHGs need-based loans were given to many members, in 33 per cent of sample SHGs need-based loan was given to few members; in 22 per cent of sample SHGs equal amounts of loans were given to all members and in 7 per cent loans were given repeatedly to a few members.

The internal lending velocity is expressed as the number of times loans has been changes members within a given period of time. The velocity of loan and primarily the fund reveals the efficiency of a unit of fund and the multiplicity uses as well as benefits of the fund to the larger benefit of many members. The more is the velocity the better is the profitability and also ensures a better chance of survival. The present study has analyzed the internal velocity under four categories namely less than one time, one to one and half times, one and half to two times and more than two times. Table 5.36 presents velocity of internal lending by SHG caste- categories. Majority of BC SHGs (40%) had velocity of one and half to two times, SC SHGs (40%) less than one time, ST SHGs (100%) one to one and half- times, Minority SHGs (66.67%) more than two times mixed-caste SHGs (39.56%) less than one time, and all SHGs combined together (37.50%) less than one time. It can be observed that minority SHGs had better velocity of internal lending than the other caste groups.

Andhra Bank, unlike all other Banks in the country, adopted a flexible and multiple loan-repayment options. Nature of loan repayment varies between single payments to payments by installments. Options for payment of principal as well as interests in installments are also made available to SHGs. The options to be given depend on the interest and credit worthiness of the SHG and portfolio of investments taken up. Analyzing the Table 5.37 it can be observed that in 83 per cent sample SHGs loan repayment is on monthly basis of which 83 are mixed groups. In 69 per cent of sample SHGs the repayment includes both principal and interest components. The mixed groups of eight have paid in single payment. Twenty two per cent of the groups paid principle also in installments. Hence, it can safely be concluded that many SHGs availing bank loan are keen in easy monthly repayment.

A more segregated analysis of the internal outstanding loan and its repayment is carried out in the current section. Going through Table 5.38, it can be observed that as high as in 85 per cent of sample SHGs less than two members in each caste-category of SHGs defaulted in repayment of bank loans. Only 3.33 per cent of SHGs the number of defaulted members in each SHG exceeded five. In 90.83 per cent of SHGs the amount of loan outstanding for more than three months was less than two per cent of total loan. Only in 3.33 per cent of SHGs this per centage exceeded 5.

## Table 5.35
## Caste-wise and Promotion-wise Distribution of SHGs by the Lending Patterns

| *Sl. No.* | *Caste category and Promotee of SHGs* | | *Lending Pattern* | | | | *Total* |
|---|---|---|---|---|---|---|---|
| | | | *1** | *2*** | *3**** | *4***** | |
| *1* | *2* | | *3* | *4* | *5* | *6* | *7* |
| 1 | BC SHGs | (5) | 2 (40.00) | 2 (40.00) | 1 (20.00) | - | 5 (100) |
| | a. Government-promoted SHGs | (3) | 1 (33.33) | 1 (33.33) | 1 (33.34) | - | 3 (100) |
| | b. NGO-promoted SHGs | (2) | 1 (50.00) | 1 (50.00) | - | - | 2 (100) |
| 2 | SC SHGs | (20) | 7 (35.00) | 5 (25.00) | 5 (25.00) | 3 (15.00) | 20 (100) |
| | a. Government-promoted SHGs | (5) | 2 (40.00) | 2 (40.00) | - | 1 (20.00) | 5 (100) |
| | b. NGO-promoted SHGs | (15) | 5 (33.33) | 3 (20.00) | 5 (33.33) | 2 (13.24) | 15 (100) |
| 3 | ST SHGs | (1) | 1 (100.00) | - | - | - | 1 (100) |
| | a. Government-promoted SHGs | (-) | - | - | - | - | - |
| | b. NGO-Promoted SHGs | (1) | 1 (100.00) | - | - | - | 1 (100) |

| | | | | | | | |
|---|---|---|---|---|---|---|---|
| 4 | Minority SHGs | (3) | 1<br>(33.33) | 1<br>(33.33) | 1<br>(33.34) | - | 3<br>(100) |
| | a. Government-promoted SHGs | (2) | 1<br>(50.00) | - | 1<br>(50.00) | - | 2<br>(100) |
| | b. NGO-promoted SHGs | (1) | - | 1<br>(100.00) | - | - | 1<br>(100) |
| 5 | Mixed caste SHGs | (91) | 35<br>(38.46) | 32<br>(35.16) | 19<br>(20.88) | 5<br>(5.50) | 91<br>(100) |
| | a. Government-promoted SHGs | (60) | 22<br>(36.67) | 20<br>(33.33) | 14<br>(23.33) | 4<br>(6.67) | 60<br>(100) |
| | b. NGO-promoted SHGs | (31) | 13<br>(41.94) | 12<br>(38.71) | 5<br>(16.13) | 1<br>(3.22) | 31<br>(100) |
| 6 | All SHGs | (120) | 46<br>(38.33) | 40<br>(33.33) | 26<br>(21.67) | 8<br>(6.67) | 120<br>(100) |
| | a. Government-promoted SHGs | (70) | 26<br>(37.14) | 23<br>(32.86) | 16<br>(22.86) | 5<br>(7.14) | 70<br>(100) |
| | b. NGO -promoted SHGs | (50) | 20<br>(40.00) | 17<br>(34.00) | 10<br>(20.00) | 3<br>(6.00) | 50<br>(100) |

*Notes:* 1. * Need - based loans availed by many members
** Need based loans availed by few members.
*** Equal distribution of loans among all members.
**** Loans extended repeatedly to only a few members in the groups.
Figures in parentheses are percentages to row totals.

*Source:* Field data.

**Table 5.36**
**Velocity of Internal Lending by SHG Caste Categories with Regarding to Latest Loan**

| Sl. No. | SHG Caste Categories | | Velocity of Lending | | | | Total |
|---|---|---|---|---|---|---|---|
| | | | < 1 time | 1-1.5 times | 1.5-2 times | >2 times | |
| 1 | 2 | | 3 | 4 | 5 | 6 | 7 |
| 1 | Minority SHGs | (3) | - | 1<br>(33.33) | - | 2<br>(66.67) | 3<br>(100) |
| 2 | Mixed-caste SHGs | (91) | 36<br>(39.56) | 20<br>(21.98) | 21<br>(23.08) | 14<br>(15.38) | 91<br>(100) |
| 3 | BC SHGs | (5) | 1<br>(20.00) | 1<br>(20.00) | 2<br>(40.00) | 1<br>(20.00) | 5<br>(100) |
| 4 | SC SHGs | (20) | 8<br>(40.00) | 4<br>(20.00) | 2<br>(10.00) | 6<br>(30.00) | 20<br>(100) |
| 5 | ST SHGs | (1) | - | 1<br>(100) | - | - | 1<br>(100) |
| | All SHGs | | 45<br>(37.50) | 27<br>(22.50) | 25<br>(20.83) | 23<br>(19.17) | 120<br>(100) |

*Note:* Figures in the parentheses are percentages to row totals.
*Source:* Field data.

**Table 5.37**
**Loan Repayment Practices by Caste - Wise SHGs**

| Sl. No. | Dimension | SHG Categories | | | | | All SHGs |
|---|---|---|---|---|---|---|---|
| | | BC SHGs | SC SHGs | ST SHGs | Minority SHGs | Mixed-caste SHGs | |
| 1 | 2 | 3 | 4 | 5 | 6 | 7 | 8 |
| 1 | Mode of Repayment of the Latest Loan | | | | | | |
| | A Single payment | - | - | - | - | 8 (8.79) | 8 (6.67) |
| | B Instalments | | | | | | |
| | (i) Monthly | 4 (80.00) | 17 (85.00) | 1 (100.00) | 2 (66.67) | 76 (83.52) | 100 (83.33) |
| | (ii) Quarterly | 1 (20.00) | 3 (15.00) | - | 1 (33.33) | 7 (7.69) | 12 (10.00) |
| | Sub-total (a to b) | 5 (100) | 20 (100) | 1 (100) | 3 (100) | 91 (100) | 120 (100) |

(Contd...)

| 1 | 2 | 3 | 4 | 5 | 6 | 7 | 8 |
|---|---|---|---|---|---|---|---|
| 2 | Nature of Repayment | | | | | | |
| | A Principal Paid Installments | 2<br>(40.00) | 5<br>(25.00) | -<br>- | 1<br>(33.33) | 19<br>(20.88) | 27<br>(22.50) |
| | B Interest Paid in Installments | - | 1<br>(5.00) | - | - | 9<br>(9.89) | 10<br>(8.33) |
| | C Principal and Interest Paid in Installments | 3<br>(60.00) | 14<br>(70.00) | 1<br>(100.00) | 2<br>(66.67) | 63<br>(69.23) | 83<br>(69.17) |
| | Sub-total (a to c) | 5<br>(100) | 20<br>(100) | 1<br>(100) | 3<br>(100) | 91<br>(100) | 120<br>(100) |

*Note:* Figures in the parentheses are percentages to column sub-totals.

*Source:* Field data.

## Table 5.38
## Borrowers' Quality of Latest SHG Loan by Caste-wise SHG

(No. of SHGs)

| Sl. No. | Dimension | SHG Categories | | | | | All SHGs |
|---|---|---|---|---|---|---|---|
| | | BC SHGs | SC SHGs | ST SHGs | Minority SHGs | Mixed-caste SHGs | |
| 1 | 2 | 3 | 4 | 5 | 6 | 7 | 8 |
| 1 | Defaulting Members (Nos.) | | | | | | |
| | A < 2 Members | 4<br>(80.00) | 16<br>(80.00) | - | 2<br>(66.67) | 80<br>(87.91) | 102<br>(85.00) |
| | B 2 to 5 Members | 1<br>(20.00) | 3<br>(15.00) | 1<br>(100) | 1<br>(33.33) | 8<br>(8.79) | 14<br>(11.67) |
| | C > 5 Members | - | 1<br>(5.00) | - | - | 3<br>(3.30) | 4<br>(3.33) |
| | D Total (a to c) | 5<br>(100) | 20<br>(100) | 1<br>(100) | 3<br>(100) | 91<br>(100) | 120<br>(100) |

(Contd...)

| 1 | 2 | 3 | 4 | 5 | 6 | 7 | 8 |
|---|---|---|---|---|---|---|---|
| 2 | SHG where extent of loan outstanding for more than 3 months (in terms of value) was: | | | | | | |
| | A < 2 Per cent | 5<br>(100) | 17<br>(85.00) | I<br>(100) | 2<br>(66.67) | 84<br>(92.31) | 109<br>(90.83) |
| | B 2 to 5 per cent | - | 1<br>(5.00) | - | 1<br>(33.33) | 5<br>(5.49) | 7<br>(5.83) |
| | C > 5 per cent | - | 2<br>(10.00) | - | - | 2<br>(2.20) | 4<br>(3.33) |
| | D Total (a to c) | 5<br>(100) | 20<br>(100) | 1<br>(100) | 3<br>(100) | 91<br>(100) | 120<br>(100) |

*Note:* Figures in the parentheses are percentages to column totals.

*Source:* Field data.

**Leadership**

Leadership is one of the structural variables of SHGs, which influence their performance. Leadership is assigned with many roles. The successful performance of which ultimately determine the future sustainability, profitability and worth of SHG. Highly cohesive SHGs guided by positive leadership leads to better performance.

Profiles of SHG leadership are discussed in Table 5.39 for Government and NGO-promoted SHGs. Average age of leaders in Government-promoted SHGs is 29 years while it is 30 years in case of NGO-promoted SHGs. Thus, SHG leadership is young in both the cases of SHGs. Average formal education of leadership in Government, and NGO promoted SHGs is 9 and 6 years respectively. As for as leadership representation from different caste groups is concerned, 46 OCs, 19 BCs, 18 SCs and 17 from minorities representing the leadership. All leaders are not necessarily equipped with similar educational background not the occupation. Analysis of the table 5.39 reveals that 52 per cent are cultivators, 23 per cent are small enterprise owners and the remaining 25 per cent are labourers. Taking into account above factual analysis, it can be concluded that leaders in majority are OCs have formal education and of cultivators.

SHG leadership is discussed in Table 5.40. There are nine different activities primarily performed by a SHG leader. Paying attention to the bottom row of the table it can be noticed that the SHG leaders across caste categories were engaged in all nine activities. Out of total 740 activities, the per centage shares of the most frequent activity is conducting meetings, and the least frequent activity is resolving conflicts in the groups.

**Table 5.39**
**Profile of SHG Leadership**

| *Dimensions of SHG Leaders* | *Leaders of Government - Promoted SHGs (No. = 140)* | *Leaders of NGO - Promoted SHGs (No. = 100)* |
|---|---|---|
| I. Average Age (Years) | 29 | 30 |
| 2. Caste Composition (Nos.) | | |
| (i) OCs. | 64 | 23 |
| | (45.71) | (23.00) |
| (ii) BCs. | 27 | 24 |
| | (19.29) | (24.00) |
| (iii) SCs. | 25 | 40 |
| | (17.86) | (40.00) |
| (iv) STs. | - | 9 |
| | | (9.00) |
| (v) Minorities | 24 | 4 |
| | (17.14) | (4.00) |
| Total (i to v) | 140 | 100 |
| | (100) | (100) |
| 3. Average Formal Educational (years) | 9 | 6 |
| 4. Occupation (Nos.) | | |
| (i) Cultivation | 75 | 28 |
| | (53.57) | (28.00) |
| (ii) Small Enterprise Owners | 32 | 20 |
| | (22.86) | (20.00 |
| (iii) Labourers | 33 | 52 |
| | (23.57) | (52.00) |
| Total (i to iii) | 140 | 100 |
| | (100) | (100) |
| 5. Annual Family Income (in Rs.) | 13,430 | 11,600 |

*Note:* Figures in the parentheses are per centages to column totals.
*Source:* Field data.

## Monitoring of SHGs

Monitoring and evaluation of SHGs is an on-going process, which is intended to improve their performance in all phases of their operation. Different functionaries of the government and NGOs are involved in monitoring and evaluation of SHGs. The more effective the monitoring and evaluation system, the better is the SHG performance.

Government promoted SHG and NGO-promoted SHGs by different persons or agencies are shown in Table 5.41. An average of 52 and 51 visits during the year 2006-07 were recorded in Government and NGO-promoted SHGs respectively. 26.42 per cent of total visits were by animator (book keeper) followed by 22.12 per cent by community co-coordinator, 17.89 per cent by village secretary and 16.15 per cent by APO/ DRDA/ Velugu. Similarly, 31.93 per cent of visits were accounted for by animator (bookkeeper) followed by 30.84 per cent visits by NGO personal at gross root level and 26.29 per cent by NGO organizers.

## Training to SHG Members

Training programmes are designed to increase the knowledge, skills and attitudes of those associated with the SHG operations. Government, NGO and bank personal impart training to SHG leaders in Different aspects of their functioning. Table 5.42 portrays the training inputs cast category-wise leaders and members received from the training agencies. Of the total 513 leaders trained, banks, others, Government and NGOs accounted for 33, 29, 25 and 13 per cent of them respectively. Of total 3161 SHG members trained, banks, others, Government and NGOs represent 30, 27, 24 and 19 per cent respectively.

**Table 5.40**
**SHG Leadership Activities**

| *Sl. No.* | *Caste-wise* | | *Leadership Activities* | | | | | | | *All SHGs* |
|---|---|---|---|---|---|---|---|---|---|---|
| | | | *1* | *2* | *3* | *4* | *5* | *6* | *7* | |
| *1* | *2* | | *3* | *4* | *5* | *6* | *7* | *8* | *9* | *10* |
| 1 | BC SHGs | (10) | 4 (13.80) | 5 (17.24) | 4 (13.80) | 5 (17.24) | 5 (17.24) | 3 (10.34) | 3 (10.34) | 29 (100) |
| 2 | SC SHGs | (40) | 16 ( 14.55) | 18 (16.36) | 14 (12.73) | 19 (17.27) | 20 (18.18) | 11 (10.00), | 12 (10.91) | 110 (100) |
| 3 | ST SHGs | (2) | 1 (20.00) | 1 (20.00) | 1 (20.00) | 1 (20.00) | 1 (20.00) | - | - | 5 (100) |
| 4 | Minority SHGs | (6) | 3 (15.00) | 3 (15.00) | 3 (15.00) | 3 (15.00) | 3 (15.00) | 2 (10.00) | 3 (15.00) | 20 (100) |
| 5 | Mixed caste SHGs | 83 | 86 (14.41) | 78 (14.93) | 83 (13.54) | 9176 (14.41) | (13.19) (15.80) | 79 (13.72) | 576 (100) | (182) |
| 6 | All SHGs | (240) | 107 (14.46) | 113 (15.27) | 100 (13.51) | 111 (15.00) | 120 (16.22) | 92 (12.43) | 97 (13.11) | 740 (100) |

Legend: 1. Provide information, 2. Collects of Savings, 3. Deposits savings in the bank, 4. Maintain all the records, 5. Conducts meetings, 6. Resolves conflicts in the group, 7. Visits bank / offices for loans.

*Notes:* 1. Figures in the parentheses in the 2nd column are number of leaders.
2. Figures in the parentheses are percentages to row totals.

*Source:* Field data.

## Table 5.41
## Monitoring follow-up of Government and NGO-promoted SHGs during 2006-07

*(No. of visits)*

| *Sl. No.* | *Persons / Agencies* | *Visits during the year* | | | |
|---|---|---|---|---|---|
| | | *Government -promoted SHGs* | | *NGO-promoted SHGs* | |
| | | *Number* | *% to Total* | *Number* | *% to Total* |
| *1* | *2* | *3* | *4* | *5* | *6* |
| 1 | Animator / Book keeper | 1071 (15) | 29.42 | 820 (16) | 31.93 |
| 2 | Community Coordinator | 805 (12) | 22.12 | - | - |
| 3 | NGO Personnel at Across Root Level | - | - | 792 (16) | 30.84 |
| 4 | Bank Officials | 189 (3) | 5.19 | 61 (1) | 2.37 |
| 5 | APO *I* DRDA *I* Velugu (Now Called Indira Kranti Patham) | 588 (8) | 16.15 | - | - |
| 6 | *MDO/MRO* | 98 (1) | 2.69 | 10 (0) | 0.39 |
| 7 | Village *Secretary* V AO | 651 (9) | 17.89 | - | - |
| 8 | NGO Organizers | - | - | 675 (14) | 26.29 |
| 9 | Others | 238 (3) | 6.54 | 210 (4) | 8.18 |
| | Totals | 3,640 (52) | 100 | 2,568 (51) | 100 |

*Notes:*

1. Figures in the parentheses are averages calculated by dividing number of visits by sample 70 and 50 SHGs in Government - and NGO-promoted SHGs respectively.
2. Averages in the parentheses are rounded off to the nearest multiple of one.
3. Monitoring visits by NGOs are confined to NGO-promoted SHGs

*Sources:* Field data.

**Table 5.42**
**Training Inputs by Training Agency**

(No. of Leaders and Members)

| *Sl. No.* | *Caste-wise SHGs* | *Training Agencies* | | | | | | | | | |
|---|---|---|---|---|---|---|---|---|---|---|---|
| | | *Banks* | | *NGOs* | | *Government* | | *Others* | | *All* | |
| | | *Leaders* | *Members* | *Leaders* | *Members* | *Leaders* | *Members* | *Leaders* | *Members* | *Leaders* | *Members* |
| *1* | *2* | *3* | *4* | *5* | *6* | *7* | *8* | *9* | *10* | *11 (3+5+ 7+9)* | *13 (4+6+ 8+10)* |
| 1 | Minority SHGs | 4 (33.33) | 20 (27040) | 2 (16.67) | 11 (15.07) | 4 (33.33) | 21 (28.76) | 2 (16.67) | 21 (28.77) | 12 (100) | 73 (100) |
| 2 | Mixed-caste SHGs | 123 (32.03) | 784 (31.64) | 37 (9.63) | 386 (15.58) | 112 (29.17) | 654 (26.39) | 112 (29.17) | 654 (26.39) | 384 (100) | 2478 (100) |
| 3 | BC SHGs | 8 (36.36) | 36 (26.67) | 3 (13.64) | 23 (17.04) | 6 (27.27) | 28 (20.74) | 5 (22.73) | 48 (35.55) | 22 (100) | 135 (100) |
| 4 | SC SHGs | 32 (35.16) | 97 (21.75) | 23 (25.27) | 154 (34.53) | 9 (9.89) | 61 (13.68) | 27 (29.68) | 134 (30.04) | 91 (100) | 446 (100) |
| 5 | ST SHGs | 1 (25.00) | 10 (34.48) | 2 (50.00) | 14 (48.28) | - | - | 1 (25.00) | 5 (17.24) | 4 (100) | 29 (100) |
| 6 | All SHGs | 168 (32.75) | 947 (29.96) | 67 (13.06) | 588 (18.60) | 131 (25.54) | 764 (24.17) | 147 (28.65) | 862 (27.27) | 513 (100) | 3161 (100) |

*Notes:* 1. Number of Leaders and members respectively are shown in 2nd column.
2. Figures in the Parentheses are percentages to row totals.

*Source:* Field data.

## SHG Governance

SHG governance primarily is focused on membership awareness levels as to SHG objectives, rules and regulation and sharing of leadership responsibilities, savings and loans, regularity of SHG meetings, level of members' attendance in SHG meetings, up to date maintenance of records etc.

SHG-governance is discussed in Table 5.43 for different SHG categories. It can be seen from the analysis that nearly 51 per cent of sample SHGs reported of being aware of the objective of SHG programme. Fifty two per cent sample SHGs all members were aware of rules and regulation, 48.33 per cent members aware of savings and loan positions, and 48 per cent of sample SHG reported of sharing of leadership responsibility by members.

Functionality of SHGs depends on the level of participation of member in the meetings. Analysis of SHG member attendance in meetings is caste along SHG caste categories in table 5.44 reveals that 10 per cent of SC SHGs, 4 per cent of mixed caste SHGs and 5 per cent of all caste SHGs attendance in SHG meeting was less than 50 per cent. A much skewed pattern of meeting attendance is shown by all caste groups. A larger per centage (34.17%) reported of attending meeting above 90 per cent; is a sound indication of functioning of SHGs.

Up to date maintenance of records is an important indicator of the health of SHGs. The study has attempted to analyze the status and is depicted the findings in Table 5.45. As can be seen from the table that 54, 68, 56, 55 and 55 per cent of sample SHGs of different caste-groups maintained up to date records with regard to membership attendance at meetings, savings collection, loan disbursements, loan repayment performance, member-wise savings and loan portfolios respectively.

**Table 5.43**
**SHG Governance by SHG Caste Categories**

| Sl. No. | SHG Caste Categories | | 1* | | 2* | | 3* | | 4* | |
|---|---|---|---|---|---|---|---|---|---|---|
| | | | Yes | No | Yes | No | Yes | No | Yes | No |
| 1 | 2 | | 3 | 4 | 5 | 6 | 7 | 8 | 9 | 10 |
| 1 | Minority SHGs | (3) | 2<br>(66.67) | 1<br>(33.33) | 2<br>(66.67) | 1<br>(33.33) | 1<br>(33.33) | 2<br>(66.67) | 1<br>(33.33) | 2<br>(66.67) |
| 2 | Mixed-caste SHGs | (91) | 46<br>(50.55) | 45<br>(49.45) | 48<br>(52.75) | 43<br>(47.25) | 47<br>(51.65) | 44<br>(48.46) | 47<br>(51.65) | 44<br>(48.35) |
| 3 | BC SHGs | (5) | 3<br>(60.00) | 2<br>(40.00) | 3<br>(60.00) | 2<br>(40.00) | 3<br>(60.00) | 2<br>(40.00) | 4<br>(80.00) | 1<br>(20.00) |
| 4 | SC SHGs | (20) | 9<br>(45.00) | 11<br>(55.00) | 8<br>(40.00) | 12<br>(60.00) | 7<br>(35.00) | 13<br>(65.00) | 6<br>(30.00) | 14<br>(70.00) |
| 5 | ST SHGs | (1) | 1<br>(100.00) | - | 1<br>(100.00) | - | - | 1<br>(100.00) | - | 1<br>(100.00) |
| 6 | All SHGs | (120) | 61<br>(50.83) | 59<br>(49.17) | 62<br>(51.67) | 58<br>(48.33) | 58.<br>(48.33) | 62<br>(51.67) | 58<br>(48.33) | 62<br>(51.67) |

*Legend:*
1*. Awareness about objectives of SH G programme
2*. Awareness about rules and regulations
3 *. Sharing of leadership responsibilities by members
4*. Awareness about member-wise savings and loan position

*Note:* Figures in the parentheses in columns 3 to 10 are percentages to number of SHGs in each category shown in the parentheses in column 2.

*Source:* Field data.

**Table 5.44**
**Level of SHG Member Attendance in Meetings by SHG Caste Categories**

| *Sl. No.* | *Caste Category of SHGs* | | *Level of Member Attendance in Meetings (per cent)* | | | | |
|---|---|---|---|---|---|---|---|
| | | | *<50* | *50-70* | *70-90* | *Above 90* | *Total* |
| *1* | *2* | *3* | *4* | *5* | *6* | *7 (3 to 6)* | |
| 1 | Minority SHGs | (3) | - | 2<br>- | 1<br>(66.67) | 3<br>(33.33) | (100) |
| 2 | Mixed - Caste SHGs | (91) | 4<br>(4.40) | 11<br>(12.09) | 45<br>(49.45) | 31<br>(34.06) | 91<br>(100 |
| 3 | BC SHGs | (5) | 1<br>- | 1<br>(20.00) | 3<br>(20.00) | 5<br>(60.00) | (100) |
| 4 | SC SHGs | (20) | 2<br>(10.00) | 4<br>(20.00) | 8<br>(40.00) | 6<br>(30.00) | 20<br>(100) |
| 5 | ST SHGs | (1) | - | 1<br>- | (100) | 1<br>- | (100) |
| | All | (120) | 6<br>(5.00) | 16<br>(13.33) | 57<br>(47.50) | 41<br>(34.17) | 120<br>(100) |

*Note:* Figures in the Parentheses are percentages to row totals.
*Source:* Field data.

## Table 5.45
## Up to date Maintenance of Records by SHG Caste Categories

| Sl. No | SHG Caste Categories | Dimensions 1* | | 2* | | 3* | | 4* | | 5* | | 6* | | 7* | |
|---|---|---|---|---|---|---|---|---|---|---|---|---|---|---|---|
| | | Yes | No | Yes | No | Yes | .No | Yes | No | Yes | No | Yes | No | Yes | No |
| 1 | 2 | 3 | 4 | 5 | 6 | 7 | 8 | 9 | 10 | 11 | 12 | 13 | 14 | 15 | 16 |
| 1 | Minority SHGs (3) | 2 (66.67) | 1 (33.33) | 2 (66.67) | 1 (33.33) | 3 (100.00) | - | 3 (100.00) | - | 3 (100.00) | - | 3 (100.00) | | 3 (100.00) | - |
| 2 | Mixed-caste SHGs (91) | 43 (47.25) | 48 (52.75) | 47 (51.65) | 44 (48.35) | 56 (61.54) | 35 (38.46) | 58 (63.74) | 33 (36.26) | 46 (50.55) | 45 (49.45) | 47 (51.65) | 44 (48.35) | 47 (51.65) | 44 (48.35) |
| 3 | BC SHGs (5) | 2 (40.00) | 3 (60.00) | 3 (60.00) | 2 (40.00) | 4 (80.00) | 1 (20.00) | 4 (80.00) | 1 (20.00) | 3 (60.00) | 2 (40.00) | 3 (60.00) | 2 (40.00) | 3 (60.00) | 2 (40.00) |
| 4 | SC SHGs (20) | 8 (40.00) | 12 (60.00) | 12 (60.00) | 8 (40.00) | 13 (65.00) | 7 (35.00) | 15 (75.00) | 5 (25.00) | 14 (70.00) | 6 (30.00) | 12 (60.00) | 8 (40.00) | 12 (60.00) | 8 (40.00) |
| 5 | ST SHGs (1) | 1 (100.00) | - | 1 (100.00) | - | 1 (100.00) | - | 1 (100.00) | - | 1 (100.00) | - | 1 (100.00) | - | 1 (100.00) | - |
| 6 | All SHGs (120) | 56 (46.67) | 64 (53.33) | 65 (54.17) | 55 (45.83) | 77 (64.17) | 43 (35.83) | 81 (67.50) | 39 (32.50) | 67 (55.83) | 53 (44.17) | 66 (55.00) | 54 (45.00) | 66 (55.00) | 54 (45.00) |

*Legend:*
1 *. Adherence to the group's bye-laws
2 *Membership attendance at the meetings
3 *. Financial decisions taken at the meetings
4 *Savings collection from member
5 * Loan disbursements
6 *Loan repayment performance
7 * Member-wise savings and loan port folios.

*Note:* Figures in the parentheses in columns 3 to 16 are percentages to number of SHGs in each category shown in the parentheses in column.

*Source:* Field data.

## Comparative Critical Rating of SHGs

In critical ratings of SHGs fourteen dimensions are used which are given weights to reflect their relative importance. The maximum possible total score is 100. Critical rating score is a single measure of operational efficiency of SHGs. Higher the critical rating score, better is the performance of the SHG.

Comparative critical ratings of SHG caste categories fourteen dimensions were used in SHG critical rating is captured in Table 5.46. Weights are assigned to each of the fourteen dimensions. Using primary data collected through questionnaires about the performance of SHGs, scores of four SHG caste categories and score of all SHGs were shown against each dimension. Overall single index of SHG performance was a sum total of scores obtained under 14 dimensions for each SHG caste category. As can be observed from the Table 5.47, the BC SHGs topped the performance with a total score of 81.60, followed by minority SHGs with a score of 78.67 points, mixed-caste SHGs with a score of 77.02 points, and SC/ST SHGs with a score of 74.76 points.

All SHGs put together had a performance score of 76.52. Compared to the performance score (76.52 points) of all SHGs put together, the performance scores of SC/ST SHGs were marginally below the average score, and score of minority SHGs and mixed-caste SHGs are marginally above the average score. The score of BC SHGs was much above that score confirms to the fact of adopting best practices for better and smooth functioning of SHGs.

## Problems and Challenges of SHGs

Self-help Groups constitute a major segment among the third sector organizations. Though the concept of SHG is not new, the linking of it to micro-finance is of recent origin.

**Table 5.46**
**Comparative Critical Rating of SHG Caste Categories**

| Sl. No. | Dimension | Weighted Average Scores | | | | | |
|---|---|---|---|---|---|---|---|
| | | *Assigned weight* | *BC SHGs* | *SC/ST SHGs* | *Minority SHGs* | *Mixed-Caste SHGs* | *All SHGs* |
| *1* | *2* | *3* | *4* | *5* | *6* | *7* | *8* |
| 1 | Feeling of Homogeneity / Solidarities | 4 | 3.0 (15) | 2.76 (58) | 2.67 (8) | 3.04 (277) | 2.98 (358) |
| 2 | Governance Issues | 6 | 3.8 (19) | 2.38 (50) | 3.00 (9) | 3.09 (281) | 2.98 (358) |
| 3 | Conduct of Meetings During Last Six Months | 8 | 7.2 (36) | 6.48 (136) | 7.33 (22) | 6.90 (628) | 6.85 (822) |
| 4 | Attendance in Meetings | 8 | 6.8 (34) | 5.62 (118) | 6.67 (20) | 6.18 (562) | 6.12 (734) |
| 5 | Financial Transactions in the Groups | 8 | 7.0 (35) | 6.90 (145) | 4.33 (13) | 6.52 (593) | 6.55 (786) |
| 6 | Member Awareness about Financial Transactions | 8 | 6.4 (32) | 5.90 (124) | 5.33 (16) | 5.96 (542) | 5.92 (710) |
| 7 | Regularity Savings | 8 | 6.6 (33) | 6.24 (131) | 7.33 (22) | 6.53 (594) | 6.40 (768) |

| | | | | | | | |
|---|---|---|---|---|---|---|---|
| 8 | Pattern of Internal Lending | 8 | 6.2<br>(31) | 5.19<br>(109) | 5.67<br>(17) | 5.81<br>(529) | 5.72<br>(686) |
| 9 | Velocity of. Internal Lending | 4 | 2.6<br>(13) | 2.29<br>(48) | 3.33<br>(10) | 2.14<br>(195) | 2.22<br>(266) |
| 10 | Repayment Terms | 4 | 3.8<br>(19) | 3.86<br>(81) | 3.67<br>(11) | 3.75<br>(341) | 3.77<br>(452) |
| 11 | Repayment Pattern | 8 | 6.4<br>(32) | 6.76<br>(142) | 6.67<br>(20) | 6.57<br>(598) | 6.60<br>(792) |
| 12 | Borrower Quality-number of Defaulters | 8 | 7.2<br>(36) | 6.86<br>(144) | 6.67<br>(20) | 7.38<br>(672) | 7.07<br>(848) |
| 13 | Asset Quality-percentage of Default | 8 | 8.0<br>(40) | 7.05<br>(148) | 6.67<br>(20) | 7.60<br>(692) | 7.50<br>(900) |
| 14 | Up-to Date Maintenance of Records | 10 | 6.6<br>(33) | 6.48<br>(136) | 9.33<br>(28) | 5.55<br>(505) | 5.85<br>(702) |
| | Total | 100 | 81.60<br>(408) | 74.76<br>(1570) | 78.67<br>(236) | 77.02<br>(7009) | 76.52<br>(9182) |

*Notes:* 1. Figures in parentheses are weighted aggregated scores.
2. Average weighted score is calculated by dividing weighted aggregate scores by number of SHGs.

*Source:* Filed data.

Significantly, the question of women empowerment has walked into the domain of the concept of SHGs and Micro-finance in recent times. This, in turn, has added a major dimension enlarging the ongoing debates on development and women empowerment in India. Given this divergent views have been expressed with regard to SHG and its role in development and empowerment. Generally, it has been widely acknowledged that economic development or empowerment need not necessarily result in socio-cultural development and empowerment of women due to existence of a large number of structural impediments, rigidities, and mediations that comes into play in any given socio-cultural milieu. Consequently, it is important that the economic activities of self-help groups in delivering micro-finance need to be examined in terms of a variety of issues, including their management and governance, concerning women empowerment.

**Constraints**

Though the SHGs proved to be very useful to their members, their families and their villages and societies and the members have strong urge to develop the SHGs as their own civil society organizations, the SHGs are facing certain constraints which may inhibit the SHGs becoming strong, sustainable and self-reliant organizations. The field interaction with multiple Andhra Bank linked beneficiaries reported of the following major constraints faced:

1. Shortage of leaders, wide gap in awareness levels of leaders and members and low internal capacities to manage the institutions.
2. Inability of members to give more time to federation work. Absence of practice of compensating the office bears for the time they put in for the federations.
3. Absence of 'operational manuals' for the functioning of SHGs and literature on good practices.

4. Ambiguity about registration and legal compliance.
5. Alcoholism of men and unreasonable restrictions at the family level are constraints at some places.
6. Non-availability of funds for on-lending and to meet the operational expenses is another important constraint.
7. Non-cooperation of local CBO (Community Based Organizers) and some officials is another major challenge.
8. Political interference is the actual and potential problem to many SHGs.
9. Constant involvement of promoters i.e. lack of role transformation is a serious problem for many SHGs.

## Issues and Concerns

It's well known that SHG movement has become one of the largest social mobilization processes in the country and is also known as the world's largest community based micro-finance program. SHGs emerged as ideal institutions that would contribute to the sustainability of the SHGs. While promotion of SHG federation requires resources, both financial and human, many SHPIs are promoting federations, with very limited resources and capabilities. In the process many vital issues remained unanswered and unaddressed. There are several issues and challenges in the promotion and functioning of SHGs. These are grouped into institutional and program related issues and concerns:

### *Institutional Related Issues and Concerns*

1. Governance, role transformation between promoters/ staff and the executive body.
2. Balance between federations and SHGs in their respective roles and responsibilities.

3. Whether the SHGs should hire professional staff from outside or develop their own members as professionals.
4. Funding is an important issue. It is not just the availability of funds, the terms of funding and the funding channels have big impact on functioning of SHGs.
5. Making SHGs financially and operationally self-sufficient.
6. Political interferences are issues of concern
7. Balancing between targets and process/quality is required. Uniform norms and by-laws as against SHG federation specific rules.
8. Capacity building–basic versus advance, for leaders/ few versus to all/many, by internal persons versus external resource persons, and within village versus outside villages. Does this lead to overburdening of women as they have to play multiple roles

***Programme and impact related issues and concerns***

1. Integration of livelihood issues with SHGs agenda.
2. Converting the financial linkages and unity among members into women empowerment and obtaining gender equity in the society and family level.
3. Developing and managing partnerships with different government departments.
4. Organizations that focus on gender and human rights are of the opinion that the SHGs and SHG federations have too much focus on financial matters and very limited attention is paid to deeper social issues like women's rights and real empowerment.

## Reasons for existence of Overdues/NPAs under SHG Finance

The study traced out several reasons for existence of overdues and Non Performing Assets under SHG finance. The most prominent reasons identified are:

- Misappropriation of SHG Credit/funds
- Migration of Members of the SHG Group to other villages and towns
- Group defunct
- Willful defaulters
- Misappropriation of funds by Group Leaders
- Lack of income generation
- Involvement of men/outsiders in the affairs of the group
- Death of members
- Lack of peer pressure,
- Officials of DRDA are not supporting / involving in recovery of loans
- All Government Programmes are routing through SHGs irrespective of their managerial abilities like Indiramma and Pasukranthi padhakam ,
- Political interference ,
- Misunderstanding among the members in repayment of interest of SHG loans and differences in internal lending, and
- Non-recovery of internal lending amount to the outsiders i.e., farmers

## Risks in SHG-Banking

Banking activity is heralded with certain risks and uncertainties. Foreseen risks could easily be managed while preparedness could be made in advance for un-foreseen risks. The risks can be minimized with systematic efforts. The study after through analysis of the different kinds and types of risks associated with the SHG finance suggested the following measures:

- Sensitizing Branch Managers on group dynamics
- Educating SHG members on risk factors.
- Establishment of Micro-enterprises
- Training the members for Skill up gradation.
- Marketing support from the Government for the groups taking up economic activity.
- Encouraging SHGs to form in to federations at village level/ Block level will empower them.
- Financing to federations will reduce the work-load at branch level, so that the branch staff can concentrate on nurturing groups.

## Challenges

A large number of SHPAs are exploring the possibility of promoting SHGs for a variety of reasons e.g. some want to promote SHGs as a withdrawal strategy; some want to promote SHGs to reduce costs; some promote SHGs realizing the need for such formal institutions to nurture the SHGs and some promote SHGs because others are doing so. The promoters should be fully aware of the advantages and disadvantages of the SHG federations and take responsibility to educate the SHG members to make informed decision. The study has carefully reviewed the findings of SHG functionality, objective of the federation and the challenged faced by all caste groups and finally captured the different challenges they are with standing. The challenges faced by the federations are grouped into the following categories, viz.

promoted or promotion related challenges, institutional building related challenges and business development related challenges:

**Promoter/promotion Related Challenges**

Some of the promoter related challenges includes:

1. Some promoters have less faith and trust in the capabilities of the women and conviction that they can achieve anything if proper facilitation support is provided. They are reluctant to handover major responsibilities to SHGs. Such mindset is a big challenge.
2. Yet another constraint related to the promoters is the limitations of promoters in terms of financial and human resources and techno-managerial capacities.
3. Promotion of SHGs in under served regions like north, north-east and western parts of the country is a big challenge.
4. In some of the areas, there is unhealthy competition among the SHGs, particularly NGOs and Government.
5. SHGs being used by Governments and NGOs to pursue their own agenda resulting in limited scope for the agenda of their members to be addressed.

***Institutional Development Related Challenges***

Institutional development, especially under the slogan of "good governance", has recently come to occupy the centre stage of development policy debate. The important institutional challenge includes:

1. Providing diverse services, especially the financial and non-financial service, is a big challenge.

2. Managing the service, which have conflict of interest (financial intermediation requires discipline and rigor while the social intermediation requires solidarity and compassion)
3. Lack of appropriate legal environment and regulatory framework.
4. Developing leadership skills of the poor women and especially making them to understand their managerial responsibilities in complex institutions like NBFIs, which they own.

***Business Development Related Challenges***

The business development related challenges include:

1. Changing the perceptions of Tribal and poor about the development and risks
2. Knowledge transfer, i.e. making the illiterate and semi-literate members as financial managers or managers of multi-task institutions
3. Harnessing potential of marketing
4. Meeting challenges posed by commercial MFIs in terms 'business competition' and 'propagation of misinformation'

## Conclusion

Promoter-wise 58 and 42 per cent of SHGs were promoted by the government and NGOs respectively. Either bankers or animators were assessing agencies in 32 per cent SHGs each in SHG-bank linkage programme. OCs, BCs, SCs, STs and minorities accounted for 33, 27, 25, 4 and 11 per cent of total SHG membership respectively. Nineteen of the SHG members are illiterates and the rest 81 per cent are educated. SHG members' turnover was highest at 15 per cent in ST SHGs and lowest at three per cent in mixed-caste SHGs. The most single important reason for drop-outs was recovery of old loans (27%). Thirty per cent of SHG members households are land less and another 35 per cent have less than one acre each. 55 per cent of these families had annual income of Rs.11,000 to Rs.13,000 each in 2006-07 comparing current volume of yearly savings to that of initial year, the highest growth rate of 71 per cent was found in BC SHGs and the lowest growth rate of 12.50 in ST SHGs.

Persistent growth in savings was noticed in 100 and 60 per cent of minority and BC SHGs respectively. Continuous savers were highest in SC SHGs (94.44%) and lowest in BC SHGs (91.18%) promoted by government. Per SHG member weighted monthly average current savings was highest at Rs.60.11 in mixed caste SHGs and lowest at Rs.30 in ST SHGs. 49 out of 70 government-promoted SHGs and 35 out of 50 NGO-promoted SHGs availed revolving fund facility from the A.P. state Government. Twenty four per cent and four per cent government-promoted SHGs and NGO-promoted SHGs respectively had four and more repeat loans. Average aggregate loan per SHG was highest at Rs.2,51,333 in minority SHGs and lowest at Rs.60, 050 in SC SHGs. Thirty six per cent of SHGs availed soft loan facility, that is, loan at three per cent interest.

Peer pressure was the most important (34% of defaulting members) action for recovery of loans. In 38 per cent of sample SHGs many members availed need-based loans.

Velocity of lending was less than one in the majority of SHGs (37.50%). On critical rating score with a maximum of 100 points, Bus scored high at 81 points and SC/ST SHGs at 75 points. The problems like regional disparities are acute in the State. Coastal Region dominates its share in comparison to other regions under the study. The over dues with SHGs are partially due to migration of members, willful defaulters and political interferences.

# 6

# Summary of Findings, Conclusions and Suggestions

## Introduction

The chapter is basically conceptualizing the entire study and finally concludes the study through delivering valuable and relevant suggestions to help improve functionality of micro-finance institutions, and programmes. The study findings are highlighted by chapters and a road map has also been drawn towards the end for future research.

## Summary of Findings

Chapter-wise findings are summarized in the following sections.

## Introduction and Design of the Study

1. There is transition from micro - credit to micro - finance by SHGs, the latter being broader than the former.
2. The enactment of the Cooperative Credit Societies Act, 1904, would be considered as the beginning of micro-finance in India.
3. From 1969 experiences of lending has been realized through Government Schemes like IRDP, Anthyodaya, SGSY etc.

4. NABARD in India is the pioneer institution in conceptualization and implementation of the concept of SHG through the SHG-bank linkage programme since 1992.
5. Micro-credit summit was a decade-long campaign that sought to ensure the delivery of credit for self-employment by 2005 to 100 million of the world's poorest families, especially the women of these families.
6. According to World Bank estimate in 1995, in the most developing countries the formal financial system reaches only the top 25 per cent of the economically active population, leaving bottom 75 per cent with no access to financial services apart from money lenders.
7. NABARD has an ambitious plan of covering 100 million poor through SHGs by 2008.
8. Out of the six micro- credit delivery models in India SHG Model is the most popular model.
9. The study is confining to three regions in Andhra Pradesh i.e. Coastal, Rayalseema and Telengana, and there are 8 districts are selected for the study having representation from each region.

**Development of Micro-finance: An Over View**

1. Grameen Bank of Bangladesh is one of world's most famous micro-finance institutions, serving more than four million borrowers annually and helping 10,000 families to come out of poverty every month. The same model is adopted in Andhra Pradesh.
2. Grameen Bank now has more than 2,300 branches that reach into 40,000 Bangladeshi villages. In 25 years it has lent more than $9 billion to 16 million borrowers. 50 per cent of them are women. In Andhra Pradesh 98 per cent are women groups.

3. India constitutes approximately one sixth of the world's total population. India's population increased from 36.7 cr in 1951 to 102.70 cr by 2001. In 1951, 82.7 per cent of the population, i.e., 29.9 crore were in rural areas. Whereas in 2001, 73 per cent of the population, i.e., 74.17 crore were in rural areas and 27 per cent of the population, i.e., 28.53 crore were in urban areas.
4. The branches of scheduled commercial banks increased from 8,262 in June 1969 to 69,471 in March 2007. The average population per branch office decreased significantly from 64,000 to 16,000 during the above period, with the share of rural branches increasing from 22.2 per cent in June 1969 to a little over 51 per cent.
5. Aga Khan Rural Support Programme's (AKRSP) savings and credit programme started off by conserving "programme savings". The initial groups formed were for a given village and had a membership of around a 100 people.
6. MFIs have also become popular throughout India as one form of financial intermediary to the poor. MFIs exist in many forms including co-operatives, Grameen-like initiatives and private sector MFIs. As on 31.03.2007 No. of SHGs linked are 29.24 lacs
7. After independence with the initiative and under guidance of RBI, vast banking network was developed. Nationalization of Imperial Bank of India in 1955 and private sector commercial banks in 1969 and 1980, and establishment of RRBs in 1975 were landmark events in vigorous extension of banking to rural sector. This institutional set-up led to multi-agency approach to rural credit.

8. MFIs are broadly categorized into formal and informal sectors. Around 1600 MFIs were found to be operating in India by the end of 1990s.
9. NGO and government-promoted and bank-linked SHGs are considered as an effective intervention strategy for poverty alleviation. In the next 10 years about one-third of Indian rural population is expected to be covered by apex-level FIs and NGOs, NGO-MFIs and NGO networks.
10. NABARD's strategy for micro-finance interalia includes forming and nurturing SHGs of poor, emphasis on thrift and its use for consumption and production needs, facilitating SHGs to access credit from formal banking channels, etc.
11. In India NABARD initiated SHGs in 1986-87. SHGs have been widely accepted as an integral part of micro-finance. Membership of SHGs should be restricted to 20 to avoid formalities of their registration.
12. With the appointment of Working Group of RBI in 1994, SHG-bank linkage in India was institutionalized. Over 24.25 million poor households are accessing micro-credit through SHG-bank linkage. Over 2,800 NGOs and 69,471 branches of 560 banks are associated with this programme.
13. Of three emerging SHG-bank linkage models, Bank-Facilitator Agency-SHG-Members (with NGOs/government agency as SHPIs) model is the most popular one accounting for 74.5 per cent of cumulative loans of banks by the end of March, 2007.
14. Southern region of India, Andhra Pradesh accounted for lion's share in total SHGs (44.82 per cent) and banks' loans to SHGs (74.95 per cent) in 2006-07.

15. Commercial banks had as high as 54.53 per cent share in total SHGs linked, and 63.17 per cent to total bank loans to SHGs in 2006-07.
16. The extent of exclusion from credit markets is much more, as number of loan accounts constituted only 14 per cent of adult population

## Micro-finance: An Experience of Andhra Pradesh

1. MYRADA-promoted and bank-linked 8 SHGs in 1992-93, marked the beginning of the SHG-bank linkage programme in A.P.
2. Up to 31-3-2008, cumulative loan amount of Rs. 5882.78 crore was disbursed in A.P. by banks
3. There are 27.85% SHGs linked to banks, 31.23% bank loans to SHGs and 29.89 % NABARD's refinance to banks in the state of Andhra Pradesh
4. As of March 2007 it is estimated that there are approximately 30,000 federations in AP i.e. 27,000 at village level, 1,000 at cluster level and 2,000 at Mandal and district level.
5. Under financial inclusion strategy of 2006, banks were permitted to utilize the services of non-governmental organizations (NGOs/SHGs), micro-finance institutions and other civil society organizations as intermediaries in providing financial and banking services through the use of business facilitator and business correspondent (BC) models.

## Micro-finance: Experience of Andhra Pradesh

1. SHG Bank Linkage Programme initiated during 1998 by Andhra Bank. Bank received the Best Performance award from NABARD consecutively for the years 2000-2001, 2001-2002, and 2003-04.

2. Andhra Bank has 1289 branches spread all over the country and 918 branches are located in Andhra Pradesh. The rural and semi-urban branches constitute 59.89 per cent of the total branches; giving an ample scope to be a forerunner in helping the poor and play a pivotal role in the mission of financial inclusion.

3. Andhra bank has financed to 71,758 groups with an amount of Rs. 718. crores during the year 2007-08. An amount of Rs. 1025 crores outstanding with 1,50,236 groups as on March 2008.

4. The quantum of loan directly given to SHGs would be in proportion of savings mobilized by the group and can be in the ratio of savings to credit 1:1 or 1:2 initially, which has been raised up to 1:10 depending on the confidence gained by the Bank. From third dose on onwards bank is following MCP (micro-credit plan).

6. The maximum limit allowed to SHGs is Rs.5.00 lacs and is with out collateral security.

7. All the groups financed by the Andhra Bank are female groups.

8. SC groups consisting of 19,290 with 17 per cent, ST groups are 9,082 with 8 per cent, minorities 14,754 with 13 per cent and other groups 70,345 with 62 per cent.

9. Bank has financed to SCs 79.68, STs 42.50, minorities 58.43 and other castes 350.63 crores.

10. Bank is following critical rating Index of category 'A' (70-100 marks) and 'B 'category (50-70 marks). "A" Rated groups are 77,160, "B" Rated groups 29,506, "C" Rated groups 5,668, and "D" Rated groups 1,137.

Bank has financed an amount of Rs403.81 crores to "A" Rated groups Rs. 95.65crores to "B" Rated groups Rs. 31.02 crores to "C" Rated groups Rs. 0.76 crores to "D" Rated groups.

11. The bank has financed to 1st dose 27,234, 2nd dose 36,315, 3rd dose, 43,114, >3rd dose 6,808 groups. The bank has financed Rs. 59.91 crores to1st dose groups, 112.57 crores to 2nd dose groups, Rs 216.72 crores to third dose groups and Rs. 142.04crores to >3rd dose groups.

12. The bank has financed Rs 50,000 and below to 63,549 groups, Rs.50,001 to Rs.1,00,000 to 43,114 groups and Rs.1,00,001 and above to 6808 groups.

13. Bank has given special schemes to SHGs like INDIRAMMA for housing and debt swapping. Under debt swapping the interest burden is reduced from 48 per cent to 3 per cent. Bank has financed 115.00 crores under debt swapping.

14. Bank has also evolved new insurance schemes like Janashree Bima for Life coverage of members and Swasthya Bima Policy for health coverage of SHG members.

15. Bank has launched a new pilot project called Andhra Bank Smart Card in Geesukonda Mandal of Warangal District where the pension payments and wage payments under APREGS are done through SHG leaders. It is an innovative step taken up by Andhra bank. So far 10,333 cards were issued in 25 villages. The bank proposed to extend the scheme to 6 districts of Andhra Pradesh.

16. Bank is extending training facilities through 10 of its rural institutes to SHGs at free of cost in Andhra Pradesh, Kerala and in bubaneswar.

17. In Andhra Pradesh out of three regions Coastal region dominates the share of linkage with 2832 crores consisting of 9 districts and the per cent of targets achievement also high with 96 per cent. The Telangana region has Rs.1844 crores performed with 9 districts with an achievement of 77 per cent. The Rayalseema area consists of 4 districts with 1152 crores and achieved 98 per cent of its targets.
18. East Godavari District has financed to 34,262 groups with an amount of Rs.483.64 crores which is Highest SHGs District in the country.
19. Chittoor District has financed to 20,353 groups with an amount of Rs 354.53 crores.
20. Visakhapatnam has financed to 18,466 groups with an amount of Rs.253.96 crores
21. Kurnool has financed to 17,177 groups with an amount of Rs.269.75 crores.
22. Karim nagar has financed to 17317 groups with an amount of Rs.206.29 crores.
23. Rangareddy has financed to 9461 groups with an amount of Rs.178.83 crores.
24. Nellore has financed to 13628 groups with an amount of Rs.234.89 crores.
25. Warangal has financed to 18,100 groups with an amount of Rs.186.71 crores.
26. All the banks in Andhra Pradesh have financed 431515 groups with an amount of Rs.588,278 lacs during the financial year.

**Performance Evaluation of SHGs-BL of Andhra Bank: Problems and Challenges**

1. In total there are 374 agencies and individuals involved in assessing government -promoted and NGO-promoted sample SHGs.

2. Model time taken for linking SHGs with banks was 6-9 months.
3. Three purposes namely obtaining loans, repayment of loans, and depositing savings accounted for above 85 per cent of SHG–bank interactions in both government, and NGO-promoted SHGs.
4. Ninety per cent of SHG members are illiterates and the rest 81 per cent have formal education.
5. Migration (12%) is the major reason member drop-outs.
6. Thirty per cent of SHG members are landless and 62 per cent are either marginal or small farmers.
7. Ninety two per cent of the SHG member households had an annual Income exceeding Rs.9,000.
8. Comparing initial and current SHG member monthly savings, it was found 43 per cent were savings-stagnating SHGs and 57 per cent savings - growing SHGs.
9. Ninety four per cent of SHG members were continuous savers and 6 per cent intermittent savers.
10. Per member weighted monthly average current savings were highest at Rs.66 in BC SHGs, and lowest at Rs.30 in ST SHGs.
11. 49 out of 70 Government-promoted SHGs and 35 out of 50 NGO-promoted SHGs availed revolving fund facility of the Andhra Pradesh Government.
12. Average amount of revolving fund support extended was Rs.11,262 in government - promoted SHGs, and Rs.11, 057 in NGO-promoted SHGs.
13. 20, 49, 15, 11 and 5 per cent of SHGs obtained first, second, third, fourth and fifth repeat loans respectively after getting the initial loans.

14. Average doses of loan in 1st, 2nd, 3rd ,4th and 5th given to SHGs are Rs.13,417, Rs.28,517, Rs.43,527, Rs.75,298, Rs.1,03,684 and Rs.1,60,000 respectively.

15. Average SHG loan amounts, including initial and repeat loans, for BC SHGs, SC SHGs, ST SHGs, minority SHGs and mixed-caste SHGs were Rs.1,22,600, Rs.66,050, Rs.1,30,000, Rs.2,51,332, and Rs.l,32,062 respectively.

16. Opportunity cost as percentage of the latest loan amount was highest at 3.65 in SC-SHGs and lowest at 0.97 in minority SHGs.

17. Only 21.63 per cent of 1.567 members got the latest loan for consumption purpose.

18. Peer pressure was the most used measure for recovery of loans (in 33.72 per cent of 86 defaulting members).

19. Weighted average critical rating scores, calculated on the bases of 14 dimensions, were 81.60, 74.76, 78.67, and 77.02 for BC SHGs, SC/ST SHGs, minority SHGs and mixed - caste SHGs respectively. The higher the critical score, the higher is the performance of SHGs.

20. Of total 360 SHG members, 59 and 41 per cent borrowed from non- institutional and institutional sources respectively.

21. Most end-use of latest loan by SHG member was for consumption and working capital (27% of the total end-uses).

22. Highest per cent of SHG member (30) used latest loan for the purpose of health, education and consumption.

23. Average member yearly saving were Rs.528 in OCs, Rs.534 in BCs, Rs.375 in SCs, and Rs.381 in STs and Rs.482 in minorities.

24. Highest 26 per cent of SHG members repaid SHG loan from agricultural income source, whereas the lowest of 0.83 from gifts.

25. Increase in wage-employment after SHG loan was highest at 67 per cent for minority SHG members and lowest at 27.59 per cent for OC SHG members.

26. After SHG loan increase in self-employment was highest at 200 per cent for ST SHG members and lowest at 64 per cent for OCs.

27. After SHG loan highest percentage of SHG members (80) had increased spending on food, whereas lowest per cent of SHG members (8) had increased spending on rent.

28. Of the total 360 SHG members, 8 per cent acted as chairman (first leaders) of SHGs, 8 per cent as secretaries (second leaders), 0.83 per cent as treasurers, 3.33 per cent as committee members, and 79 per cent as members only.

29. With regard to benefits from the government schemes, 19, 17 and 84 per cent of SHG members got benefited under housing, supply of cooking gas, ration cards schemes respectively.

30. The income level access to formal institutions has shown noticeable improvement of 70.5 per cent and 67.5 per cent respectively. Significant improvement has been made 42 per cent in habit of living.

31. Cast categories of ST,SC,BC,OC, Minorities have shown moderate to significant change of 76.5 per cent,77 per cent, 84.4 per cent,92.6 per cent, 88.2 per cent respectively.

32. Employment generation was significant of 55 per cent from third linkage onwards.

33. Freedom from money lenders has shown significant improvement of 62 per cent in 2nd linkage. and the caste category of BCs have shown 64.5 per cent

34. Habit of saving has been stated from 1-2 years itself since it is linked to thrift.

35. Majority of the members are having TVs at their houses after they entered in to the linkage.

36. Reduced the incidence of poverty through increase in income, and also enabled the poor to build assets and thereby reduce their vulnerability. It is also observed with the increasing the age of the SHGs, the performance in respect of poverty reduction is improving.

37. Contributed to a reduced dependency on informal money lenders and other non institutional sources. The share of loans borrowed from moneylenders with high interest rates was significantly reduced and came down in the post-SHG situation to low levels.

38. There was remarkable improvement in social empowerment of SHG members in terms of self-confidence, involvement in decision-making, better communication, etc.

39. Consumption patterns have also reported to be increased substantially with the highest consumption recorded for food followed by festivals/recreations, Clothing, Education, Health.

40. Through participation of group activities members also became more assertive in confronting problem situations social evils like, Drinking, Gambling, Wife beaten by husbands.

41. Social evils like dowry, child marriage are less among members of SHGs

## Conclusions

Development of weaker section and alleviation of poverty is call of the day. Empowerment of women through financial inclusion is also adopted as fruitful strategy by many of the formal financial institutions in India. There are many formal, informal and semi-formal institutions working on mF route of poverty alleviation. Andhra Bank is one among them.

Andhra Bank is the premier institute in the state of Andhra Pradesh and is accredited for fund disbursement of all government initiated projects and programmes. Indiamma Housing programmes, Velugu programme and all other development funds are rooted through Andhra Bank following the self-help group.

It is found that there are many institutions engaged in formation, capacity building, skill development, record keeping and overall management. IKP through Velugu programme, Forest department for water-shed programme and DRDA's formed many SHG in the state. Similarly, some NGOs also formed several self-help groups to organize poor, vulnerable and marginalized community to commonly fight for eradication of poverty and hunger.

Following the NABARDs' view of financial inclusion and the directives of RBI, Andhra Bank has extended fund support to many self-help groups to take up livelihood activities. The institutions is not bias towards loan sanction to the NGO promoted SHGs or Government promoted SHGs, rather fund disposal depends on the kind of project, type of activities decided through Micro Credit Plan (MCP).

Similarly, the study looked at the difference between SHG categories as to continuously and intermittently saving shows that there is hardly any difference between the sources of formation of SHG and the savings of them. However, pattern of saving in the origin year and current year with the bank is highly correlated.

The study also reported that there is a statistically significant difference between two SHGs categories as to agencies/individuals involved in SHG bank linkage and hence the null hypothesis is rejected.

The functionality of SHG is more or less regulated by the caste group of its formulation. SHGs of mixed groups are more vibrant than the other communities. Looking at the loan repayment ST and OC self-help groups are more serious of repayment in comparison to the other groups.

A glance at the loan use shows that significant proportion of loan is used for day-to-day consumption followed by purchase of milk animal.

Andhra banks operation is quite open and suits the requirement of local groups organized for carrying out income generation programmes. Analysis of regional performance of the MFIs and the Andhra Bank reveals that coastal region dominates in the micro-finance scene than the other regions under the study.

Micro-finance operation through SHG root's of Andhra Bank has shown high degree of impact on the life of the women of the state of Andhra Pradesh. Vulnerability level has been reduced, dependency on money lenders is reduced, family members of SHG are accessing better health and education facilities, and women are taking part in household as well as village level decision making.

## Suggestions

In India only certain pockets have shown tremendous growth in SHG bank linkage. Andhra Pradesh is one among the leading SHG-root of micro-finance operating State in the south region. In AP the East Godavari District linked the maximum number of groups. Micro-finance operation is not limiting to the banks and that to Andhra Bank only and hence, there whole lot of institutions and organizations do participate in the process of execution of the micro-finance programme.

The present research is purely on the evaluation of Andhra Banks functionality on SHG-BL programmes, however, the impact of all other institutions do matters in the execution of the programme. The interaction with beneficiaries of Andhra Bank linked programmes shows that policies of the state government and all other institutions do influence the operation of the programme. Hence, the study has comes out with suggestions for improvement of SHG-BL programme of Andhra Bank exclusively along with some suggestions applicable for functional improvement of all other institutions partly responsible for micro-financing activity. The suggestions are as follows;

**State Governments**

a. *To cover in other districts:* In Andhra Pradesh the linkage is success in coastal Districts than Telangana and Rayalseema Districts. Hence, Government to pay more attention to these areas.

b. *Cover all BPL women:* Ensure coverage of all poor family members under SHG bank linkage.

c. *Strengthening of Supervision:* SHGs in AP are not effectively integrated horizontally and vertically to reap the benefits of synergy. Supervision should be strengthened by the Government over SHGs and their federations at various levels so as to make SHG-bank linkage programme effective and sustainable.

d. *Control over end-use of the loans:* The practice of extreme lending by SHG members is often noticed, which should have curbed by better control over end-use of the loans by SHG leadership and community coordinators.

e. *To take up more economic activities:* The State Governments to see that SHGs should take up the new economic activities than the traditional activities to generate better income. SHGs should innovatively take up add-on cluster of economic activities apart from credit delivery so as to augment incomes of their members. Activities relating to agro based, service oriented and business related may be encouraged.

f. *To study the skills of SHGs:* The Government to study the skills of SHGs and encourage in their activity.

g. *Awareness of various schemes*: Awareness of various schemes is by the members is low. So attention by State Government is required pay focus on it. It is observed that there are no active social workers at field level.

h. *Appoint active social workers:* The Government should appoint some active social workers.

i. *Provision of default risk fund:* A fund is to be created towards the default in payment of loans. CGTSME guarantee also may be extended for SHG loans.

j. *Study on economic activities:* A study to be conducted on number of SHGs who have taken up economic activities and type of economic activities whether they are remunerative or otherwise what activity to be taken up by them to get better income.

k. *Recoveries of loans:* The State Government to appoint active animators so that they can collect the money at village itself and pay the installments by animators only so that the branches will not be crowded and the braches can do the other business.

**Central Government**

1. *Area coverage:* Coverage of SHG-bank linkage programme is poor in North-eastern states where tribal population is more and Northern states where incidence of poor is high.

2. *Micro-finance Act*: Expedite the Act of micro-finance and see that micro-finance bill is implemented.
3. *Regulation of MFIs:* MFIs are to be regulated and suitable legislations

**Banks**

1. *Awareness on the schemes:* Awareness of various schemes has to be made from time to time to keep all staff informed about the schemes and the operation mechanism.
2. *Don't thrust too many schemes on SHGs:* Care should be taken to ensure that too many programmes and schemes are not executed at a time with the same intent and spirit.
3. *Increase velocity of lending:* Low velocity of lending resulted in small loan volumes to SHGs and consequently to their members.
4. *Provide higher volume of loan amounts:* To ensure higher volume of loan amounts, SHG-banks should lend to SHGs in greater multiples of their corpus funds.
5. *Enhancement of the limit:* The existing loan limit of Rs. 5.00 lacs is not sufficient at present due to launching of various schemes like INDIRAMMA and debt swapping etc., the limit may be enhanced to Rs.7.50 lacs without collateral security.
6. *Continuous policy in credit delivery:* Further, there should be some policy of continuity in credit delivery to SHGs.
7. *Greater scope for Bank-promoted groups:* Bank promoted groups performed relatively more in institutional loan repayment. There is greater scope for bank promoted groups for improving the conduct of SHGs and capacity building of its members.

8. *Streamlining of Methods and procedures:* Methods and procedures in SHG-banks should be streamlined so as to reduce time period between clearance of the previous loan and grant of repeat loan.

9. *To Constitute Committee:* Though SHG rating is available at the branch level, it is also necessary to constitute a committee to study the growth and inspect. Since the bank linkage is most successful model, banks have to frequently study the groups.

10. *Over-dues and NPAs:* Recovery should be geared up to avoid overdues and NPAs further.

11. *Understanding of SHG concepts by the banks:* Improve understanding and internalization of SHGs concepts among banks staff to increase functional efficiency of the staff and bank.

**NABARD**

1. NABARD should evolve a special policy to strengthen SHG-bank linkage programme in these states.

2. *Improve capacity buildings:* For greater acceleration of rate of economic empowerment, future strategy must focus more and more on training and capacity building of members besides ensuring adequate linkage supports.

3. *Regulation of NGO sector:* NGO sector should be regulated either by NABARD or state governments to avoid repetition of unhealthy practices of high rates of lending, forceful recollection of the loans, etc.

**Reserve Bank of India**

1. RBI, being regulatory of credit, should evolve policy guideline to have general control over the operations of MFIs and SHGs in their fold to avoid crises in micro-credit.

2. NGO sector should be regulated either by RBI or State Governments to avoid repetition of unhealthy practices of high rates of lending, forceful recollection of the loans, etc.

**Non-Governmental Organizations**

1. Where banks are not available NGOs have to go and finance to SHGs.
2. Where the bank branches are functioning avoid double financing.
3. Area demarcation is necessary while financing by banks/ NGOs/MFIs etc.,

**MFIs**

1. Interest rates should not be very high.
2. Avoid double financing so that SHGs should not become overburdened for payment of multiple loans.
3. No forcible recovery of loans.

**SHGs**

1. **Regulation of savings:** SHGs are expected to promote thrift and the study reveals that 43 per cent of SHGs were stagnant in monthly savings. This disturbing trend needs to be reversed by better end-use of loan for income generating activities.
2. Identify causes of drop outs and address them
3. Improve financial management, record and accounts maintenance
4. *Define performance standards:* SHGs, in particular, need to be helped to define performance standards for themselves, so that they internalize self-assessment processes and practices, and are provided with the capabilities required to reach those performance standards.

5. *Involve more in developmental programmes:* SHGs role may further be enhanced through its involvement in developmental programmes implemented in the areas.
6. *Strengthening the existing groups:* While expanding the programme for wider coverage, efforts also need to be focused on strengthening the existing groups and institutional building such as federal structures. Defunct groups may be activated.
7. Improve rotation in leadership positions: Rotation in leadership positions is to be improved.
8. *Distribution of bank loans among members:* Avoid large loans to only a few members. Loans to members only on entitlement (pro-rata) basis without reference to nature of need - equal distribution of bank loans.
9. *Repayment of bank loan through other sources:* SHGs should not repay of bank loan installments by raising loans from other sources like MFI loans etc

**Future Outlook:** Growth Strategies for SHG Movement in Andhra Pradesh

## New Approaches in Social Mobilization

The most critical task in organizing self help movement is social mobilization of poor. It requires a number of imaginative themes and techniques for motivating the society to form collectives for common good. In the case of self help movement, thrift and credit is the entry point activity. While campaign approach (movement) is a tempting suggestion indeed to bring every possible BPL family within the ambit of self help movement, here time-scale and magnitude of outreach becomes the paramount considerations rather than addressing critical questions of efficiency and effectiveness of social mobilization efforts. No doubt, Andhra Pradesh has largely benefited out of campaign approach, but the quality of social mobilization needs improvement. Induction of massive numbers in a campaign necessitates a unified organizational and communication strategy which may in fact run counter to diverse indigenous aspirations and social processes. Campaign approach further limits number and type of actors involved and initiatives for product development or system innovations. Further, the approach also limits the number and type of actors who can be involved coupled with near absence of role clarity among them.

The extent of group mobilization in Andhra Pradesh under various thrift and credit programme is estimated to be in the order of 4,50,000 groups involving nearly 6.75 million households. Out of these, a large number groups formed in DWCRA, IMY, SAPAP and some NGO sector largely conform to SHG concept of NABARD, except that quite many groups have weak management structure and loose financial dynamics resulting in severe internal stress. The groups formed by ITDAs' have rudimentary SHG characteristics and those formed under Joint Forest Management and Watershed Development Programmes do not have thrift and credit focus for the present. However, they do have potential for converting into SHG with minor modifications in their structural and functional configurations. Similarly, some group formations coming under MACS mode do not completely match the group configuration envisaged under SHG concept especially in terms of collective decision making, risk sharing mechanisms, etc. Nevertheless, they present close generic resemblance to SHG mainly on account of thrift-first-credit-next maxim.

Perhaps, '*mission approach*' may be more appropriate solution to induct numbers into the movement, with particular emphasis on the left out and deprived sections of rural communities. It is actually further scaling up the present programme without compromising on the fundamental objectives and related processes. The mission approach envisages consensus and pooling of resources coupled with synchronized efforts of all participants in a determined pursuit of clearly laid down goals and objectives. At the same time, the approach provides, for ample flexibility in contextualizing methods and processes to local requirements. Considering the involvement of several departments/agencies and the admixture of their programmes, a healthy synthesis of roles and functions of every actor in the movement is not only imperative but also beneficial to obtain necessary synergies. Clarifying the roles and responsibilities of partners and upgrading their skill is in itself a challenging task.

**Capacity Building of Self-help Movement**

Well conceived capacity building programme is the key to sustainable development and growth of SHG that is juxtaposed to the state of group development and objectives of movement. Imaginative sequencing of various components of capacity building programme with stress on empowerment of civil society is another area of concern. In the anxiety to document successes in the short run, there is marked tendency to hand down unrelated tasks on SHG resulting in the malady of task overload. It is not the carrying capability of community that is under question, but it is the capacity of groups to sustain and maintain new responsibilities without commensurate increase in their managerial abilities. While ignorance and illiteracy among members are often posed as major handicaps in managing knowledge delivery efforts of Self-help Promoting Institutions, it must be admitted that rural poor do possess native wisdom and adequate numeracy skills, enough to manage their lives and livelihoods.

Considering the large mobilization of SHG in Andhra Pradesh separate initiatives are required for restructuring and strengthening weak groups on one hand and fastening credit and non-credit linkages on the other.

**Groups Restructuring Programmes (weak groups)**

Intensive group restructuring and strengthening exercises must be taken up by associating lead agencies like DRDAs, NGOs, NGO Networks, Banks, Training and Consultancy Organizations particularly for reconstructing and strengthening DWCRA, IMY, MACS, JFM and Watershed groups. The major activities involved in the area would include:

i. SWOT Analysis of group configuration
ii. Assessment of training needs
iii. Identification of trainers and formulation of training strategy
iv. Preparation of comprehensive training modules focusing on self management
v. Preparation of training materials and aids using innovative communication techniques
vi. Structured cross sharing of experiences
vii. Visit to successful groups and higher organizations
viii. Informed guidance to groups and other structures on development related aspects
ix. Awareness building of socio-politico environment to sustain group development

**Group Maintenance and Upkeep (matured groups)**

Perhaps, the greatest need of the hour is to ensure stability of group dynamics and consolidation of internal financial control systems to enhance group effectiveness calling for conscious efforts for group maintenance functions. Based on strengths and weaknesses the strategic route could be pursued for sustained group action includes:

a. Organization development for participatory group monitoring

b. Finance and accounting control and related audit mechanisms

c. Credit Plus activities like project opportunity guidance, skill training and linkage support

d. Imaginative capacity building for community involvement in self help movement

The accent of capacity building exercises must be on injecting those set of processes and practices that seek to involve and empower communities to own, manage and control self help movement. This calls for skilful documentation of human processes related to different stages in life cycle of SHG and their relationship with society at large which can also serve as a document on best practices. Process documentation will also yield evolutionary pattern of SHG which will contribute immensely to resource planning and task planning efforts of promoting agencies in a systematic manner. Further, community involvement in process build up will greatly reduce monitoring expenditures for process monitoring and is a reflection of self monitoring and tool for training needs assessment.

**Standard Accounting Package (SAP)**

It is mentioned that the total corpus of the SHGs aggregated over Rs.1500 crore by the end of March 2003. Increasing savings and building up of the sizeable corpus of a large number of SHGs underscore the importance of proper and reliable accounts at each SHG level. Safety of the savings of the poor, particularly the net savers among them is of paramount importance for the banks and SHPI alike. The state of maintenance of records and accounts at the level of majority of the SHGs leaders much to be desired. The SAP essentially comprises three core books viz., Transactions Sheets, Thrift-cum-loan Register and Minutes Book. The transaction sheet is unique feature of the SAP as it simultaneously supports the functions of cash management, financial control, audit and MIS at group level. NABARD has conducted a series of training programmes for trainers, master book-keepers, etc. for putting in the place the package among the SHGs. It has been decided by the DRDAs to implement the SAP among the SHGs in a gradual and phased manner. Adoption of SAP ensures uniformity in record keeping by all SHGs in the state and enables building up of management information system with transaction sheet as a basic information unit.

## Economic Agenda for Self-help Groups

With a view to making thrift and credit activity perpetual and to secure increases in their income levels, the groups must be encouraged to deploy their fund base in investment or income generating activities. A first step towards economic empowerment of such groups should necessarily place emphasis on increasing their accessibility to productive assets and credit facilities concomitantly enhancing their managerial abilities. One must be clear about the suitability and compatibility of wage employment or self employment approaches while converging anti-poverty programmes with SHG mechanism. It must be realized that the groups may be effective in tackling social or economic dimensions of poverty simultaneously only in a few favorable pockets and as such the entire management of anti-poverty efforts cannot be trusted upon them, especially when the target group comprises individuals from destitute class. Moreover, the mobility of individuals in SHG system is determined by individual entrepreneurial ability and success of business ventures, irrespective of groups' support and contribution. How many doses and quantum of loan capital triggers the entrepreneurial behavior among members of SHG is a question that needs to be analyzed in detail. But there is strong evidence to show that members of SHG do chart a course leading to micro-entrepreneurship. Training in business skills, enterprise management, financial management, project opportunity guidance coupled with delivery of credit plus inputs all contribute to such graduation process. Most studies reveal particular preference for small trading businesses in SHG and investment in farm operations. Furthermore trading activities indulged into by SHG members is in itself a training ground to infuse in them the required confidence for business management and risk taking. Group strengths are also frequently put to use to combat business crises. Moreover, contrary to our expectation, the individual members do not avoid financial risk sharing in Self Help Groups even when they graduate into micro entrepreneurs. Perhaps, the situation may differ when asset creation is envisaged through group action.

***Farm Sector***

The community action can be promoted through collective efforts and investment in the form of both capital and labour in the areas of infrastructural development, maintenance of community assets that are essential to sustain the developmental process in the chosen field. Since such community action will pervade the entire community over a large agro-climatic geographical unit (e.g. watershed area), it is necessary that the possession and management of the entire land mass of that given area is brought within ambit of group's functioning. Towards this end, the Government should take initiative to give perpetual/usufruct rights to the community represented by such groups over the surplus land, government land and Panchayat lands so as to enable them to execute comprehensive plans for securing all round development of the project area. Similarly, the capability of the groups in planning and executing the developmental plans needs to be enhanced, for it required objective appraisal of endowments, high degree of technical skills, financial expertise and inter-personal relationships. At times, the investments for development of necessary infrastructure like water harvesting structures, bunding, etc., coupled with soil and water conservation measures may be required, the benefits of which may not accrue equally to all the contributors where Self-help Promoting Agencies/groups can devise suitable conflict resolution mechanism to secure voluntary participation of the entire community concerned. Perhaps the government can think of funding such investments having large labour component through programmes like Swarnajayanti Gram Swarozgar Yojana, Janmabhoomi, NREGS etc. with active involvement of the local people.

To sustain the development process considerable amount of perseverance with the recommended package of practices by individual farmers is necessary besides adoption of environment friendly livestock management system. The farmers in the project area may, therefore, require diversification of their economic pursuits to insulate the households from vagaries of monsoon. For this purpose, funding from group's corpus could be explored. They may initially be encouraged to take up quick income generating activities like nurseries, bio-fertilizer units, backyard poultry, etc., at individual or group levels commensurate with their native abilities to supplement their farm incomes. In the long-run the investments in silvipasture, dry land horticulture, can be encouraged to increase their incomes.

The community groups can also be actively involved in forestry development. Similar to area development programmes like Watershed Development and Forestry Development also requires comprehensive action by harmonizing diverse needs and interests. A prerequisite for executing such plans is community vigilance on forestry resources, access to efficient technologies of energy use and investments to regenerate forest cover, overcoming man-animal conflict situation. They can effectively function as environmental ombudsman to protect the indigenous rights of the local community while preserving equity. Perhaps they could be provided quasi-judicial powers with necessary checks and balances for prevention of environment related offenses. In the initial stages, the groups can place emphasis on agri-waste management, use of bio-manures, bio-fuels, restrained pastoral habits and prevention of forest fires. State Government can consider giving possession of forest lands, surplus lands and other Panchayat lands in the vicinity to such groups to take up comprehensive development of forest areas. While doing so they may clearly demarcate the boundaries of different land forms and water bodies to prevent any distortion in ecological equilibrium. The groups can be given the right to collect local taxes and fees to maintain the forest tracts. Similarly they can be encouraged in harvesting of timber forest produce and minor forest produce collection which will serve as powerful incentive for them to make community investments in the sector. Over a period it is possible to handover the entire joint forest management programme to the local community through micro credit mechanism, particularly the Self Help Groups. But, this requires rigorous technical and training support in addition to supportive legal framework.

***Non-Farm Sector***

Recognizing the limited absorption capacity of surplus labour in farm sector and the need to insulate the farming community from instability of income levels, there is an immediate need to promote non-farm sector activities through micro credit interventions. It has been observed that stable and matured SHG help develop entrepreneurial quality and leadership behaviour among the members which can be harnessed to promote entrepreneurship in Non Farm Sector. Initially micro credit users are expected to set up small business enterprises often with low investment size commensurate with their managerial ability. With the increased fund availability and experience gained, the enterprises also grow in terms of both scale and magnitude of operations, requiring further investments. It is imperative for the group to develop relevant technical and marketing skills to appraise the individual loan proposals besides rendering necessary assistance to their members for identification of suitable project opportunities. As micro credit structures get consolidated a few coalitions are likely to emerge which will specialize in a specific or a group of related activities in manufacturing, processing or marketing sectors. Already groups formed by weavers and potters are emerging in micro credit scene. Government may, therefore, encourage growth of such coalitions and entrust them with the task of developing appropriate infrastructure and strengthen the support services to such clusters. In fact the training infrastructure could also be handed over to specialized Non Governmental Organization networks to develop specific training facilities for the micro credit users. Similarly "*market consortia approach*" could be attempted through SHG Federations/NGOs to provide market access to member artisans. As regards technology up gradation and dissemination, industry-SHG linkage can be evolved through ancillarisation arrangements, wherever considered feasible.

Preference could be given to a few matured groups to set up large sized group based projects under group lending scheme under SGSY that may help develop appropriate infrastructure for the smaller decentralized micro enterprises. Private industrial estates, craftsmen complexes and showrooms by SHG Federations for providing necessary backward and forward linkages to member enterprises will also greatly benefit the movement.

## Social Agenda for Micro-Credit Users

Empowerment of rural poor will not be complete without social agenda. It is, therefore, necessary that literacy, health care, nutrition, primary education, savings and income generating activities are all integrated and convergence obtained at group level. Voluntary sector will have to play a major role in this regard. Perhaps, voluntary sector will be another big employment opportunity for vibrant and resourceful groups. Mature and stable groups and their coalitions can take up the role of NGOs and develop a suitable mechanism to pursue the social agenda. In fact their familiarity with local aspirations, responsive administration, flexible methods of operation and their identification with target groups put them in an unenviable position to discharge such tasks.

### Operational Strategy for Accelerating SHG Bank linkage Programme

The short-term operational strategy for 2000-01 will aim at further intensification of SHG bank Linkage in the State. Major emphasis will be placed on inducting new partners particularly new bank branches (non starters) in the programme to ensure its balanced spatial and institutional spread. The proposed strategy will broadly cover the following critical areas:

(1) Incorporate micro-finance programmes in Annual Credit Planning (ACP) process of banks.

(2) Formulate a coherent training strategy for entire matrix of development and banking institutions involved in micro-Finance sector. Designing and implementing customized training modules for sensitizing various actors for ensuring common understanding of SHG concepts and linkage practices. Perhaps, it may be quite essential to promote gender concerns through these modules especially when nearly 99 per cent of the groups are women groups.

(3) Attempt saturation of training efforts for stepping up credit linkage of SHGs in areas supported by APDPIP,

particularly Adilabad, Anantapur, Srikakulam and Vizianagaram districts.

(4) Accelerate financing of mature DWCRA groups conforming to SHG norms in potential districts of Cuddapah, Guntur, Kurnool, Nalgonda, Nizamabad, Nellore, Prakasam, Visakhapatnam and West godavari districts.

(5) Ensure complete coverage of women groups promoted through South Asia Poverty Alleviation Programme (SAPAP) of UNDP under credit linkage programme in Anantapur, Kurnool and Mahabubnagar districts.

(6) Increase space for Non Governmental Organization sector in SHG-Bank Linkage processes both as facilitators and credit retailers.

(7) Explore alternate financing routes through Non Banking Financial Intermediaries like BASIX in districts like Cuddapah, Anantapur, Srikakulam, Vizianagaram and Visakhapatnam districts.

(8) Encourage cooperative banks for financing Self Help groups, particularly in Chittoor, Guntur, Krishna, Kurnool, Nalgonda, Nellore, Nizamabad, Visakhapatnam and West Godavari districts.

(9) Encourage financing of SHG federations and Mutually Aided Cooperative Societies through select intermediaries like Andhra bank, State Bank of Hyderabad, BASIX and a couple of Regional Rural Banks.

(10) Strengthen and activate institutional mechanism of SLRCCDI for mutual information sharing and coordination between micro-Finance practitioners.

With a view to make thrift and credit activity perpetual and to secure increases in their income levels, the groups must be encouraged to deploy their fund base in investment or income generating activities. A first step towards economic empowerment of such groups should necessarily place emphasis on increasing their accessibility to productive assets and credit facilities concomitantly enhancing their managerial abilities.

**Lessons for the Future**

It can be observed that in Andhra Pradesh the organizational energy that grew with the total literacy campaign leading to the anti-arrack movement of the women was channeled to steer the savings and credit movement. Many organizations, government and non-government took part in this. Large number of women got organized around thrift and credit, forming a very large number of women's groups. Though most of these groups are involved in savings and credit activities, there is substantial variation in their design.

This experience clearly demonstrates that it is possible to make financial services available to a large number of people from the disadvantaged sections of the society, primarily the women. At this juncture, when most other states in India recognize that extending financial services is a critical step towards poverty alleviation, but where the savings and credit activities have not yet taken the form of a movement, it may be worthwhile taking a look at some of the factors that has made it possible in AP.

Majority of NGOs in Andhra Pradesh are basically involved in provision of social service to their target beneficiaries and their attitudinal orientation, methodology adopted and systems and procedures are so designed that they require social mobilization in large scale. Now with their diversification in economic sphere especially in thrift and credit activities, their resourcefulness needs to be harnessed and synthesized with SHG-Bank Linkage Programme. But, there exists another dimension to the said diversification which relates to their competence and capability to handle new assignments notwithstanding the financial and manpower commitments to their existing programmes in social sector. Perhaps, there is a need to design a comprehensive training strategy for personnel of NGOs in various aspect of managing SHGs to secure proper focus. Similarly, District Administration in several districts of the State is promoting thrift and credit groups under DWCRA programme which are akin to SHGs. A UNDP supported South Asia Poverty Alleviation Programme has been implemented in the districts of Anantapur, Mahabubnagar and Kurnool, which envisages to use the thrift and credit group promoted under the project as conduit for channelising their health, nutrition, education and other development programmes under an approach called "Community Based Convergent Services". However, the induced formation of groups needs to be cautiously pursued without undermining the autonomy of groups - a critical element to ensure effective functioning of SHGs. Nevertheless, the groups so formed do provided the opportunity to financing banks to expand their exposure to SHGs.

There is also an imperative need to enlarge the coverage of SHGs in the advances portfolio of banks as part of their corporate strategy, to recognize perceived benefits of SHG financing in terms of reduced default risk and transaction costs. In the meanwhile, the banks may have to devise suitable policy guidelines for appraisal, monitoring and supervision of SHG advances together with necessary documentation. Further efforts may be required to internalize these guidelines and build confidence in their operating personnel before their strategy gets going. SHG financing means not only direct financing of SHGs, but also coverage of SHGs through financial intermediaries, including the emerging clients – SHGs federations/MACS.

## Micro-finance to micro-enterprise

Deepening Services - “Enabling graduation of SHG members from micro-finance to micro-enterprise” to achieve this linking to local and distant markets is necessary. Market linkages were considered very crucial for promotion of micro enterprises. As globalization is redefining local markets, it is important that linkages of SHG products are established to both local and distant markets.

## Conclusion

As we enter the twenty first century, we must take along an active people centered and growth oriented poverty alleviation strategy - a strategy which seems to incorporate people’s aspirations, dynamics and involvement and that is distinctly different from the ones implemented during last five decades. It is envisaged that SHG will play a vital role in such strategy and already people have begun the process of grassroots organizational development for forming cohesive, dynamic and vibrant groups. It is, therefore, imperative that the promotional agencies particularly credit institutions must recognize the strong undercurrent across the country and harness its potential through suitable adjustments in their programme contents and delivery mechanisms to assimilate the new development.

Perhaps, a mission type approach will be more useful to assist and support such coalitions till they develop necessary competencies to handle their affairs independently, rather than campaign type approach that deals only with figures, targets and results. A fact that must be admitted is that thrift and credit activity will continue to be the life line of Self Help Groups but will eventually remain hidden as they embark upon the economic social agenda.

Further, many groups have formed many networks, undergoing structural reorientation to suit requirements of new business. Credit strategies must take cognizance of such adjustments and realignments and devise innovative credit delivery systems and offer flexible financial instruments to meet their socialized credit requirements. Such funding mechanism could involve government resources available under Watershed, Yuvashakti, Joint Forest Management, Swarnajayanti Gram Swarozgar Yojana and Janmabhoomi Programmes. Synthesis of government programmes and thrift and credit activity of SHG to facilitate informal interface between the two entities is, therefore, the need of the hour.

# Bibliography


A *Study of SHG Bank Linkage in Andhra Pradesh* by AP MAS 2006.

Andhra Bank, 161 Agenda book of SLBC, 2007.

*Andhra Pradesh Urban Services for the Poor* – Project document. 2004.

Anjugam, M and Alagumani T, Impact of Microfinance Through Self-Help Groups: A Case Study, Indian *Journal of Agricultural Economics,* Vol. 56, No.3, 2001, pp.458-459.

Annual Report of APMAS, 2006-07.

APMAS, Self Help group Bank linkage programme- A recurring study in AP, 2007.

Audit Sampling Microfinance Portfolio-at-Risk Mark Schreiner, Prepared for *Micro Rate* for a document produced by CGAP, 2000.

Bandhyopadhyay, D., B N Yugandhar, Amitava Mukherjee, "Convergence of Programmes by Empowering SHGs and PRIs", *Economic and Political Weekly,* June 29, 2002, p.2556.

Banerjee, Dr. G.G., Evolution Study on Self-help Groups *Agriculture*, Vo1.34, No.2, April-June 2002, pp.38-40.

Basu, Kishanjit, Krishnan Jindal, *Microfinance: Emerging Challenges,* Tata Me Graw Hill Publishing Company Limited, New Delhi, 2000.

Basu, Priya, Pradeep Srivastava, Exploring Possibilities: Microfinance and Rural Credit Access for the Poor in India, *Economic and Political Weekly*, Vol.XL, No.17, pp.1747-1756.

Chatterjee, Shankar, *Development of Rural Poor Through Groups,* Mudrika Graphics, Hyderabad.

Chavan, Pallavi and R. Rama Kumar, "Micro-Credit and Rural Pave, *Economic and Political Weekly,* March 9, 2002, p.963.

Chavan, Pallavi and R. Rama Kumar, Micro-Credit and Rural Poverty: An Analysis of Empirical Evidence, *Economic and Political Weekly,* Vol. 37, No.1 0, March 9th, 2002, pp.9-5-965.

Choudary. R.C., N. Mohanan, P. Purushotham, K.P. Kumara, A. Mohinuddin, D. R. P Reddy, *Micro-credit for micro-enterprises,* NIRD, Hyderabad Publications, 2001.

Das, R, Barman RN and Baruah PK, Performance of Self- Help Groups in Sonitpur District of Assam, *Indian Journal of Agricultural Economics,* Vo1.56, No.3, 2001, p.466.

Das, Rimijhim Mousmi, Microfinance Through SHGs: An Boon for The RI Poor, *Kurukshetra*, Vol. 52, No.4, February 2004, pp.43-45.

Discrimination in Instalment Lending by Retailers of Consumer Durables, In Apartheid South Africa Mark Schreiner, Douglas H. Graham, Manuel Cortes-Fontcuberta, Gerhard Coetzee, and Nick Vink. (1996) *Development Southern Africa,* Vol. 13, No. 6, pp. 847-860.

Fisher, Thomas and M.S.Sriram: *Beyond Micro - Credit, Putting Development Back into Microfinance,* Visitor Publications, New Delhi, 2002.

GOAP, *Annual Report Dept of Rural Development,* 2005.

Gupta, S.K. and Shrivastava A, A Study of Working of Self - Help Groups in Madhya Pradesh, *Indian Journal of Agricultural Economics,* Vo1.56, No.3, 2001, pp.470-471.

Harper, M, Self-Help Groups Some issues from India, *Small Enterprise Development,* 2001, Vo1.7, No.2. pp.36-41.

Harper, Macoln, *Practical Microfinance: A Training Guide for South Africa, to Women,* Financing Vistar Publications, New Delhi, 2003.

Harper, Malcolm, *Microfinance Evolution, Achievements and Challenges,* ITDG Publishing, London, Sanskrit Publishing, New Delhi, 2003.

Jayaraman, B., Microfinance Retrospect and Prospects, *Occasional,* NABARD, Mumbai, 2001, pp. 5-10.

Jha, TN, Micro Credit Finance Models in Bangladesh: Lessons for India, *Yojana*, Vo1.46, No.2, February 2002, pp.23-30.

Joshi, Deepalipant, Microfinance: Need of the Hour, *Agriculture,* Vo1.34, No.2, April-June 2002, p.25.

Kaladhar, K., Microfinance in India: Design, Structure and Governance, *Economic and Political Weekly,* vo1.32, No.42, October 18-1997, pp.2687. 2706.

Kale, Alankar, *Microfinance: Experience So far.*

Kallur, MS, Empowerment of Women Through NGOs: A Case Study of MYRADA Self-Help Groups of Chincholi Project Gulbarga District Kamataka State, *Indian Journal of Agricultural Economics,* Vo1.56, No.3, 2001, pp.465-466.

Kalpana, *The Shifting Trajectories in Microfinance Discourage: A Critic al Reading of the Anti-Poverty Dimensions of Microfinance Programmes,* MIDS, Chennai, June, 2004, pp.7-8.

Karmakar, K.G., *Rural Credit and Self-help Groups Microfinance Needs and Concepts in India,* Sage Publications, New Delhi, 2002, pp.177-178.

Khandelwal, Anil K., Microfinance Development Strategy for India, *Economic and Political Weekly,* Vol.XLII, No. 13, March 31,2007, p.I-131.

Kumaran, K.P., Role of Self - Help Groups in Promoting Micro-Enterprises Through Micro-Credit: An Empirical Study, *Journal of Rural Development* (Vo1.21, No.2, April-June 2002, pp.231-250.

Lal, Meera, *SHG bank linkage in India –Empowerment & sustainability,* 2007.

Mishra, J.C. and R.K.Thanvi, Indian Banking System and Microfinance, *Kurukshetra,* Vo1.52, No.4, February 2004, p.12.

Mishra, R.K., Self-help Groups and Micro-Credit Movements in Orissa: Issues and Options, *Indian Cooperative Review January*, 2002, p.189.

Mohan, S., "Micro-credit and Empowerment NGOs", *Yojana,* February 2000, p.22 .

Mohanan, N., Micro Credit and Enterprise Development by the Paper, *Workshop Background Papers,* NIRD, Hyderabad, 2000.

Mohanan, S, Micro-credit and Empowerment of Women: *Yojana,* Vo1.44, No.2, February 2000, pp.21-23.

Moorthy, Krishna, A., *Workshop on Micro Enterprises*, NIRD, Hyderabad, 2000, pp.26-27.

NABARD, Andhra Pradesh State Focus Paper 2006-2007, Hyderabad, December 2005.

NABARD, Banking with the poor, Financing SHGs, 2005.

NABARD, Banking with the Poor, Hyderabad, 2003, pp.I-4.

NABARD, Development Initiatives, Annual Report, Mumbai, 2006 pp.50-90.

NABARD, *Microfinance for Micro-enterprises*, 2007.

NABARD, NABARD Banking with the Poor: Financing Self Help Group, Hyderabad 2005.

NABARD, Potential Linked Credit Plan, 2006-07, Hyderabad.

NABARD, Progress of SHG-Bank Linkage in India 2004-05, Mumbai.

NABARD, Progress of SHG Bank Linkage in India-2005-06

NABARD, State Focus paper 2008-09.

NABRD, Ground level credit: SHG Bank linkage Programme, Hyderabad.

Nair, Ajai, Sustainability of microfinance self help groups in India: would federating help? *World Bank Policy Research Working Paper No. 3516,* Feb. 2005.

Nair, Tara S., "Institutionalizing Microfinance in India", *Economic and Political Weekly January* 27, 2001, p.400.

Nair, Tara S., "Rural Financial Intermediation and Commercial Banks" *Economic and Political Weekly,* Vol. XXXV, No.5,January, 29, 2000 p.299.

Nair, Tara S., Institutionalizing Microfinance in India:Strategic Issues, *Economic and Political Weekly, Vo1.36,* No.4, January 211 2001, pp. 399-404.

Nair, Tara S., The Transforming World of Indian Microfinance, *Economic and Political Weekly,* Vo1.XL, No.17, April 23-29, 2005, p.1695.

NIBM, A Study on SHGs linkage programme, 1999.

NIBM, Innovative Approach of Oriental Bank of Commerce to micro-finance, 2000.

Pandian, Punithavathy, R. Eswaran, Empowerment of Women Through Micro-Credit, *Yojana,* Vo1.46, No. 11, November 2002, pp.47-50.

Patel, A.R., Microfinance and Microfinance Institutions: Need for Banks, Initiative and Commitment, *Financing Agriculture,* January-March 2000, pp.8-12.

Patel, Amrit, Micro-Credit and Role of Banks, *Kurukshetra,* Vol.52, No.4, February 2004, p.6.

Prakalpa -*The Journal of Commerce* Feb. 2008.

Raju, Y.B. and Firdousi AA, Women's Development: Issues, Concerns and Approaches, *Journal of Rural Development,* Vol.16, No.1, 1997, pp.113-122.

RBI, *Guidelines on Total Financial Inclusion,* 2006.

RBI, *Report on Trend and Progress of Banking in India,* Mumbai, 2007.

Reddy, G. Narayana, Empowering Women Through Self-Help Groups and Micro Credit: The Case of NIRD Action Research Project, *Journal of Rural Development,* Vol.21, No.4, Oct-Dec., 2002, pp.511-535.

Sa-Dhan, Microfinance Resource Centre, An Introduction to Microfinance Delivery Models in India, New Delhi, and Second Edition: 2005, pp.I-21.

Sa-Dhan, *Maturing microfinance emerging challenges* 2007.

Sarkar, AN., Innovations in SHG-Led Microfinance Development Programmes: Sharing of Global Experience, *Indian Cooperative Review,* Vol.41, No.1, July 2003, p.8.

Sarker, Debnarayana, A Study of SHG-NGO and SHG-Non-NGO Models of Rural Micro financing in West Bengal, *Indian Journal of Agricultural Economics Vol.56,* No.3,2001, pp.454-456.

Seibel, H. D. and Shyam Khadka, *SHG Banking: A Financial Technology for Reaching Marginal Areas and the Very Poor,* 2005.

Seibel, Hans Dieter, Financial Systems Development and Microfinance, *Deutsche Gesells Chaft fur,* D-65726, Eschborn, pp.51-52.

Seibel, Hans Dieter: History matters in microfinance Small Enterprise Development – *An International Journal of Microfinance and Business,* June 2003.

Shahidur, R. Khandker, *Fighting Poverty with Micro Credit Expenditure in Bangladesh,* Oxford University Press, New York, N.Y. 10016, 1998.

Sinha, Frances, *Impact Assessment of Microfinance in India* and Impact assessment team, 2004.

SLBC of AP, Andhra Pradesh District profiles, 2007.

SLBC, *Highlights of Annual State Credit Plan 2007-08.*

Srinivasam, Girija and P. Satish, Networking for Micro Credit Delivery, Journal of Rural Development, Vol.20, No.4, 2001, pp.635-671.

Srinivasan, Girija and D.S.K.Rao, Financing of Self-Help Groups by Banks-same issues, workshop on *Micro Credit and Enterprises,* NIRD Hyderabad, 2000, pp.40-58.

Stephen, Agrnes and A. Seilan, "SHGs and Micro Finance-creating Linkages with Banks", *Social Welfare,* July 2005, pp.33-34.

Subhash, C. Wadhwa, Sustainable Micro Credit Model for Poverty Alleviation and Empowerment, *Financing Agriculture,* Vo1.31 3/4, July-September 1999, p.111.

Synghal, Sudarshan, Taking Micro-credit. *Agriculture,* Vol.34, No.2, April-June, 2002, pp.3- 7.

*The Asian Economic Review,* Dec.2007.

*The Journal of accounting & Finance,* Apr- Sept.2007.

Thingalaya, N.K., Microfinance and Poverty Alleviation: Some issues, *Financing Agriculture,* Vol. 34, No.2, April-June 2002, p.16.

Thorat, Usha: Inclusive Growth - *The Role of Banks in Emerging Economies,* 28.02.2008.

Vasimalai, MP and K. Narender, Microfinance for Poverty Reduction: The Kalanjiam Way, *Economic and Political Weekly,* Vol. XLII, No. 13, March 31,2007, pp.1190-1195.

Wednesday, Jun 26, 2002,Hindu, India's National Newspaper CM seeks direct funding from NABARD for SHGs.

Working Women forum Annual Report 1995.

# Index